2012

Sta

The Goddess

Stalking
The Goddess

Mark Carter

MOON
BOOKS

Winchester, UK
Washington, USA

First published by Moon Books, 2012
Moon Books is an imprint of John Hunt Publishing Ltd., Laurel House, Station Approach,
Alresford, Hants, SO24 9JH, UK
office1@o-books.net
www.o-books.com

For distributor details and how to order please visit the 'Ordering' section on our website.

ISBN: 978 1 78099 173 3

A CIP catalogue record for this book is available from the British Library.

Design: Stuart Davies

Printed and bound by CPI Group (UK) Ltd, Croydon, CR0 4YY
Printed in the USA by Offset Paperback Mfrs, Inc

We operate a distinctive and ethical publishing philosophy in all
areas of our business, from our global network of authors to
production and worldwide distribution.

CONTENTS

PREFACE

In the last sixty years, mainstream religions have faced a unique problem, which even their most farsighted leaders never anticipated. The so called "big three" of mainstream religion, Christianity, Judaism and Islam, have all suffered encroachments from a growing religious minority. Some members of this minority call themselves witches and research medieval witch trials for their spiritual inspiration. Others consider themselves druids and study ancient Celtic culture. Still others draw upon classical Rome or Greece for their spirituality. Their sources and reasons vary, but the label of *pagan* can be applied to this group collectively.

Nearly sixty years ago Robert Graves penned his classic work of paganism, *The White Goddess*. His study of goddess worship and pagan poetics has since become a masterpiece of alternative religion. As the Western pagan movement has grown from a handful of British eccentrics and Californian hippies to over two million strong, *The White Goddess* has ascended to near liturgical status. With this rising appreciation come all the problems of liturgical texts. Many pagans consider Graves's work like the goddess herself; awe inspiring but distant and impenetrable.

Literary critics have long recognized the significance of Graves's works but have little incentive to examine the impact of *The White Goddess* on the development of paganism. Such a study must originate within the pagan community. Yet, few pagans realize the full extent of Graves's impact and even fewer are aware of the earlier sources from which Graves draws. The way in which the book shifts between ancient history and Graves's personal poetic system is maddening and no single reader can evaluate the entire body of pagan literature and place Graves in his proper context. This study makes no claim to do so but is merely a step in that direction.

Stalking the Goddess explores the bewildering forests of historical sources, poems, and Graves's biographical details to reveal both his unorthodox claims and entrancing creative process. Relentlessly stalking down these paths we will explore the uncharted woods and reveals the few and subtle signposts Graves has posted. The hunt for the goddess spans an antique family library, the battlefields of France, the British museum, and the Balearic Islands. En route, we encounter not only the goddess herself but her three sacred animals, dog, roebuck, and lapwing. Perhaps the muse cannot be captured on her own grounds, but now at least there is a map.

CHAPTER I

THE FOREWARNING

Once upon a time an intellectual poet, mystic, and expatriate penned a book, which changed the world. He poured into this work, years of classical and occult education alongside his own life altering experiences. The result was a tour de force explanation of mythology, ritual, and history. Four publishers rejected the book, considering it too deep and controversial for publication. The world was at war and books challenging mainstream religion or examining obscure historical problems were unpopular. The book was only published after it was championed by another visionary poet. Upon publication, the book earned a small following of dedicated supporters.

Experts of Greek, Roman, and Celtic history were confounded by its arguments. Biblical scholars labeled it heretical. Theologians considered it a return to a primitive faith, which denied the last two thousand years of Western thought. Readers argued whether the book was to be taken literally or as poetic metaphor. The book inspired contemporary poets and its themes recurred in their works. Lost souls who could never classify their spirituality suddenly found their unorthodox beliefs depicted with uncanny accuracy and some treated the book as holy writ. Many of them flooded the author with letters and pilgrimages to his secluded island home.

This incredible book was written during the tail end of World War II. The author was British poet and novelist Robert Graves and the book became his most famous nonfiction work, *The White Goddess*. Since its publication in 1948, *The White Goddess* has been recommended reading for those interested in pagan religions. In its early years the book's audience may have been limited mainly to mystical poets, self-proclaimed druids, and even some simple parlor

3

room occultists. However, with the 1954 publication of Gerald Gardner's *Witchcraft Today* a new subculture was defined, bridging the gap between occultism and spirituality. These people were the modern pagans. Wicca may have origins shrouded in controversy, but its future was clear from the outset. It became the meeting ground between groups such as The Golden Dawn and those holding séances in darkened rooms. It was this community of Wiccans and other pagans who popularized *The White Goddess* and made it what it is today.

Naturally enough, we cannot understand *The White Goddess* without actually reading it. The scope and magnitude of the book defies summary or simplification and its thesis and main points often vanish amid the history, mythology, and secret ciphers, which Graves uses to support his arguments. This alone leads many would-be critics to avoid the book or any of its points of contention. Thus, an early review of the argument may be helpful.

The thesis of *The White Goddess* is revealed in its Forward: "My thesis is that the language of poetic myth ... was a magical language bound up with popular religious ceremonies in honour of the Moon-goddess, or Muse, some of them dating from the Old Stone Age, and that this remains the language of true poetry" (Graves 1993, 9-10). It may not be an oversimplification to say that Graves's thesis is that *all* poetry derives from pre-Christian goddess worship. Graves believes that all "true poetry" draws either directly or indirectly from these pagan traditions. The corollary of this belief is that all poets are pagan in spirit, if not in their actual religion. There are Jewish and Christian poets, Graves argues, but they are either poor poets writing hack verse or poor representatives of their proclaimed religions.

Graves offers several smaller points to uphold this thesis. Among these is the claim that all primitive cultures were originally matri-archal and worshiped a great mother goddess in the three forms of maiden, mother, and crone. This triad corresponds with the phases of the moon, her most potent symbol. The twenty-eight day lunar cycle was likened to the cycle of menstruation. The waxing and waning of the moon was linked to the growing seasons, and the "death" and "return" of the moon, along with the progression of the growing season, was taken as evidence of reincarnation. These ideas, plus several others which Graves examines, comprise the body of this pagan poetic tradition, which he argues all true poets draw from.

Other traits of this pagan tradition include the worship of a lesser male deity who constantly battles a rival male (or *tanist*) for the right to be the consort of the goddess. These two male deities are sometimes considered brothers, sometimes as father and son, sometimes as twin aspects of the same individual, yet there are always two and they are always at conflict. They compete in an endless cycle of life and death, constantly killing each other to be reborn from the goddess in alternating succession. These two gods symbolize the seasons of summer and winter and the waxing and waning lunar phases. The deaths of these males occur at periodic intervals, which may coincide with either the solstices or equinoxes, or may be extended for a predefined number of years.

This dying and reborn god is the divine model for early kings of these matriarchal cultures. Thus, we find many ancient pagan cultures where the king is subservient to the queen and is allowed power only through his marriage to her. These kings are often sacrificed at periodic intervals, just like their divine role model. This entire theory is best explained in Frazer's *The Golden Bough*, a book that heavily influenced much of Graves's work. Another characteristic of this pagan tradition is the holy reverence given to nature and especially to certain trees. Tree worship and tree symbolism permeate this goddess religion and underlies the pagan poetic language that Graves argues is the only true foundation to poetry.

This tree symbolism achieved its highest development with the creation of the *ogham* or *Beth-Luis-Nion*, a secret script, which served as both an alphabet and mnemonic calendar. According to Graves, this secret alphabet was universal among ancient goddess-worshiping pagans and was inseparable from tree symbolism. Graves argues that all goddess-worshiping pagans used this tree symbolism and used ogham to transmit secret pagan doctrine. The ogham itself was an expandable framework, which could include any type of symbolism needed. Thus, not only did a tree ogham exist, but there were also oghams of precious stones, foods, city names, and countless other ways to represent the characters of this secret alphabet. The universal goddess, her twin lovers, lunar symbolism, tree symbolism, and the ogham variants are the foundations of the pagan poetic tradition, which *The White Goddess* examines. Briefly, this is the theory Graves attempts to support.

Having stated what he believes to be the original religious beliefs of these pagan cultures, Graves then explains how this goddess religion was corrupted, and eventually overthrown, by a monotheistic patriarchal religion. Numerous factors contributed to the overthrow of this goddess religion and much of *The White Goddess* attempts to document the downfall of this goddess culture.

The most significant factor was the discovery of the relationship between sexual intercourse and reproduction. Until this link was established, women claimed that reproduction was a magical act under their exclusive control. This belief placed women closer to divinity than men, gave them claims to higher magical powers, and improved their social and economic status as well. It could be argued that the entire theory of ancient matriarchies rested on the claim that women controlled reproduction. Once males realized their reproductive role, this claim to exclusive control was shattered and men demanded equal status. Indeed, Graves believes that men inverted the early claim of women and now claimed that the males were the most important part of reproduction. Women were then degraded into sexual objects to be controlled by men. Marriage became a contest where men competed for the most nubile female, who could ensure reproduction and therefore preserve *his* lineage and allow *his* sons to inherit *his* property. In short, men realized that they could control society by controlling reproduction. This initiated a chain of events, which ended matriarchy in most ancient pagan cultures.

Other factors that weakened this hypothetical matriarchy and its goddess religion include warfare and economic difficulties. Various tribes in Greece, and later in parts of Celtic Europe, suffered economic hardships and were driven to support themselves through warfare rather than agriculture and hunting. As the need for warriors grew the status of men rose accordingly. Eventually, a warrior class developed beliefs, which idealized violence and aggression. These warrior beliefs and images of violence dominated their mythology and slowly overpowered the more passive aspects of goddess worship. In their struggles to find new lands to pillage, these warrior tribes became nomadic, carrying their patriarchal system of violence to the surrounding peaceful tribes. These peaceful tribes were either slaughtered, forced into slavery, or became warrior tribes themselves.

So says Robert Graves. We must remember that the above model is only a general theory and in no way can we accept it as accurate. Indeed, even as Graves wrote, it was considered a faulty model of prehistoric Europe and serious historians had already abandoned it. Graves retains this model mainly because it provides a suitable framework to support his own poetic style. Much of Graves's poetic style developed because in his early career he had read authors who supported similar models. Earlier authors such as Frazer had suggested various theories of prehistoric matriarchy when the theory was popular. Graves quickly absorbed these ideas and began developing his poetic system around their implications. The result was that Graves perfected his style years after such theories were considered outdated.

These theories were not Graves's creation but he had supported them for at least twenty years before publication of *The White Goddess*. He had believed in ancient matriarchies as early as 1924 and probably favored the idea even earlier. Graves's first wife, Nancy Nicholson, was considered an extreme feminist in her time and had once said that Christianity was "rot" because it viewed God as male. This view helped Graves alleviate his own religious anxieties (Graves 1957, 270). By 1926, Graves had refused to attend church for a decade and believed that organized religion was the enemy of freedom itself.

Graves's ancient matriarchy, which worshiped a mother goddess, the associations of the moon to women, the seasons and reincarnation, the twin gods who alternately died in service to the goddess, the sacred king who imitated the gods, the rise of warrior tribes, the eventual downfall of the goddess religion and its secret survival, are all interrelated factors within *The White Goddess.* To understand the book we must remember all this simultaneously with whatever else Graves chooses to throw at us in our long hunt through his tangled woods. Forgetting any of these factors, results in getting lost while hunting. Nor is Graves a reader-friendly author in his chase. He manipulates his arguments with total disregard to the reader's ability to follow until we suspect that this is intentional. He is struggling to reveal his ideas to poets while simultaneously complicating the issue enough that critics eventually lose the trail. Put simply, Graves believes he is revealing the true nature of poetry and it will only be revealed to poets who can survive the chase. Anyone else reading for any other reason, especially critics, are meant to get lost in the woods. As one critic said, "Graves does not feel the casual reader is worth stopping for and can be purposely difficult when he chooses to be so" (Mehoke 78).

Once we understand Graves's theory of ancient goddess worship and its downfall we can examine just how he believes portions of this pagan tradition have survived into our own times. His main argument is that much of pre-Christian paganism has passed directly into European literature to become preserved in poetry and fiction. Pre-Christian literature in Greece and Rome was profuse. Similar pagan texts also came out of the Middle East. Celtic Europe produced no true examples of pre-Christian texts; however, medieval manuscripts prove the existence of a long-standing oral tradition. These combined sources laid the foundation for Graves's pagan poetic system and often placed poets and fiction authors at odds with the church. It's in this literary form that Graves believes the goddess religion is best preserved.

Graves claims individuals and small groups who remained loyal to the goddess intentionally cultivated this survival of pagan ideas. These groups, sects, or cults became pockets of resistance against a more patriarchal system of paganism and eventually against the arrival of Christianity. The two most significant of these groups were the witches of the Middle Ages and the poetic schools of Wales and Ireland. Graves argues that both groups followed a surviving form of goddess worship and used ogham to secretly transmit their heretical teachings.

To support his theory that Celtic poets retained this goddess worship Graves examines the works of several Celtic authors. He particularly examines two thirteenth century bardic poems in which he claims pagan religious ideas are secretly encoded. These poems are *Cad Goddeu* and *Hanes Taliesin*, both of which can be found in their original Welsh form in the collection of early Welsh poetry *Myvyrian Archaiology*.

Armed with these poems, and with a rough idea of Graves's theories, we can enter his forest of research. We have the foundation on which his arguments are based and we have the poems he cites. We already know many of the points he supports and conclusions he attempts to reach. This is more than what most readers are given. With this brief outline serving as a map, we may attempt to hunt the roebuck Graves conceals in his thicket of scholarship.

CHAPTER II

PUBLICATION AND IMPACT

In 1943, Robert Graves frantically scrawled out the first draft of *The White Goddess*. At the time, Graves was in his late forties and had already published over fifty works ranging from poetry and fiction to translations and an autobiography. He had fought during World War I, had been severely wounded and prematurely pronounced dead. He had already married Nancy Nicholson and abandoned her for poet Laura Riding, whom by 1939 had abandoned him. He had served shortly as Professor of English Literature at the Royal Egyptian University, Cairo and, finally, moved to Majorca to focus exclusively on his writing. By 1943, he had already published his autobiography *Good-bye to All That* and his classic novel *I, Claudius*.

While writing during a temporary stay in Devonshire, England, Graves was overtaken by the urge to write what became *The White Goddess*. To hear Graves tell it, the image was overpowering. He was busy working on a series of maps to be included in his *Golden Fleece* when he was suddenly overtaken by the desire to explain early Greek and European goddess worship. Something in his research had clicked with facts and myths he had collected over the years and he suddenly saw the relationship between poetry, mythology, and religion clearer than ever. That Graves suddenly saw mythology and history in a new light at this time is not surprising. The massive amount of research undertaken to write *Hercules* could easily have changed his outlook. Douglas Day states that this research was "exhaustive" and that Graves consulted over a dozen ancient Greek and Roman authors (Day, 154-155).

It was clearly a time of enlightenment for Graves and for years afterwards, he claimed that he scrawled the rough draft of *The White Goddess* in a frenzied, almost trance-like state. He was already familiar with this state and had written about it as early as 1922. He induced this same poetic trance while writing poetry and he claimed that from this state he could recover lost historical events. It was during the research phase of *The White Goddess* that Graves was finally able to label this process, calling it *analeptic* memory. Additionally, he claimed an opposite mental state also existed which allowed the entranced poet to predict the future rather than see the past. Despite the similarity of this state to automatic writing Graves firmly denied that it was supernatural or had any connections to occult powers.

Using this analeptic state as his main inspiration, he claimed to have finished the first draft of *The White Goddess* in about three weeks. Yet, nine years after writing the postscript Graves claimed that the draft took six weeks rather than three. The manuscript reached 70,000 words, or about 110 typed pages, that he dubbed *The Roebuck in the Thicket*. The title derived from the idea that the roebuck, symbol of the Muse, was actually a unicorn. In 1946, he returned to his home in Majorca, where he revised *Roebuck* into *The White Goddess*. Therefore, Graves claims *The White Goddess* was the product of a poetic frenzy, which lasted three to six weeks.

Yet, could such a book be the result of poetic frenzy? Graves said yes and maintained this view his entire life. However, we've already seen that he had been researching exactly these subjects for an earlier book before this frenzy began. Nor did many of the points of *The White Goddess* flash into Graves's head spontaneously; in a letter dated September 5, 1946, Graves wrote that he had been pondering the meaning of "true poetry" since at least 1943 and had concluded that poetry was the last remnants of an ancient European religion. He suggests that this religion had been the faith of the Minoans, had been overpowered by waves of Aryan invaders, and finally by the arrival of Christianity (O'Prey 34). His grafting of this theory onto a Celtic framework was inspired by his reading of Celtic historians Edward Davies, John Rhys, and David Brynmor-Jones in December of 1943.

It's noteworthy that 1943 saw the publication of *The Reader over Your Shoulder*, which Graves had co-authored with Alan Hodge. *Reader over Your Shoulder* was subtitled *A Handbook for Writers of English Prose* and intended as an instructional manual for fellow authors. Before writing this book, Graves and Hodge had discussed authoring a manual on poetic standards as well. Hodge anticipated problems with this project and politely bowed out. He later admitted that this poetic manual seemed a very personal project to Graves and that it would become "a kind of myth" (R.P. Graves 1995, 73). Graves had wanted *Reader over Your Shoulder* to serve as a "yard-stick" for measuring prose; possibly he intended that he and Hodge would next write a yardstick for poetry. *The White Goddess* bears the subtitle *A Historical Grammar of Poetic Myth* and sounds suspiciously like a follow up to *A Handbook for Writers of English Prose*. This implication is strengthened by the mention of a poetic "yard-stick" in the first paragraph of *White Goddess*.

Graves submitted various drafts of *Roebuck* to four publishers before finding a buyer. J.M. Dent, Jonathan Cape, Cassell and Oxford University Press all rejected the book. Still not discouraged, Graves submitted the draft to T.S. Eliot at Faber and Faber. They had already accepted *The Long Week-End* and Eliot wrote to Graves claiming that he was interested in seeing a revised draft of *Roebuck*. Graves immediately began an immense list of revisions and expansions which threatened to push the book into two volumes and turn Faber against it. On July 25, 1946, Graves wrote that he was making final additions to the book. Near the end of the same year, Graves was still correcting the proofs. The revision process lasted into the next year and in a letter dated Feb. 15, 1947 Graves wrote that he was still making changes. On March 23, 1947, Graves wrote to inform Eliot that he was nearly finished with the job.

The revisions lasted into late 1947. In a letter to Joshua Podro dated Dec. 15, 1947 Graves claimed that he was still revising proofs and had also discovered much new material (O'Prey 50). Thus, not only was Graves correcting proofs at this point, but he was still doing new research and attempting to squeeze his findings into the final draft. Among these changes was a change in title and *The Roebuck in the Thicket* officially became *The White Goddess*. Again, we see that the book wasn't the product of three or six weeks of frantic work but was the result of a long process of editing and revisions. Despite their disagreements on poetry, and the size of the book, Eliot still favored it after reading the final draft. He went so far as to describe *The White Goddess* as a "prodigious, monstrous, stupefying, indescribable book" in the Faber catalog and it was finally released to the public in May of 1948 (M. Seymour 312).

In America, Creative Age Press published it despite expectations of poor sales. They had recently become Graves's primary American publisher and were willing to take what they considered a low profile book if it guaranteed their future with Graves. To their surprise, *The White Goddess* became a steady seller. The book had appeared in America on Aug. 26, 1948 and sales were 2,837 when their vice-president wrote to Graves in early January, 1949. The letter also stated that Creative Age expected the book to sell "quietly" for at least a few years (Seymour-Smith 1982, 417).

Supporters of *The White Goddess* frequently claim that it isn't a scholarly study of poetry, paganism, or the goddess but rather an inspired poetic inquiry into these subjects. They often hide behind this claim when charges of bias or inaccuracy are leveled against Graves. They claim that Graves himself stated that the book was such an inspired metaphor and sometimes quote him to support this view. Admittedly, there is much evidence favoring this argument. Graves had once openly denied that the book was a scientific book and instead claimed that it addresses "how poets think". He claimed: "it's not a scientific book or I'd have given it notes and an immense bibliography of works I hadn't read" (Seymour-Smith 1982, 405). In later lectures, Graves again reiterated that the value of *The White Goddess* didn't rest upon its historical claims (R.P. Graves 1995, 268).

One supporter of Graves's metaphorical argument is Margot

Adler. Adler cites not only *The White Goddess* but also Graves's *Watch the North Wind Rise* and *King Jesus* as having a high impact on paganism (Adler 59). While all this is true, it doesn't prove Graves's intent or determine his level of accuracy. Graves often downplayed the book's enormous influence on Wicca's development, crediting Wicca's spread more to Murray's works rather than his own. He said in 1964 that Wicca "attracts hysterical or perverted characters" and that its structure was prone to "schisms and dissolutions" (Graves 1964, 553). Nonetheless, Wiccans were a good group with the right ideas who only needed a good leader to organize them properly. However, he refused to be that leader.

Adler argues that Graves knowingly wrote *The White Goddess* as a poetic metaphor. However, it can be seen by his other works and interviews that he clearly believed *The White Goddess* to be literally true. Isaac Bonewits, founder of Ar nDraiocht Fein, North America's largest druidic organization, believes that Graves took his work too literally. Bonewits accuses Graves of "sloppy" research, complains that *White Goddess* inspires faulty anthropology among pagans, and concludes the book is an inspirational metaphor which Graves interpreted too literally (Adler 59). Later pagan authors, such as Edred Thorsson, agree with Bonewits and complain that Graves allowed "poetic truths" to displace authentic history (Thorsson xi). Ronald Hutton also believes Graves wished his work to be taken as an "authentic work of history, an accurate portrait of the Old Religion" (Hutton 42). Many Wiccans believe that *The White Goddess* alludes to knowledge of Wiccan beliefs and question if Graves had early access to Gardner's material. It would be more accurate to say that Gardner was influenced by Graves and not vice versa. Gardner mentions Graves's 1949 novel *Seven Days in New Crete* (a.k.a. *Watch the North Wind Rise*) in his own *Witchcraft Today* and while there is no evidence that Gardner also read *The White Goddess* at this point, it seems likely. The two books are only a year apart and complement each other well. *Seven Days* was Graves's vision of a world living by the beliefs outlined in *The White Goddess*. Gardner had clearly read *The White*

Goddess before publishing *The Meaning of Witchcraft* in 1959; it appears in his bibliography along with Graves's *King Jesus* and *Wife to Mr. Milton*.

Nor is Gardner the only pagan leader to incorporate Graves's material into his religious beliefs. Janet and Stewart Farrar's Wiccan text *Eight Sabbats for Witches* mentions Graves over a dozen times. Aidan Kelly, founder of the New Reformed Order of the Golden Dawn, was clearly influenced by Graves and it shows in the rituals he created (Adler 163). Ed Fitch, publisher of *Crystal Well* magazine and cofounder of Pagan Way, also lists Graves among his influences despite that (like Bonewits) he calls Graves "sloppy" (Adler 43; Fitch 146). Wiccan author Herman Slater uses the term *white goddess* as an actual goddess name in various published rituals alongside terms such as "Old Ones", drawn from H.P. Lovecraft, and the phrase "fear is the mind killer", taken from Frank Herbert's *Dune* (Slater 2, 3, 26, 62, 137). Just as Slater allows fictional works to influence his paganism, so paganism has also influenced fiction. Morgan Llywelyn cites *The White Goddess* as a primary inspiration for her novel *Bard* and Marion Zimmer Bradley's *Mists of Avalon* also utilizes Graves's model of pagan Europe.

Fred Adams, founder of Feraferia, was particularly influenced by Graves's utopian novel *Seven Days* (Adler 239). Adams went so far as to meet Graves personally in 1959. Gerald Gardner also visited Graves at Majorca in January 1961 (M. Seymour 398). By this time however, Wicca's popularity had spread and Gardner no longer monopolized its content. Gardner's publishing career was over at this point and any influence from this meeting would only have impacted his own coven.

Celtic historian John Matthews states that Graves's historical evidence is "shaky" (Matthews 2002, 85). Casey Fredericks, Douglas Day, and J.M. Cohen have attacked the book more violently. Cohen denies *The White Goddess* is a scholarly work but confesses that perhaps Graves never intended to be so (Cohen 95-96). Daniel Hoffman agrees that Graves is too free with his sources and accuses him of bending evidence (Hoffman 211). Graves himself had called the book "heretical in the extreme" (O'Prey 75). In the Forward Graves gives a warning to the reader with a "rigidly scientific mind", implying that the book will offend such readers because of its nonscientific approach.

While it's true that Graves makes this claim he also makes contradictory claims both in the text of *The White Goddess* and in other sources. The Forward also states that a study such as *The White Goddess* "has never previously been attempted, and to write it conscientiously I have had to face such 'puzzling questions'..." (Graves 1993, 9). Here, Graves implies that much research went into the text.

Graves knew that his unorthodox conclusions and lack of references prompted heavy criticism and offers *White Goddess* as supporting evidence for his earlier works. This implies that Graves intended to show every step in his argument and provide references. It also reveals that Graves realized the criticism that his analeptic method caused him. Instead of being another inspired poetic work, he intended *The White Goddess* to be the final proof that his poetic examinations in his other works were historically valid. *The White Goddess* would vindicate the "tree alphabets" which Graves utilized within *King Jesus* and prove them to be logical suppositions. In a letter to T.S. Eliot, Graves again claimed that "in *The White Goddess* I justify all, or practically all, the mythological theory I introduced into it" (O'Prey 37).

The Forward also admits that Graves faced the same disturbing questions, which troubled Socrates and confesses that he is "a very curious and painstaking person" (Graves 1993, 11). Here again Graves implies that *White Goddess* wasn't the product of poetic trance but was the result of painstaking research. In the Postscript, Graves even claims to distrust his intuition unless given opportunity to cross-check it. Whether this is an honest statement from Graves or an attempt to backpedal away from his analeptic method after receiving criticism is questionable. Either way, Graves apparently believed *The White Goddess* was a well-researched book. A final suggestion that

Graves took his research seriously can be seen from another letter to Eliot in which Graves states that he has cross checked his "phonier-seeming theories" (O'Prey 43).

Graves therefore believed *The White Goddess* to be a historically accurate text and not a product of poetic trance or inspiration as he sometimes claimed. A few critics have realized this. Hoffman implies that Graves interpreted his work historically when he suggested that Graves "resented the suspicion of having manipu-lated...texts nobody but he could understand" (Hoffman 137). Hoffman realized that the accusation of manipulation offended Graves because it implied dishonesty.

The White Goddess began as a rough draft in 1943 titled *The Roebuck in the Thicket* and this was the inspired poetic investigation that Graves sometimes mentions. It may well have been one of his many analeptic works and could have been furiously drafted in three weeks of entranced brainstorming. Upon completing the draft, Graves realized that much of what he hastily wrote while in Britain now sounded unhistorical when read leisurely in Majorca. This surely contributed to its many rejections because many publishers couldn't imagine the finished product looking better than the draft. If the book were to be published it would have to be expanded and better documented. T.S. Eliot, a poet himself, naturally saw the potential of *Roebuck* and encouraged Graves to revise and expand it. Amid his personal library, Graves was able to bolster his finished argument with a greater array of mythic examples much as Frazer cataloged hundreds of specimens to prove a handful of arguments. This was the revision phase, where *Roebuck* slowly became *The White Goddess* and the frantic musings of poetic inspiration slowly became a detailed study and, eventually, *A Historical Grammar of Poetic Myth*.

Therefore, the claim that *The White Goddess* was written as a poetic examination rather than a scholarly work is untrue. Yet, the claim allows Graves to ignore historical inaccuracies, which would ruin his thesis. An identical motive drives Graves's novels to employ minor characters, which are removed from the novel's context. *King*

Jesus claims to be written by Agabus near the end of the first century. *Hercules* is recited by the oracular ghost of Ancaeus, last survivor of the voyage. *Count Belisarius* was likewise told by a minor character. Lastly, *I, Claudius* is presented as a surviving text written by Claudius directly to the modern reader. Each novel avoids historical complexities by presenting the tale a few years removed from its true context or via the use of a speaker speaking to readers several centuries removed from himself. Graves seldom speaks as the main character or even a fairly important one and never speaks to contemporary readers. This allows him to use historical sources but leaves room for error or the necessary fictionalization required to make his tales enjoyable. *The White Goddess* also depends upon necessary fictionalization but, being a nonfiction book, Graves couldn't place it in the mouth of a minor character removed from the context. Instead, he creates the story of an entranced Robert Graves scribbling out the book in a few short weeks. This deception was required to fulfill Graves's dual purpose of historical examination and poetic inspiration.

Graves was attempting to revive poetry in his age and this required the creation or re-creation of a valid mythology for poets, a mythology that faltered under closer investigation. His claim also helped to put the more logically or scientifically minded readers off the trail. In order for Graves's theory to work for poets, it must elude the scholarly or scientific crowd. Just like any mythology or religion, Graves's creation would die and become useless if it were examined too critically. Like the roebuck in so many fairy tales, Graves had to keep his book one step ahead of the critics and partly concealed in the thicket.

CHAPTER III

THE USUAL SUSPECTS

Although *The White Goddess* challenges many popular beliefs the basis for its arguments are not wholly original. Like any historian, even an unorthodox one, Graves built on earlier literary sources. Admittedly, Graves quotes out of context, builds non sequitur arguments, and resorts to personal attacks. Yet, he drew from an impressive list of earlier sources. Many of these authors may have been surprised at the conclusions reached from their material, but Graves was certainly well read in the appropriate subjects.

Casual readers of *The White Goddess* may overlook the depth of Graves's research and we suspect this is exactly what Graves wants. Downplaying his research allows Graves to claim the book was written in a short frenzy. While most authors seek to properly document their sources Graves attempts to confuse the matter. The most obvious tactic in this plan is his refusal to include a bibliography. A tally of the works mentioned within *White Goddess* reveals over 160 titles, not counting poems or historical manuscripts. If these works are included, the number reaches nearly two hundred. From his comment regarding "an immense bibliography of works I hadn't read" we suspect that Graves knew his lack of bibliography would trouble some readers. It's unlikely that Graves had fully read all of the books cited. Like any author, he did the research needed, found the required passage in his sources, and cited the book. Yet, unlike other authors, Graves refused to list those sources. His reasons for doing this are unknown but at least two factors can be assumed.

First, he wanted his argument to stand on its own. *The White Goddess* was intentionally written in a non-scholarly tone because he felt that the book must stand or fall on its own claims, not the sources used to bolster those claims. Graves was making a statement and he wanted that statement credited directly to himself. Citing all the evidence and providing a complete bibliography may have seemed apologetic to Graves, as if he were required to justify his every statement. Graves was speaking on history, but speaking as a poet, and he probably felt that citing his evidence would only weaken his poetic authority.

Secondly, Graves realized his bias. In chapter nineteen, he implies that much of *Hanes Taliesin* baffled him and most of his answers relied on "poetic intuition" verified by later research. This proves Graves began writing *White Goddess* with strong preconceptions. He already knew the points he supported and consulted only those sources confirming his theory. Thus, a bibliography was irrelevant to him. He would have reached the same conclusions regardless of the books used. A bibliography would reveal the extent of his bias rather than his research. Graves faced a similar problem when researching *King Jesus* and confessed that a bibliography would be "more impressive than helpful". What would have impressed readers, in either book, wouldn't have been the works he had consulted but the works he had *not* consulted. Those, which he ignored, revealed as much about his methods as those he used. Logically, Graves used those sources, which were most likely to support his theories. Yet, unlike most other authors, Graves sometimes used these sources out of context and completely ignored those sources, which contradicted him. Ultimately, he gives an argument, which is mostly one sided.

This problem is compounded by his reader's inability to evaluate his claims. This was true in 1948 and is truer today considering the decline of classical education. Few lay readers, even those who consider themselves poets or pagans, have a firm grasp of the fine details of etymology, Greek, Roman, and Celtic history, or the development of the ogham. These are specialized fields of knowledge, which require years of study and access to rare and costly books. Few pagans have the time, money, or desire to study the *Myvyrian Archaiology* or obscure books from the Celtic Revival of the nineteenth century. Such readers are forced to take Graves at face value, never realizing the massive amount of evidence against him. Although Graves can't be blamed for the ignorance of his readers, he should be more understanding of their position and the fact that he isn't implies that he wishes to be taken at face value.

The White Goddess is often the first in depth book on these difficult subjects the reader may encounter and as he is forced to accept its premise, it becomes the standard which later sources are compared against. This had led to the book becoming akin to Holy Scripture in some circles. This process had begun even within Graves's lifetime and had prompted him to claim, "There are some hopeful young people in California who have taken my book *The White Goddess* as their Bible" and that there were "various *White Goddess* religions started in New York State and California" (Kersnowski 95, 156).

Nor is the lack of bibliography Graves's only method of concealing his sources. Within the body of the text he cites over 160 sources in a casual and inconsistent manner and following up on many of his citations is difficult. Graves never gives a full citation, including title, author, and year of publication. Instead, he makes brief mention of his sources: sometimes omitting the author, sometimes abbreviating the title, and sometimes giving an incorrect title altogether. This method of citation may work for commonly known books such as the Bible or Frazer's *Golden Bough*, but is insufficient in most other cases.

Perhaps the most significant aspect of Graves's sources is the ages of the works cited. A listing of Graves's sources reads more like a catalog of museum manuscripts than a bibliography of contemporary research. There are at least three reasons for this. First, Graves drew from his Father's antiquarian library. Secondly, much modern research contradicted Graves and he was forced to cite outdated material. Lastly, Graves's classical education predisposed him towards the ancient historians and the older translations of these historians, with which he was familiar.

In *Good-bye to All That* Graves claims his childhood home contained nearly five thousand books, including "an old-fashioned scholar's library bequeathed to my father by my namesake" (Graves 1957, 29). This library was central to Graves's early education and some of these books played a more direct role in writing *The White Goddess*. Besides owning the "old-fashioned scholar's library" Alfred Perceval Graves was a Welsh Bard at the 1902 Bangor Eisteddfod. He was active in the Irish Literary Society, collected books on Celtic culture and folklore, and had published translations of Celtic poems. To say that Robert Graves came from a literate family with a Celtic predisposition would be a vast understatement and it seems Graves had at least a rudimentary grasp of Celtic mythology even as a child. As if to confirm this, the back cover of the first edition of *The White Goddess* stresses that Graves's education began within his family library. Chapter two of *White Goddess* reveals that Graves had read Taliesin's legend in his childhood, probably in Guest's translation. A fascination with Celtic material recurs in Graves's poetry long before 1948 and it's obvious that Graves was well aware of Celtic themes early in his career.

The second reason for Graves's antiquated sources is more revealing. By the 1940's, many of Graves's theories were already outdated. As we've seen, Graves supports a model of prehistoric Europe and the Mediterranean which included both widespread goddess worship and the more untenable idea of large-scale political matriarchies. In holding this theory, Graves commits a non sequitur, which experts had already abandoned: the assumption that widespread goddess worship implied widespread matriarchies. Graves retained this model due to the impact of those earlier authors who originally supported them in the late nineteenth and early twentieth centuries. Yet, even these authors refused to carry the argument as far as Graves.

Frazer attempted to undermine Christianity by drawing parallels between it and earlier pagan religions. His comparisons proved the old cliché "nothing new under the sun". He implied that the goddess was superior to the god because the god must constantly die and be reborn while the goddess is eternal. He admitted to widespread prehistoric goddess worship but shunned the idea of matriarchies. His theories on sympathetic magic and the idea of "like produces like" were his primary tools for dissecting myths and rituals from various pagan cultures. Many of his claims were later discredited but not before they had their impact on the literary world. Even after critics had done their worst, his ideas lingered in popular belief.

Although Graves claimed he couldn't recall the first time he had read *Golden Bough*, evidence indicates that he discovered Frazer before 1920. In *Fairies and Fusiliers* (1917) Graves included poems of seasonal life and death cycles and images from Greek and Celtic myth. While this isn't condemning proof of Frazer's influence, it echoes his ideas. We suspect poems such as *Bough of Nonsense* were reactions to Frazer. In this poem, we find mention of a famous bough in a thicket of oaks. Within this forest, poets seek a nest built of skulls and flowers. It's a short step from this nest to the nest of the Night Mare found in chapter one of *The White Goddess*. There, Graves describes the Night Mare as one of the ferocious aspects of the goddess and reveals that her nest is built from various ominous objects, including entrails and jawbones. Apparently, the image of the goddess as a destructive and prophetic bird is one that Graves had developed for years and what started off as an image in a nonsense poem was modified by ideas from Frazer, Shakespeare, and the Bible to make its final appearance in *The White Goddess*.

His *On English Poetry* (1922) makes a direct reference to *The Golden Bough* and *A Survey of Modernist Poetry* (1928) shows influence from Frazer, while *Mockbeggar Hall* reveals ideas from both Frazer and Margaret Murray. By 1935, Graves was writing of druids and stone circles in *Claudius the God*, and drawing on archeology and Celtic literature (Graves 1962, vi). By 1948, his poetry and fiction had been immersed in Frazer's ideas for years. In his poetic system, Graves used Frazer's view of paganism to support certain aspects of eighteenth century romanticism such as the noble savage and the divinity of nature.

Most readers of *The White Goddess* are aware of Frazer's influence but few are aware of the full extent. In a way, *The White Goddess* is a counterpart to *The Golden Bough*. Frazer spends nearly his entire book developing the theory of the divine king-hero-god who is victimized by a queen-goddess. He tells the story from the viewpoint of the divine king and focuses on the male aspects of the pagan mystery cults. Graves tells the same story from the female viewpoint, focusing on the queen-goddess and her mystery cults.

Margaret Murray also postulates a prehistoric goddess religion and believes women held positions of greater power before the fall of this hypothetical matriarchy. However, she still claims the god of her witch-cult predated the goddess (Murray 1970, 15, 65). Her three books *The Witch-Cult in Western Europe, God of the Witches*, and *The Divine King in England*, claim that witchcraft was the last remnants of a dying pagan religion. Contrary to popular belief, Murray was not the first historian to make this suggestion; she was actually the last and merely the most popular. Ten years before *Witch-Cult*, Dr. John MacCulloch's *Religion of the Ancient Celts*, one of Graves's lesser sources, had said the same thing (MacCulloch 175). Others, including Girolamo Tartarotti, Walter Scott, Karl Jarcke, and Franz Mone had also anticipated this claim (Murray 1996, 4; Hutton 136).

Murray tentatively suggests that this cult descended from druidism. Using Frazer's theories of sacred kingship, fertility cults, and sympathetic magic, she concludes that the victims of the witch persecutions were members of a fertility cult, which had existed in Europe, under various forms, since prehistoric times. This fertility cult was based on the beliefs of a pre-Celtic people of Europe but showed corruption from classical Greek paganism. Like Frazer, she was uncritically accepted for a while but eventually refuted. Murray's theories appealed to Graves's sense of romanticism. Secret rituals, magic, and the survival of the "true" religion of the ancient British undoubtedly attracted Graves's attention shortly after *Witch-Cult's* publication.

Murray's alleged witch-cult contained several conflicting elements. At times she depicts it as the pagan religion of "inarticulate uneducated masses" and claims it survived "among the illiterate" and "in less accessible parts of the country", especially among women (Murray 1970, II, 29). The members of the cult may have been illiterate as late as the reign of Rufus, yet they somehow penetrated the highest government offices. Murray claims that several English kings were members of the cult and were sacrificed in its service. Yet, paradoxically, she claims that often the upper classes and nobility were Christian while the lower classes remained pagan. She explicitly states that the Norman invaders were Christian in their nobility but the masses remained pagan. Graves makes virtually the same statement in *The White Goddess* (Graves 1993, 23-24). In the end, Murray clearly favors the witches she writes about and creates a romantic image of them, which she then defends.

Murray's influence on Graves was deep and judging from his works we suspect that he knew her theories by 1922, a year after *Witch-Cult* was published. By the time he published *Whipperginny* (1923) Graves was familiar with Celtic myth and had been reading accounts of witch trials. His 1924 poetry collection, *Mockbeggar Hall*, includes the poem *The Witches* and an excerpt of a 1591 book, which inspired the poem. Therefore, Graves was reading both Murray and earlier accounts of witch trials. Readers should note that while Graves refers to the "witch-cult" (a term borrowed from Murray) he never refers to *Wicca*.

Jane Harrison fared slightly better, if only because her theories were slightly less shocking than Murray's. Harrison applied Frazer's method to ancient Greek artwork and painted a very unconventional image of early Greek paganism. Like Murray, Harrison held that goddess worship and matriarchies predated patriarchal religions, but also claimed that the shift from matriarchy to patriarchy was inevitable and beneficial. Harrison believed that a great deal of Greek myth was misunderstood by later Greeks and grew into the Olympic mythos remembered today. In her *Mythology and*

Monuments of Ancient Athens (1890) she suggests that mythology derives from misunderstandings of ancient rituals. According to Harrison, beneath the elegant mythos of Homer is an older, more primitive and chthonic religion of fertility, death, restless spirits, and even human sacrifice. This is the religion depicted on Greek artifacts and pottery and the classical interpretations of them drawn from Olympic mythology are late inventions by a more advanced Greek culture. Indeed, a reading of Harrison's *Prolegomena* is like a precursor to *The White Goddess*. Both books make radical interpretations of mythology, contain weak etymology, have no bibliography, and labor under the long shadow of Frazer.

In his introduction to *Prolegomena*, Robert Ackerman says the book "is neither 'safe' nor 'neat'; it was written at white heat, as much to discharge her teeming brain and achieve mental clarity" (Harrison xiv). The same is true of *The White Goddess*. Indeed, Harrison's influence on *The White Goddess* is second only to Frazer and like Frazer, Harrison was a controversial author that Graves had read early in his career. He refers to Harrison's *Ancient Art and Ritual* in his own *Poetic Unreason* twenty years before he began the rough draft of *White Goddess*.

The importance of Frazer, Murray, and Harrison cannot be overstated. If Graves does have any truly primary sources, it is these three authors. Many books cited within *The White Goddess* could have been easily omitted and may have been consulted simply because Graves had them on hand but Frazer, Murray, and Harrison are exceptions. Removal of their works would cause *The White Goddess* to collapse. Each of them postulated ideas of extensive hidden or misunderstood religious ideas and their methods of interpretation are the foundation of Graves's own theories.

The third reason for Graves using these older sources is easily explained. Graves, like any well-off British gentleman of his time, held a classical education. In today's high tech world, we sometimes forget that it was only a couple of generations ago that classical education was considered standard and twelve-year-old children learned Latin, not Java. Graves had been educated from the great historians of Greece and Rome. He had been raised on Homer and Virgil and wrote complex Celtic *englyns* in his spare time. He read Roman historians in both their native language and in Victorian era translations, which are often just as alien to us as the Latin originals.

These combined factors led Graves to cite many older sources besides Frazer, Harrison, and Murray. It was these three authors who most impacted Graves's views on anthropology and one critic has said of Graves that he is "the living writer most deeply affected not only by *The Golden Bough* but by the whole corpus of Frazer's writing" (Vickery 1). However, there are other minor characters to consider. Indeed, we may consider these three to be the "usual suspects" behind Graves's book, yet there remains a host of lesser players to encounter. These lesser authors didn't write monumental books like Frazer or Harrison. Nor did they suggest controversial witch-cult theories like Murray. Yet these lesser-known authors were considered the experts of their time within their fields. Most of them dealt with Celtic history and literature and have since been forgotten by everyone today, other than the modern experts whose predecessors they are.

Foremost among those Celtic experts which Graves consulted was Edward Davies, author of *Celtic Researches* (1804) and *The Mythology and Rites of the British Druids* (1809). Graves had discovered these books in December of 1943 and began incorporating their research into his own works immediately. Graves considered Davies "hopelessly erratic" but even this is an understatement (Graves 1993, 38). Others have referred to Davies's theories as "eccentric in the extreme" and gone so far as to say he had an "unbalanced" mind (Matthews 1995, 13; M. Seymour 310). Peter Ellis is more tactful, yet even he admits that Davies possessed "imperfect knowledge" and his works have been ridiculed since the mid nineteenth century.

Davies believed that the druids built Stonehenge, a common misconception of his time, and suggested that British stone circles were used in pagan rituals as late as the twelfth century. Davies was a Christian before he was a historian and his historical views suffered accordingly. He regarded the Bible as "a correct epitome of the most ancient periods" and dedicated the entire second and third chapters of *Celtic Researches* to proving its historical validity (Davies 1804, 6). He often put biblical views before all other evidence and sometimes before common sense itself. He twisted much of his evidence to support earlier theories of the *Helio-Arkite* religion.

The Helio-Arkite theory had been suggested by Jacob Bryant in his *A New System; or, an Analysis of Ancient Mythology* (1774). According to Bryant, this Arkite religion was a type of universal patriarchal paganism, which worshiped Noah and the ark under countless symbols and forms. This faulty theory allowed a reconciliation between history and Christianity and allowed eighteenth century readers to overlook historical inaccuracies within the Bible. Furthermore, by extending the Arkite symbolism to fantastical extremes Bryant was able to "prove" that various pagan cultures were actually derived from biblical worship. This not only reinforced biblical authority but allowed modern Greeks and Romans to accept the glory of their own pagan ancestors while at the same time asserting that they practiced something at least vaguely related to biblical worship.

Davies cleverly incorporated Bryant's Arkite theory into British history. According to Davies, the British Arkite religion was founded by Noah's descendants after landing the ark in the British Isles. Noah's descendants eventually came to worship him as the savior of mankind and the ark as the vessel of their salvation. This worship supposedly became idolatry in which the horse and bull were sacred and the sun was the primary symbol of God. Davies claims this Arkite religion survived to influence the druids and lasted into medieval times. King Arthur and the mythic Welsh hero Hu Gadarn were worshiped as incarnations of Noah and their legends were supposedly worked into mystery plays commemorating the flood. This Arkite religion also had supposed connections with Bacchus,

Ceres, and Isis. In other words, Bryant and Davies drew from the best-known pagan cultures to create their insane theory.

Helio-Arkite theories were strengthened by the fact that Noah's descendants were assimilated into some medieval Welsh manuscripts as the Welsh struggled to derive their own history from biblical authority. The lost tribes of Israel and the complex genealogy of Noah's descendants allowed the Welsh to connect with the Bible at a time when its historical accuracy was unquestioned. The resulting confusion spurred the Helio-Arkite theory and the related Anglo-Israelite movement. Graves was fully aware of these spurious theories. In the opening of chapter four, he denies being one of the "British Israelite" in an attempt to distance himself from historians such as Davies.

Davies fanatically declared that the poems attributed to Taliesin were true examples of sixth century poetry that had passed through oral tradition until they were recorded in the medieval *Book of Taliesin*. Davies believed that not only were these poems truly ancient but that they were written by a historical Taliesin and contained hidden elements of druidic religion. Much of his work attempts to extract this druidic religion from the poetry, much as Graves attempts in *The White Goddess*. However, Davies's works can't be depended on for any sort of historical accuracy. He was a crackpot theorist and *Celtic Researches* was already over 140 years outdated when Graves read it.

The reasons why Graves favored such outdated and inaccurate sources are many. Most significantly, Davies believed that early Celtic poetry concealed druidic teachings. The very basis of *The White Goddess* is that *Cad Goddeu* and *Hanes Taliesin* contain secret druidic beliefs hidden in a cryptographic method. Davies supported a similar view and argued that *Cad Goddeu* wasn't a poem about a physical battle but dealt with a conflict of language. He suggested the link between *Cad Goddeu* and letters, which became central to Graves's work.

Graves's reliance upon Davies extends beyond his interpretation of Celtic poetry or history and influences Graves's attitude towards poetry in general. Near the end of chapter one, Graves compares English poetry to Arabic *kindling* poems; the poet begins with stereotypical images of poetic beauty and then quickly turns to philosophical subjects. Graves states that this fast switch enables the poet to cleverly include statements of "the shortness and uncertainty of human life". Almost 140 years earlier Davies had complained of the same method within Celtic *tribanau* or metrical sentences and mentioned that this method allowed the bard to express "the shortness and frailty of human life" (Davies 1809, 78).

Graves also preferred Lady Charlotte Guest's 1849 translation of *The Mabinogion* when more recent translations existed. *The Mabinogion* is a well-known collection of medieval Welsh legends, which originated from a much older oral tradition. Lady Guest's translation of these adventure tales became the standard English versions partly because hers was the most vibrant translation thus far, and partly due to her extensive notes on the sources, origins, and alternate versions of the stories. The footnotes to Guest's translations comprised nearly a third of her work and are an introduction to Welsh mythology in themselves. Graves admits to a careful reading of these notes in a later essay. Considering its popularity, Graves is justified in using the dated Guest translation. However, he may be held accountable for not also using more recent translations to throw additional light on the subject.

Another of Graves's sources, which has already received brief mention, is the 1801 *Myvyrian Archaiology*. Herein lies the original poems and stories, which Guest translated for her *Mabinogion* and, like Guest's *Mabinogion, Myvyrian Archaiology* became a standard for those studying Celtic literature. We should remember that although *Myvyrian Archaiology* is the ultimate source of much of Graves's material, he couldn't read Welsh and was required to consult English translations. Which translations Graves used and why he used them will reveal interesting factors later in our study.

For his information on ogham, Graves used at least four sources.

Most significantly, he drew upon Robert Macalister's 1937 *The Secret Languages of Ireland*. Although Graves and Macalister disagree regarding the origin of ogham, Graves still found much in Macalister's book, which he worked into *The White Goddess*. *The Secret Languages of Ireland* only dedicates a single chapter to ogham, but significantly, it also dedicates a chapter to cryptology, and applies many of its methods to the ogham. Graves was so inspired by Macalister's works that he eventually wrote to him regarding the ogham alphabet. Macalister's reply mentions the variation between early ogham sources and advises Graves to treat these sources with caution.

Graves supplements his ogham theories with material from Rodrick O'Flaherty's 1775 *Ogygia*. Exactly where Graves found a 170-year-old Irish history book is unknown but his Father's library is the most likely source. Graves's grandfather, Charles Graves, was a historian specializing in ogham research; his name appears in the subscribers list of Davies's *Celtic Researches*. He wrote a series of articles about the ogham in which he claimed that it was used "only by the initiated". It's likely that *Ogygia* and these articles were among the contents of A.P. Graves's library. Alternately, Graves may have depended on the wealth of second hand accounts of *Ogygia* taken from Patrick Joyce's *Social History of Ancient Ireland* and Davies's *Celtic Researches*. Graves's use of O'Flaherty is negligible and could have been culled from these sources alone.

Our last ogham source could probably be found in the family library as well. The *Auraicept Na N-Eces* was a medieval Irish manuscript used for the training of the Irish *fili*, or master poets. Versions of this text occur in both the *Book of Ballymote* and the *Yellow Book of Lecan*. It contains multiple lessons regarding the ogham, its usage and history, and other nuggets of Irish poetic lore. George Calder translated this work from its original Gaelic to English in 1916 under the title *The Scholar's Primer* and this translation became the standard. It's revealing that Graves draws on the *Auraicept* repeatedly in *The White Goddess* and never gives the correct title.

Instead he cites it as a "manual of cryptography" or sometimes incorrectly as *Hearings of the Scholars*. This conflict of titles suggests that Graves bypassed Calder's translation and went directly to the manuscripts, from which Calder worked.

However, Graves's suggestion that the alphabet was invented in Achaea reveals that he did use Calder's translation. Graves claims that Achaea became corrupted to Accad and Dacia in some of the manuscripts (Graves 1993, 237). Calder makes an identical observation in his introduction (Calder xxxiii). Furthermore, chapter seven of *White Goddess* mentions that the Edinburgh copy of the *Auraicept* lists *Salamon* as an alternative name for *Salome* or *Salia*. A footnote in Calder's translation notes the same fact (Calder 20). Lastly, *King Jesus* cites the *Auraicept* as Calder's *Hearings of the Scholars*. For whatever reason, Graves has consulted Calder's translation and consistently substituted *Hearings of the Scholars* for *The Scholar's Primer*. In later works, Graves adds to the mystery by citing Calder's translation by its correct title (Graves 1969, 5).

The *Auraicept*'s theme obviously draws from non-Celtic sources. The central plot revolves around a confused account of the building of the tower of Babel and the resulting confusion of language. Irish Celts used this tale to uphold their belief that the Gaelic language was superior to all others. This belief was difficult to reconcile with biblical claims that Israel was God's chosen people and that language was intentionally confused by God at the tower. Irish intellectuals faced the problem of retaining their oral traditions while simultaneously acknowledging biblical authority. Their solution to this contradiction was not entirely original but did display the usual Celtic love of the fantastic and extravagant.

The *Auraicept* claims that a poet named Fenius Farsaidh, a descendant of Noah, traveled to the plain of Shinar after the tower's collapse. He brought with him seventy-two assistants and together they intended to learn the seventy-two languages, which God had created to confuse men. Fenius intended to merge these languages into a single superior language using the best parts of all known tongues. However, Fenius's students failed to learn the seventy-two languages at Shinar and Fenius dispersed his followers over the world to find and learn these languages. Meanwhile, Fenius founded a school at the fallen tower and awaited their return. Ten years later the seventy-two men returned and Fenius merged their languages into a superior tongue reserved for the elite alone: Gaelic was invented for the Celts. Henceforth, the *Auraicept* depicts Gaelic as a superior language intended to supersede all others. Just as God had formed a covenant with the Jews in Hebrew, he now established a new covenant with the Celts in Gaelic. Hebrew is conveniently disregarded as a language that "some say...the people of heaven had" (Calder 17). Whatever language was spoken in heaven was irrelevant to the authors of the *Auraicept*; Gaelic was superior here on earth.

Furthermore, the *Auraicept* reduces the importance of racial origins and instead stresses the importance of language and culture. The Celts themselves were identified more by their language than their race and they despised the Old Testament notion of a special covenant based on racial membership. Instead, the *Auraicept* supports language as the definition of a people and allows Celts to retain both their language and their loyalty to a Hebrew God. By using language as their connecting point, Irish authors were also able to utilize Latin grammarians and graft their works to earlier ogham traditions.

Obviously, the authors of the *Auraicept* were familiar with biblical themes such as Nimrod's tower. Speculation over when this story reached Ireland is irrelevant. It was current long before the *Auraicept* and we need not wonder that fourteenth century Irish scribes were familiar with it. Conversely, the references to Jewish cabalism are surprising and reveal that Irish poets were in contact with the contemporary Jewish mysticism, which swept across Spain and France from the thirteenth century onward. The belief in a secret oral tradition inherited by Noah's descendants, the school centered around Nimrod's tower, and the recurrence of the number seventy-two all suggest a cabalistic impact on fourteenth century Irish poetry. The *Auraicept's* attempts to derive the Gaelic language from Middle Eastern knowledge indicates a desire to compare Irish oral traditions to Jewish oral teaching of the Torah.

For whatever reason, Graves completely ignores the cabalistic influence within the *Auraicept*. Certainly, the connection occurred to him; he was familiar with cabalistic symbolism by at least 1946. *King Jesus* contains strains of Jewish mysticism and strives to merge ogham to Jewish interpretations of *Ezekiel's* chariot vision. His wide range of reading also reveals Jewish sources such as the *Zohar*, *Talmud*, the visionary *Book of Enoch* and the cabalistic *Steganographia* of Trithemius.

Accepting the cabalism of the *Auraicept* would have strengthened Graves's argument that certain Irish tribes originated in Spain. Spain was one of the world's largest cabalistic centers between the twelfth and thirteenth centuries, during the height of Jewish mysticism. However, confronting the cabalistic material within the *Auraicept* would force Graves to admit the flow of information between Spain and Ireland dated to the high point of the Middle Ages. This effectively ruins his later theory of patriarchal invasions spanning from the Middle East to Ireland before the arrival of Christianity. Instead, Graves depends upon the works of Patrick Joyce and Edmund Spenser to support theories of earlier Irish-Spanish contact.

Next on our list of Celtic sources is David William Nash's 1858 *Taliesin, or, The Bards and Druids of Britain*. The history and legends surrounding the Welsh poet Taliesin is central to *The White Goddess* and Nash's book was the definitive treatment of Taliesin, despite its age. Nash translates over fifty pieces attributed to Taliesin, including *Hanes Taliesin* and *Cad Goddeu*. While Graves never cites Nash's book by its title he does mention Nash repeatedly and we can rest assured that Graves is referring to *Taliesin, or, The Bards and Druids of Britain* any time he cites Nash. It's unclear why Graves refused to mention Nash's book by title, despite his numerous references to the book. One possible reason may be that Nash's ideas on *Cad Goddeu* were damaging to Graves's theory.

Nash questioned the validity of *Cad Goddeu* and believed the importance of Taliesin in Welsh tradition was highly exaggerated. He argued that *Cad Goddeu* and *Hanes Taliesin* were products of the medieval era. These poems dated only to sometime after the twelfth century and contained no conclusive references to ancient druidic religion. Nash argued that the Taliesin poems "probably did not contain the mythological jargon extracted from them by Mr. Davies" (Nash VIII). He further argued that although there may have been an authentic Taliesin in the sixth century virtually none of his works survive and most of what is attributed to him was written by medieval Christian bards as a tribute. He observed that there is roughly 600 years between the era when the Taliesin poems were supposedly written and the earliest surviving copies. Nash also claimed the Welsh bards had no alphabet except the usual Latin and no secret alphabet that linked trees to letters (Nash 234-235).

Nash placed Graves in a difficult position. Graves, under the influence of Edward Davies, sought to prove that Taliesin's material was ancient and did contain druidic beliefs. If Graves could ignore his disagreements with Nash, he could still use his translations to support his own argument. After all, Nash claimed *Cad Goddeu* and *Hanes Taliesin* were written at the same point at which Graves believes someone stumbled onto druidic secrets and began writing under the already established name of Taliesin. Ultimately, Graves was forced to draw only what he could use from Nash and quietly pass over the rest. This may explain why Nash's book is never properly cited.

The above books are the most influential of the Celtic sources behind *The White Goddess*. Other sources are of lesser importance and will be introduced as they arise. Yet, there is another author who deserves attention before turning away from the high profile sources of *The White Goddess*. He wrote no books, which Graves cites directly, but his works have earned him a rather notorious place in the history of Celtic studies.

Edward Williams, who wrote under the name Iolo Morganwg, was a Welsh mystic *par excellence* and had collected an impressive number of rare medieval Welsh manuscripts. He had once written that "the poems of Taliesin in the sixth century exhibit a complete system of Druidism". What he didn't mention was that where he couldn't find this druidic system he would resort to forgery to create it. Morganwg may have been inspired by James Macpherson's Ossianic forgeries of the 1760's. Where Macpherson revived interest in ancient Irish paganism by way of forgery, Morganwg sought to do the same for the Welsh. Morganwg sometimes provided fellow researchers with unique translations from his private collection without producing the original manuscript he claimed to have translated. By concealing both his own works and authentic manuscripts, he made it easier to perpetrate his forgeries. Suspicions arose within his own lifetime and his own son, who himself wrote under the name Taliesin, admitted his father's sources were questionable. Nash implicates Morganwg when he mentions that many Welsh poems have been intentionally translated to support theories of concealed druidism while others have been outright falsified, and even the eccentric Edward Davies provides detailed evidence of Morganwg's forgery (Davies 1809, 33-36). It was always difficult to know when Morganwg drew on authentic sources and when he was resorting to forgery to support his ideas. Any material he contributed, and which couldn't be independently verified, was potentially suspicious.

Morganwg's influence on Celtic studies dates to at least 1792, when he contributed material to Dr. Owen's *Essay on Bardism*. He also contributed to the *Myvyrian Archaiology* and the Guest *Mabinogion*. Just how much of his contribution was forgery is unclear but it's significant that he was a primary source for the later section of Guest's Taliesin chapter.

Undoubtedly, Morganwg's greatest deception was to produce the papers which Rev. Williams Ab Ithel later published as *Barddas*. This two-volume work was subtitled "a collection of original documents, illustrative of the theology, wisdom, and usage of the Bardo-Druidic system of the isle of Britain". Put simply, it was a manual on how to become a bard. Morganwg claimed it was based on authentic medieval manuscripts, some of which preserved ancient oral traditions and some, which were more recent creations by medieval bards. In reality, it was a combination of authentic Welsh manuscripts and earlier forgeries from Morganwg. Morganwg drew from several authentic manuscripts, but fleshed out the system with typical Neoplatonic philosophy of the romantic era. In an attempt to conceal his alterations, he then attributed his forgeries to those bards whose names appear in *Myvyrian Archaiology.*

Nowhere in *The White Goddess* does Graves admit to drawing from *Barddas*, although he does cite other Morganwg material, possibly including those which Morganwg later incorporated into *Barddas*. This material includes a document called *Anthony Powel of Llwydarth's Manuscript*, which offers an alternate version of the Taliesin story. Graves admits that this alternate version may be a late forgery, yet this may not be the only time Graves draws from Morganwg and those other times may have slipped past Graves himself. We are left wondering just how much material Morganwg contributed to *Myvyrian Archaiology* and the Guest *Mabinogion*. Was that material forged too and, if so, was Graves aware that he was drawing indirectly from Morganwg by using it? Lastly, did Graves draw from *Barddas* without acknowledging it? We have no direct evidence but he repeatedly cites information that is found there. These points of agreement are so numerous that it seems likely Graves was familiar with either *Barddas* or Morganwg's earlier poetry book, which contained some of the same material.

After addressing these known sources we enter into a less confident arena and begin to guess at which books *might* have influenced *The White Goddess* despite Graves's failure to mention them. Such speculation is risky but worth pursuing nonetheless. Indeed, there are a few titles missing from the book, which we can almost be sure Graves had read.

Foremost among the absentees is Robert Briffault's 1927 *The*

Mothers. Graves had over twenty years to find *The Mothers* between its first edition and the first edition of *White Goddess* yet he didn't read the book until after starting his *White Goddess* research (Seymour-Smith 1982, 387). The superficial similarities between Graves and Briffault make the absence of *The Mothers* even more impressive: both men had been children of their father's second wife, both had a classical education and were well versed in Latin and Greek, both served in World War 1 and were gassed in France, both loved poetry and did translating work for extra income, both considered their novels potboilers, and both were disciples of James Frazer and Dr. W.H.R. Rivers, the eminent psychologist of their age. Ironically, both came to reject their mother's religious views in order to support their own feminist opinions. Considering that Graves started his feminist line of thought early, it seems he would have met Briffault's book, if not the man himself, at some earlier date.

Briffault's thesis is that the mother and child relationship is the basic social unit of all primitive cultures. He claims this relationship was the original family unit at a time when fatherhood was unrecognized and that all other social units grew from this mother and child relationship. Like Graves, Briffault believes in a prehistoric matriarchy in which women held political and religious power, and which worshiped a great mother goddess. This theory was nothing new. Johann Bachofen had made a similar argument as early as 1861 in his *Das Mutterrecht*, beginning a controversial debate in which Briffault and Graves were latecomers.

Briffault argues that originally only women were allowed to serve in this goddess religion and that its symbolism was tied directly to lunar worship, fertility, and menstruation. In Briffault's prehistoric model, the overthrow of this goddess religion and the substitution of men for women in the priesthood was an early step towards patriarchy. Additionally, Briffault suggests that Hellenic Greece was a matriarchal society and wrote of the relationship between metal smiths and magicians. Both of these were ideas Graves later developed.

Another early feminist book, which Graves fails to mention, is M. Esther Harding's *Women's Mysteries Ancient and Modern*. To the pagan of today, it seems incredible that this book was written in 1935. Even by today's standard the book is impressive and although it isn't a specifically pagan book it serves as an excellent introduction to pagan ideas. Harding examines worldwide lunar myths and uses Jungian methods to reveal their concealed meaning. In Harding's hands, these moon legends deal exclusively with ancient goddess religions and prehistoric matriarchies. In her study, Harding draws from Jung, Briffault, Frazer, Harrison, and Murray. In short, she collects her material from the same usual suspects, which Graves cites. Yet, she doesn't stop there. In a move, which rings more of Yeats than Graves, she also consults Hermetic texts, in particular those translated by G.R.S. Mead, and which have had a significant impact on early occult groups such as the Golden Dawn and Dion Fortune's Fraternity of the Inner Light. Lastly, she cites Jessie Weston, author of *From Ritual to Romance*, a book which inspired T.S. Eliot's *The Waste Land*.

Harding's final product, after intermingling these sources, would have intrigued Graves. She expounds on the link between lunar cycles and menstruation, the significance of a triple goddess, the linking of bull-horns to the crescent moon, and the symbolism of the unicorn. All of these appear in *The White Goddess*. This in itself doesn't prove that Graves read Harding, but proves both authors were pursuing the same subjects within a few years of each other. For now, we can simply state that *The White Goddess* and *Women's Mysteries* deal with nearly identical subject matter.

We'd think that Graves would have read such a book, cited it within *The White Goddess*, and that from there it would become a staple book in pagan circles. Harding's book has become a staple within the more educated pagan groups and has gone on to influence such feminist pagans as Starhawk. However, the story of how Harding became popular with pagans doesn't include Graves. Instead, the book was popular with Charles Seymour, a member of the Fraternity of the Inner Light during the late 1930's. Seymour eventually wrote the inspirational essay *The Old Religion: A Study of the Symbolism used in Woman's Mysteries*. In this essay, Seymour cites our usual suspects. He also includes a triple goddess, prehistoric matriarchies, and images of the Celtic god Cernunnos. He read the same Mead translations of Hermetic texts Harding had read and cites the works of Professor Rhys and Charles Leland. Seymour appreciates the mystical side of the Celtic Revival and was inspired by Yeats's *Celtic Twilight*. Like Harding, he studied Jung and speaks of initiation not as a ritual but as a process of life.

Seymour's essay remained unpublished until 1968, long after the publication of *White Goddess*. However, it circulated within occult circles before this time and it's possible that Gerald Gardner had encountered it. If so then Seymour's work may have contributed to the creation of Wicca. Graves, on the other hand, probably never read Seymour's essay. If he did, it didn't offer anything new to a veteran poet with a classical education.

However, Graves possibly read Harding's *Women's Mysteries*, despite his refusal to cite it. If so Graves's refusal to credit Harding may relate to Harding's use of Jung. Graves detested Jung and had once written, "I am anxious to rescue myth from the ignorant Jungian psychologists" (O'Prey 109). Graves also attacked Jung in his introduction to *The Greek Myths* and was offended when Randall Jarrell had applied Jungian methods to *The White Goddess*. Harding, on the other hand, uses Jung as her primary source and draws from him on nearly every page.

The possibility that Graves read *Women's Mysteries* is enforced by his descriptions of two images. In chapter eleven of *White Goddess*, Graves describes an Assyrian sculpture depicting two goats flanking a stylized tree of thirteen branches. In his description of this image, he also briefly mentions a Babylonian tree image containing five leaves. Graves reveals that both images derive from Felix Lajard's 1847 *Sur la Culte De Mithra*. However, both images also occur in Harding's *Women's Mysteries* on consecutive pages and Harding also credits them to Felix Lajard's work within her caption. The possibility that Graves found these images in Harding's book rather than in Lajard's more scarce 1847 work shouldn't be overlooked. Harding offers both images in a wider collection of images (nine in all) within a chapter titled "Emblems of the Moon" (Harding 179-80). Her scant comments reveal almost nothing regarding the meaning of these images and leaves Graves free to speculate upon them. Graves may have either read Harding's work or simply leafed through the book and became interested in its illustrations.

The possibility that Graves merely studied the illustrations is supported by his similar treatment of other sources, including Cook's three-volume *Zeus*, Sir Arthur Evans's four volume *Palace of Minos*, and *Bilderatlas* by Hans Haas. Repeatedly we notice that where Graves cites Cook there is usually an illustration involved. Graves's mention of the Phrygian bronze votive statue, the Etruscan mirror depicting Ixion, Nemesis's statue, and Europa seated in a willow tree are prime examples (Graves 1993, 63, 173, 197, 255). Evans is only mentioned twice; both times in relation to illustrations, he provides (Graves 1993, 233, 387). Haas appears only once; in relationship to a gemstone described in his work (Graves 1993, 151). The possibility that Graves merely skimmed these books to study artwork is enforced by his interest in mythic icons and his theory of iconotropy. This also explains how Graves consulted these books and fails to discover significant supporting evidence not tied to their illustrations.

Just as surprising is the absence of William Skene's *Four Ancient Books of Wales* (1868). It seems that this would be a primary source for Graves considering that his argument depends so much on Welsh poetry and Graves himself couldn't read Welsh. Skene's book is an English translation of all of the major medieval Welsh poetry, including most of the poetry Graves cites. Skene offers English versions of the poems found in four medieval Welsh manuscripts entitled *The Black Book of Carmarthen*, *The Book of Aneurin*, *The Book of Taliesin*, and *The Red Book of Hergest*. The history of these four manuscripts is beyond the scope of this book and, for the most part, irrelevant to our study, but we should note that any time Graves refers to any of these four manuscripts he could have easily found their translations in Skene. However, it seems that Graves never read Skene's book, or if he did, he attempted to hide the fact. Why Graves would avoid the most complete and popular translations of the very poems he was interested in is unclear.

If Graves had read Skene and refused to mention him, the reason may lie in Skene's theories on the Taliesin material. Skene took the middle ground between the arguments of Edward Davies and William Nash. Skene asserted that Taliesin, Aneurin, and Myrddin were real sixth century people and agreed with Davies that the Taliesin poems were ancient, but he agreed with Nash that they contained no druidic material. Skene had written, "It would probably be difficult to find a stranger specimen of perverted ingenuity and misplaced learning than is contained in the works of Davies" (Skene 8). Interestingly enough, Skene disagrees with Nash's translation of *Cad Goddeu* and the conclusions he drew from the poem, but he felt Davies's druidic ideas were even further from truth than anything Nash suggests. Although Skene believes that *Cad Goddeu* commemorated the alliance of Celtic tribes he believes this union occurred in the fifth century and his theory would never allow Graves to push the subject of the poem back into the first Belgic invasion.

Thus, Graves was placed in a difficult position. He needed to draw from Nash, and perhaps Skene, as part of his research, yet he needed to maintain a position similar to Davies. In the end, Graves draws heavily from Nash, neglects Skene, and refuses to name either of their books. Perhaps Graves was loath to admit he was drawing from sources, which disagreed so strongly with him. He had already confessed to a disagreement with Macalister regarding ogham's age and perhaps he felt that to reveal disagreement with other primary sources would weaken his stance. Admittedly, this is offered only as a tentative suggestion. To suggest that Graves read Skene and then concealed the fact seems unfair. Yet, the *Four Ancient Books* was the most complete edition of these manuscripts at the time and Graves's research would have eventually led to it. Skene's work is referenced in several of Graves's known sources.

So far, we have only addressed those books Graves read or may have read because he agreed with them in some way. But it seems there was at least one book Graves took issue with and which likely influenced his theories. William Butler Yeats's *A Vision* was Yeats's most mystic work, and his most obscure. Like *The White Goddess*, it contained a system of poetic symbolism with highly spiritual overtones. Also like *White Goddess*, it defies simplification or summary, which makes it difficult to deal with in any brief criticism.

A Vision (1925) was an explanation of the underlying beliefs Yeats expressed in his poems. It was a summing up of his symbolism, mythology, and philosophy into a (supposedly) coherent system, which divided mankind into groups based on lunar phases. Yeats claimed that the book was "channeled" by his wife and written in automatic writings, which Yeats later revised. Graves may have been thinking of *A Vision* when he complains of automatic writing and spiritualism (Graves 1993, 441). Yet there is a fine line between Graves's poetic trance and automatic writing, and comparisons between *A Vision* and *The White Goddess* are valid. Graves's insistence that analeptic memory differed from automatic writing may derive from his desire to distance his own poetic trance methods from those of Yeats.

The basic tenets of *A Vision* conflicts with *The White Goddess* in several places and this likely contributed to Graves's dislike of Yeats. Graves disliked Yeats on several grounds but the greatest thing he held against him was Yeats's occultism. Yeats had been a member of the Golden Dawn and had socialized with such men as S. L. MacGregor Matthers and Aleister Crowley. Yeats had also studied Hinduism, which Graves probably considered akin to occultism. Lastly, Yeats had studied various Hermetic texts. *A Vision* contains hints and traces of this study, and sometimes delved into Hermetic symbols such as the unicorn and cosmic egg.

Why Graves rejected Yeats on the grounds of occultism isn't clear. While Graves claimed to detest occultism, he was equally as guilty of it as Yeats and had once even consulted a fortune teller (R. Graves 1995, 203). Graves's interest in the occult was so widely known that occult researcher Colin Wilson visited Graves at Majorca in 1969 and later dedicated his comprehensive study *The Occult* to Graves. Graves was one of the many people who denounced astrology yet continued to read his horoscope and sometimes gave astrological advice to others. He distrusted automatic writing but he believed in the powers of séances and derides Yeats for his "dabbling in spiritualism" (Graves, Hodge 201). *Good-bye to All That* criticizes those who hold séances and while he clearly implies that he disapproves of spiritualism, he also implies his belief in its powers (Graves 1957, 233). Nor did Graves disregard the existence of ghosts, as his poetry and autobiography show.

He mentions in his autobiography that Laufzorn, his Grandfather's manor in Germany, was supposedly haunted and that while he never saw ghosts there he admits to seeing ghosts of dead soldiers during WW1 (Graves 1957, 24,120). In 1918 Graves and his first wife lived in what they claimed was a haunted house where strange sounds and sights were recorded. Nor was this the only haunted home Graves occupied. While living in Egypt he shared a flat with Laura Riding, who claimed the flat was haunted. We can be sure that Graves agreed; a haunted Egyptian flat occurs in *Seven Days*. Graves's interest in ghosts could be traced back to his membership to the Charterhouse debate team, where he debated *against* the existence of ghosts and spirits (R.P. Graves 76). Other works showed his belief in telepathy and suggested that hauntings could be caused by radio waves, magnetic fields, or emotional shock (Graves 1991, 91; Graves 1969, 38, 50). Indeed, Graves admits that he hails from a fairly superstitious family and his shunning of Yeats on occult grounds seems hypocritical in this light.

Yet, there may be another reason Graves detested Yeats: sheer jealously. Yeats had after all, beaten Graves to the punch by writing *Celtic Twilight* shortly before Graves was born. Yeats revived Irish tales of fairy abductions, cattle raids, and wizards long before Graves and this made Graves appear as a latecomer to many. To these people, *The White Goddess* was only a complex rehashing the same mystical Celtic themes that Yeats had explored decades earlier. Although being born in the height of the Celtic Renaissance may have shaped Graves's views, it also meant that his own works would appear too late to ride the wave of interest that earlier writers like Yeats had created. Graves knew this. He had spent his early years under the influence of his father's generation and then, in his late teens and early 20's, struggled to throw off the long shadow they cast over him.

In the end, we have no proof that Graves read *A Vision*, yet he attacks exactly the sort of symbolism it contains. It would seem unusual for Graves to read the most cryptic book by his most hated poet, yet Graves was no fool. It's unlikely that he would dismiss a fellow poet without attempting to understand his position. Incidentally, we know that Graves had read at least some of the Hermetic texts like those Yeats cites because Graves mentions the medieval Hermetic *Book of Lambspring* and Agrippa's *Vanity and Uncertainty of Arts and Sciences* within *The White Goddess*. Considering how Graves deals with images like the cosmic egg and the unicorn in exactly opposite terms of Yeats we must assume that Graves understood Yeats's stance.

CHAPTER IV

EARLIER PAGANS

Regardless of the tremendous impact that *The White Goddess* had on the emerging pagan movement, it would be wrong to assume that Graves created the entire movement alone or that nothing existed before 1948. The term neopagan had been used as early as 1891 to describe romantic authors who drew their inspiration from earlier Greek paganism and a reverence for nature (Hutton 28). Yet, this use of the word is only a faint shadow of the definition given to it by pagans today. There were romantic poets and naturalists before *The White Goddess,* but were there actually people practicing religious beliefs, which could be termed witchcraft or paganism by current definitions?

Interestingly enough, there was a proven increase in occult interest before 1948 and Graves knew it. *The Long Week-End* reveals that the National Laboratory for Psychical Research was founded in 1925 to study psychic phenomena. Spiritualism was a common topic of the British *Daily Mail* and was frequently attacked by the church (Graves, Hodge 59, 116, 287). In the same book, Graves also mentions the popularity of occult authors Sax Rohmer (Arthur S. Ward), Ouspensky, and Gudjieff, and attacks the "theosophical incoherence" of Madame Blavatsky (Graves, Hodge 50, 197, 203). Graves may not have been intimately familiar with these authors but his research for *The Long Week-End* meant that he was at least marginally aware of some of the best-known occultists before 1948. Aleister Crowley, Dion Fortune, Helena Blavatsky, and the groups they created or joined all predate Graves's entrance into pagan culture.

Crowley's *Magick in Theory and Practice,* reveals exactly what sort of occult books were available at the time and the appendix reveals that Crowley was required to draw heavily from Eastern spiritual works. The lack of quality Western material forced him to utilize Western fiction instead. The first reading course Crowley suggests contains Eastern titles such as *The Yi King, Tao the King, The Upanishads, Bhagavad-Gita, The Shiva Sanhita,* and *The Dhammapada* (Crowley 209-10). Following this Crowley offers a secondary reading list of "books, principally fiction, of a generally suggestive and helpful kind". This list contains more Western sources, but relies primarily on fiction and poetry. The list includes Pope's *Rape of the Lock,* Stoker's *Dracula,* Malory's *Le Morte d'Arthur,* and works by Lewis Carroll, Arthur Machen, Shakespeare, and Blake (Crowley 212-14).

Despite the lack of good source material, there was a genuine, grass roots pagan movement struggling alongside the more esoteric groups founded by Crowley, Fortune, and Blavatsky. In New York, Russian immigrant Gleb Botkin founded the Church of Aphrodite in 1938. Botkin regularly preached tenets of goddess worship to about fifty church members and further expounded his beliefs in a handful of novels written in the late 1930s (Adler 233-234). Aidan Kelly provides evidence of a pagan group called the Harpy coven as early as 1932 and suggests that other pagan groups existed in Kentucky, New York, Alabama, Georgia, and California (Kelly 21-24). Yet Kelly depends upon secondhand accounts and questions their accuracy.

Additionally, Ronald Hutton mentions John Williams, who came forward in 1996 to claim he belonged to a group on the island of Mons who worshiped Gwydion symbolized by a stone head. Williams claimed his group had 1200 members who were lead by priestesses commonly regarded as witches. Via independent research, Hutton concluded that Williams did belong to an occult group founded sometime in the early twentieth century (Hutton 303-305). Hutton also recounts the foundation of youth groups such as the Boy Scouts and Woodcraft Indians and reveals the pagan bias behind their "back to nature" teachings. As early as 1921, one Woodcraft group had celebrated the Celtic holiday of Lughnasadh in a ritual circle complete with central fire and typical Neoplatonic symbolism.

Before *White Goddess,* books on authentic Western paganism were scarce and those on witchcraft in particular were little more than lurid tales of impossible black magic or repetitive accounts drawn from testimony of medieval witch trials. Such books were written by the credulous and marketed towards the uneducated who thrilled to ghost stories and accounts of torture. There was little, if any, true paganism recorded in them. The only possible exceptions to this rule were the works of Margaret Murray, whose ideas were so radical that they must be considered separately.

The oldest examination of witchcraft Graves cites is Joseph Glanvill's 1689 *Saducismus Triumphatus.* This, Glanvill's most famous work, is a defense of typical witchcraft beliefs. Glanvill attempts to prove the existence of witches and thereby establish the existence of Satan. This, in turn, implies the existence of God. In short, Glanvill attempts to prove the existence of God via the reality of witches. This was no new argument and had appeared as early as 1484 in *Malleus Maleficarum.* Indeed, the *Malleus* states that a disbelief in witches implied a rejection of the spiritual world and therefore a rejection of God. Glanvill, using similar logic, attempted to bring people to God by attesting the reality of witchcraft. Unfortunately for Glanvill, his arguments are contradictory and he often pleads ignorance regarding the supernatural as an excuse to relieve himself of further explanation. *The White Goddess* cites *Saducismus Triumphatus* only once and it's possible that Graves only knew the work secondhand from similar citations in Murray's books (Murray 1996, 89).

Most witchcraft books before Murray were of the Glanvill type. They included alleged satanic pacts, ghosts, werewolves, and supernatural legends. Popular witchcraft tales often involved the occurrence of strange or ironic events, which the author claims were foretold years in advance by either a famous seer such as Mother Shipton or that staple character of tabloids, Nostradamus. Such tales were second only to the more lurid accounts of the alleged black mass and the ritual sexual abuse of young virgins. Such stories have little relation to pagan definitions of witchcraft but do serve as a gauge to popular opinion on the subject at the time of Graves's writing.

Before the 1940's books on witchcraft reinforced these negative images and few authors beyond Murray suggested that witchcraft contained any truly religious concepts. Before Murray witchcraft was an elusive term used to label a wide range of supernatural occurrences taken from various cultures and eras. This witchcraft literature roamed the world and spanned the years between Virgil's *Aeneid* and the Salem witch trials. The very definition of witchcraft was vague and included nearly any supernatural event falling beyond the commonly accepted religion practiced at that time, in that location. Medieval Christians defined witchcraft differently than ancient Greek pagans yet both agreed that it was something sinister and beyond the norms of their culture. Basically, witchcraft was any unexplained and undesired supernatural experience and witches were anyone who intentionally courted such experiences.

In reality, "witchcraft" was an umbrella term, which applied to such a wide range of actions and beliefs that it was nearly worthless as a label. It completely failed to describe those actions to which it was applied and merely created a spurious connection between unrelated rituals or traditions. However, the church, being hostile to (or ignorant of) these traditions merely lumped them together under the label of witchcraft. The resulting admixture of beliefs and practices was not a true religion. It was merely a Frankenstein's collection of dismembered traditions and pagan religions of an earlier era. There was no cohesive belief or theology between these traditions.

Murray narrowed the scope of witchcraft by focusing only on medieval European trials. To her, witches were Europeans who practiced either a satanic rejection of Christianity or a surviving form of paganism. Her works helped reinforce the stereotypical image of the witch as a white European female who rode a broom and stirred a cauldron. This allowed Graves to postulate his own link between Celtic paganism and European witchcraft and also set the stage for Gardner's *Witchcraft Today* and enabled Gardner to elaborate on both Murray and Graves.

However, Murray's theories of a secret witch-cult didn't immediately catch on. In the early 1940's, both Charles Williams and William Seabrook published books entitled *Witchcraft*. Williams mentions all the cliché arguments of witch trial historians including accusations from children and confessions taken under torture or from the mental ill. He summarizes the best-known witchcraft trials including Dame Alice Kyteler, Major Weir, and the Salem incident. He neither supports or denies Murray's theories and makes only a single mention of her works (Williams 1971, 112). Overall, Williams's book is a rehashing of common occult themes, which adds nothing to the pagan revival.

Seabrook fares slightly better in his attempts to prove that witchcraft survives in Europe and America. Repeatedly, he offers personal observations taken from his travels and recounts tales of black magic in Europe, America, and Africa. Yet his stories read more like tabloid sensationalism. He cleverly conceals vital facts in an attempt to protect his sources but readers suspect that he's also creating a smoke screen allowing him to exaggerate his tales beyond credibility. Nearly a fourth of Seabrook's *Witchcraft* is devoted to vampires and werewolves and the remainder examines black magic and Satanism among the jet set, with which he associated. In all, his witchcraft looks nothing like that presented by Murray, Graves, or Gardner. It's possible that Graves read Seabrook's *Witchcraft*, but if so it seems to have had little impact on either Graves's work or the development of Wicca.

Although criticizing authors such as Williams and Seabrook is easy, we should remember that Murray's works were equally flawed. Her suggestion that witchcraft was a lingering pagan cult is historically weak and depended heavily on a handful of carefully selected trial documents. Her study focused on certain localized outbreaks of

witch persecution. From these isolated instances, she created gener-
alizations about European witchcraft as a whole. Rossell Hope
Robbins calls Murray's works "speculative and unscholarly"
(Robbins 558). Earlier works to undercut Murray included Elliot
Rose's *A Razor for a Goat,* Norman Cohn's *Europe's Inner Demons,* and
works by Adler and Luhrmann.

Not surprisingly, the publication of *White Goddess* and Gardner's
Witchcraft Today helped increase acceptance of Murray's witch-cult
theory despite the fact that neither Graves nor Gardner offered any
fresh evidence. Instead, they postulated what Murray's witch-cult
might have been like in the past and suggested what witchcraft may
become in the future. By doing so, they gave a flesh and blood image
to Murray's theory and made it appear more possible without
offering any new proof.

What is most noticeable to readers is the lack of actual religion in
Murray's witch-cult. To Murray, witchcraft is a cult in the most
derogatory sense and she depicts witches as cultists who are no
longer sure exactly what their religion entails. Murray suggests that
the witch-cult was in a constant state of decay and fails to explain
any of its finer theological points or ethical issues. She depicts
witches blindly worshiping a horned god whom they know to be
only a man in a mask and their requests to him involve mainly
wishes for a good harvest, health, and wealth. Alternately, Murray's
witches occasionally pray for evil to strike their enemies. In the
lowest state of their decay, witches actually perform mundane acts
of rebellion such as stomping down crops and destroying bridges.
We seldom see a real religion within Murray's witch-cult.

Once Graves and Gardner had elaborated on Murray's theories,
other authors joined the debate. Few of these authors were trained
historians. Finally, after years of rejection by expert historians,
Murray's theories were winning popularity with the average reader.
The fact that her theories were shunned by historians and
championed by lay readers only increased their acceptance in the
pagan revival. Many witchcraft authors realized the schism between

experts and lay readers and tried to pander to both crowds. Popularizers such as Seth, Tindall, and Holtzer openly discredited Murray but their own subsequent conclusions revealed that they retained large portions of her model.

Ultimately, we see that there were a handful of people practicing paganism before *White Goddess,* and even before *Witch-Cult.* Yet, their pagan practices were widely divergent. They drew from many non-European sources and from witchcraft stereotypes, which extended beyond the Middle Ages. Murray and Graves redefined witchcraft into a religion with an actual theology, which offered something of value to the modern seeker standing outside of Jewish or Christian belief. Murray formed the goddess from the primordial myth, Graves breathed life into her, and Gardner became her first high priest.

Thus, Graves's impact on later pagan literature is proven; but what impact did early pagan literature have on Graves before 1948? Was Graves an outsider who assured his place in pagan history with *White Goddess,* or was he firmly entrenched in pagan literature before the 1940's? Graves had already read Murray and Davies, but these were historical works with possible religious interpretations. Did Graves also read Crowley, Fortune, or any other occult authors?

Graves's rejection of occultism and his dislike of Yeats on occult grounds suggests a negative answer. Yet, Graves wasn't wholly ignorant of occult literature. He specifically cites the Hermetic *Book of Lambspring.* Superficially, Graves's mention of this book appears to be a casual reference but deeper investigation of *Lambspring* reveals something else.

The *Book of Lambspring* is a late sixteenth century Hermetic text, which became popular with Hermetic students by 1625. Such Hermetic texts were inspired by earlier Greek and Latin texts which expressed philosophical themes of the early Roman Empire, and which were commonly attributed to Hermes Trismegistus. Many authors, including Davies, dated these works as contemporaneous with Moses. Most of these texts actually dated to about the fourth century AD and are Neoplatonic in philosophy. As they became popular in medieval Europe, late imitations such as the *Book of Lambspring* surfaced. Many of these Hermetic books addressed religious and philosophical problems in obscure allegories dealing with fantastical creatures or attempts to turn lead to gold.

As these books became more obscure the allegory was forgotten by less observant readers. The result was many Hermetic students who took these texts literally and descended from philosophy to the more occult pursuit of alchemy. Many readers became sidetracked into actual experiments of obtaining eternal life or turning lead into gold. Graves had attacked these occultists in a 1927 essay and again in *White Goddess*. Later Hermetic texts catered to this crowd, sometimes ignoring religious or philosophical problems entirely to focus on ritual magic. The problem was compounded further when authors began to use these chemical experiments as allegory for spiritual problems, and thus the symbolism had run full circle. The result was a collection of enigmatic books, some being complex spiritual allegories and others lost amid misunderstandings, ritual, and hocus-pocus.

While *Lambspring* is a sixteenth century text, it seems to retain the original philosophical slant and has not descended into alchemy. The book contains fifteen allegorical images, their accompanying captions, and poetry. It's interesting that Graves read such a book. Its mystical images, poetry, and extreme allegories all relate to his views on religious symbolism.

Graves particularly cites the third image of the book, which depicts a unicorn and a deer peacefully meeting in a forest. The caption reads, "Hear without terror that in the forest are hidden a deer and an unicorn". The accompanying poetry says:

The Sages say truly
That two animals are in this forest:
One glorious, beautiful, and swift,
A great and strong deer;

The other an unicorn.

They are concealed in the forest,

But happy shall that man be called

Who shall snare and capture them.

The Masters shew you here clearly

That in all places

These two animals wander about in forests

(But know that the forest is but one).

If we apply the parable to our Art,

We shall call the forest the Body.

That will be rightly and truly said.

The unicorn will be the Spirit at all times.

The deer desires no other name

But that of the Soul; which name no man shall take away from it.

He that knows how to tame and master them by Art,

To couple them together,

And to lead them in and out of the forest,

May justly be called a Master.

From the poetry, Graves correctly identifies the unicorn and deer as spirit and soul. The message of *Lambspring* is that the student must reconcile both spirit and soul within himself. To many readers these terms are fairly synonymous and the lesson's meaning becomes obscure at best. Thankfully, we are not as concerned with the original meaning as we are with Graves's interpretation.

Graves reinterprets both the unicorn and his horn. To him the horn symbolizes the linking line between the earthly king and the zenith or central point of the heavens. This stresses the king's divine link to the other world and his dominion over our world through his divine right. Further associations of the unicorn in *White Goddess* include "immortality-through-wisdom" (Graves 1993, 255). This immortality is poetic immortality and comes only through wisdom and spiritual integrity. This recalls the belief held by many romantic poets that only a morally good person is able to write good poetry.

Thus, to Graves the unicorn represented unblemished purity of thought and deed. This purity allowed the sacred king to rule and poets to gain eternal life through the spiritual act of writing poetry.

Other meanings of the unicorn are dismissed by Graves as unsatisfactory, including the meaning given in *Lambspring* and the Bible. The unicorn symbolizing spirit as separate from soul is dismissed as worthless Hermetic musings. Graves paints a negative picture of these Hermetic students by claiming their system was patched over with misunderstood fragments of true bardic tradition.

Notice that Graves fully understands the allegory of *Lambspring* and refutes it anyway. This is not a typical case of a modern reader becoming confused with Hermetic symbolism and dismissing it all as mumbo-jumbo. Graves understands the intended meaning, Hermetic symbolism, alchemical experiments, and the date of the book itself. This implies that he has done more than a casual reading of Hermetics. Exactly how this reading influenced *The White Goddess* is revealing.

The three most significant animals mentioned in *The White Goddess* are dog, roebuck, and lapwing. Graves argues for a connection between the roebuck and unicorn and in the end, their symbolism is synonymous. Nor is the unicorn the only one of Graves's three animals mentioned in *Lambspring*. Plate five of the book depicts a dog fighting a wolf and the message of the text is similar to that of the deer and unicorn: internal unification. Later images include two birds fighting in midair. Interestingly enough, the text reads:

In India there is a most pleasant wood,
In which two birds are bound together.
One is of a snowy white; the other is red.
They bite each other, and one is slain
And devoured by the other.
Then both are changed into white doves,
And of the Dove is born a Phoenix,

Which has left behind blackness and foul death,

Several features stand out in both the image and the text. Notice that one bird is "snowy white" while the other is red. These birds combine to form a phoenix: "Which has left behind blackness and foul death". This combination of red, white, and black is typical of Celtic mythology and although *Lambspring* isn't a Celtic tale it's unlikely that Graves missed the three colors of the Celtic other world in this passage. *Lambspring*'s symbolic treatment of the unicorn, dog, and red and white birds likewise caught Graves's eye. Lastly, we encounter the phoenix, a bird Graves deals with in chapter twenty-three, immediately after the unicorn.

Is there further reason for Graves's interest in this work? Starting with image eleven, *Lambspring* tells the story of an "old father of Israel, Who has an only Son" and the spiritual guide who the father assigns to the son. The father, son, and guide become a male trinity and *Lambspring* says of them, "Know that the three are body, soul and spirit". After a series of travels the son and guide return home to the father who, in an extreme case of allegory, swallows the son whole. Next, the father falls sick and awaits the rebirth of his son through his own body. The father prays to God for assistance and then the text claims, "There is now a glorified and beautiful Father, And he brings forth a new Son". The power of a male trinity and prayers to a male god allow a father to give rebirth to his son without female intervention. Yet, "The Son ever remains in the Father, And the Father in the Son". The implication is that the father and son have both undergone a spiritual rebirth through this process and the final image of *Lambspring* is of the father, son, and the guide sitting on thrones and laughing at death.

Is it any wonder that Graves was offended by this book? Beneath the surreal images of unicorns, fighting birds and cannibalism is an allegorical story of spiritual rebirth based on the all male trinity of Christianity. The underlying message is that man can reach spiritual perfection without female intervention. No mention of woman is made throughout the book and even images of birth are ridiculously attributed to man. The concept that man is spiritually and physically self-sufficient contradicts the story of Taliesin's rebirth from Caridwen and assuredly offended Graves's feminist viewpoint; he explicitly attacks the idea of male conception in chapter nine of *White Goddess*. In conclusion, Graves may have felt obligated to address the images in *Lambspring*. They were too offensive for him to pass over silently. He was bound to liberate the dog, deer, and unicorn from *Lambspring's* patriarchal and philosophical viewpoint.

CHAPTER V

ICONOTROPY EXPLAINED

Although *The White Goddess* contains many tangled threads, the main thesis of poetic language has already been stated. This is the keystone to the entire book as well as much of Graves's other works. He argues that this language was corrupted by invaders from central Asia who changed the myths from matriarchal to patriarchal systems. These invaders intentionally altered or misinterpreted the myths, symbols, and rituals to reflect their male views of divinity. This is the process that Graves termed *iconotropy* and it plays a large role in *The White Goddess* and Graves's later works.

Graves first introduced the idea of iconotropy in his 1946 *King Jesus* and retained the theory for use in later works such as *The White Goddess* and *The Greek Myths*. It was in *King Jesus* that Graves first defined the term by labeling it "deliberate misinterpretation of an ancient set of ritual icons" (Graves 1984, 423). When defining iconotropy in chapter twelve of *The White Goddess,* Graves refers readers back to his comments in *King Jesus* and explains that iconotropy twists the meanings of icons to give myths new relevance. This change is usually one from matriarchy to patriarchy and Graves had suggested as early as *Hercules* that all images of the goddess had been misunderstood by later pagans. Upon publishing *The Greek Myths,* Graves admitted that not all examples of iconotropy were intentional and accidental misinterpretation of images or rituals could be just as disastrous as willful corruption. After introducing the term in *King Jesus*, Graves increasingly depends on iconotropy to explain why his own ideas deviate from popular opinion. Iconotropy plays a small part in *King Jesus*, a considerably larger part in *The White Goddess*, and finally, it dominates nearly every myth within *The Greek Myths*, until Graves is finally free to recreate ancient Greece based on his own model.

Graves believes in a double or hidden meaning in nearly every myth or poem he reads. *Cad Goddeu* and *Hanes Taliesin* are only two examples. Others exist throughout *White Goddess* and also appear in his other works, especially *The Greek Myths*. Exactly why Graves believed in this hidden history of religion, traces partly back to his own shaken religious beliefs. When Graves was demobilized from the Welch Fusiliers he favored agnosticism and only the idea of Jesus as a perfected man and a few ideas from classical Greek and Roman paganism kept him religious at all. He claimed that organized religion was incapable of addressing the intense emotional and spiritual problems of reality. Yet he realized that Greek, Roman, and Celtic paganism, and even Christianity, had served their cultures well for generations. Thus, he postulates that each of these religions had its own past golden age but had since fallen. Their downfall was due to their inability remain contemporary and the falling educational standards of the followers.

This ignorance led to iconotropy. Iconotropy may be intentional or accidental but it eventually implies that a few elite followers may intentionally conceal the true religious ideas within contemporary myths and poetry. Of course, to Graves, these elite were poets and therefore he was qualified to disentangle the iconotropy and reveal the true meanings. As unlikely as this sounds, it provided Graves with immense comfort to think that modern poets could still find spiritual value in old mythologies, even if they required deeper digging to reach it.

For our purposes, iconotropy can be defined as the accidental or intentional misinterpretation of mythic or religious symbolism in order to uphold a competing mythic or religious idea. Put simply, it is the perversion of one group's myths to suit another group's needs. Also guilty of this crime are the Greek philosophers such as Socrates who favored logic over myth, hence Graves's attacks on Socrates' school.

Graves argues that Greek and Roman philosophers are partly

responsible for the corruption of mythology from its pure state. Davies had suggested as early as 1804 that the mythologies of Greece and Rome were so confused that even ancient writers were sometimes unable to explain them and philosophers felt justified in rejecting mythical traditions. By 1911 Albrecht Dieterich had concluded that the downfall of Olympian paganism happened in part because of the rise of Greek philosophy and Cook mentions that "philosophers and sophists" offended the common Greeks with their views (Cook 1: 165; 2: 2). However, this is unlikely. Despite the number of philosophers remembered today, we must realize that at the time of their writing educated philosophers were a minority and their works had little impact on paganism. Most of them studied philosophical concepts that the average Greek or Roman couldn't understand, let alone evaluate. The pagans of classical Greece weren't like today's pagans who study history, philosophy, and theology. Classical Greeks followed their pagan cults mainly out of tradition, fear of punishment, and hope for material success, mostly in the form of a good harvest. Their education was limited and the lofty ideas that philosophers addressed hardly changed their age-old pattern of worship and belief. Basically, the common man's argument for tradition was stronger than the philosopher's argument for higher education and more meaningful theology. It also seems that in Greece the link between mythology and pagan ritual wasn't as strong as in other pagan cultures. This allowed philosophers to criticize mythology while remaining loyal to the pagan cults that taught religious ritual and the theological concepts behind them.

Evidence of this comes from those philosophers and historians who discredited mythology but whom themselves were members of pagan mystery cults. Plutarch, a philosopher, historian, and priest of Isis, is a prime example. He found no conflict in these three positions. To him, his duties to Isis and his loyalty to Plato coincided perfectly. Upon the death of his young daughter, he comforted his wife with lessons drawn from Dionysus's mysteries, despite claiming that most people didn't believe these myths. Plato himself spoke against cult aspects of pagan religion, but was considered "out of tune" with his times and his philosophy was unpopular with the masses during his lifetime. Neither he, nor Pythagoras had significant impact on pagan cults (Lane-Fox 70, 88, 96). The fact that the temple of Delphi employed Platonic philosophers as prophets in the third and fourth centuries reveals that philosophy clearly meshed with pagan religion of the time. Roman examples of such philosophers and priests include Marcus Aurelius whose Stoic philosophy did not prohibit his belief in an afterlife. This dual approach was revived in Europe during the fifteenth and sixteenth centuries with the rediscovery of the Hermetic texts. Giordano Bruno confessed that he sometimes wrote his philosophical poetry from a trance state and saw no conflict with being both philosopher and poet.

It has been suggested that philosophy actually contributed to pagan religion rather than degrade it. Harrison repeatedly lumps poets and philosophers together as if to imply that they worked together to create the Greek mythos (Harrison 285, 396, 508). Some philosophers may have considered myths as allegory and spoken of the existence of a single all-powerful god, but they still respected the individual's right to join multiple cults. By the mid third century, public officials were still being commemorated in inscriptions as both poets and philosophers, and by the fourth century Constantine was attacking the corrupting influence of both philosophers and poets in the same public speech. If poetry and philosophy were indeed separate languages, then a great many people were fluent in both. In the end, philosophers may have driven more people into paganism by raising disturbing theological questions.

In reality, it's this unity of pagan poetry and philosophy that Graves resents. While the merger of poetry and philosophy do date to classical times, it's only logical to assume that there was a time when myth and pagan poetry existed devoid of any deeper philosophy. The question isn't did philosophy corrupt mythology in classical times. The question Graves asks is how far back must we go to find mythology without philosophy. If it can be shown that philosophy and paganism merged in classical times with little consequence, then Graves is determined to search for "true poetry" in an even more remote age.

In doing so, Graves echoes Harrison's claim that classical mythology of Greece and Rome was late and superimposed over a more primitive and chthonic paganism. It's this time frame, in man's most remote and darkest prehistory, that poetry was not yet corrupted by philosophy. However, in order to find this point, Graves has taken readers back to man's most savage period. Myths were taken literally and poetry was a vivid and thriving oral tradition, but men lived in constant fear of natural forces, and sacrificed each other to ensure a meager subsistence through hunting and gathering.

Graves claims that the origins of poetry lie in the rituals of this matriarchal age and that this is the era in which poets were most respected. We've already seen our usual suspects support the theory of such an age and place it in the furthest prehistory of mankind. In chapter twenty-five of *White Goddess*, Graves states that nobody can hope to understand poetry unless they have had visions of this primitive matriarchal age in which entranced dancers circle their victims while screaming for blood. Clearly, Graves wishes to push poetry back into a time when it was a passionate, emotional art without the overindulgence of intellectual reflection, which has become associated with modern poets.

Surely, Graves doesn't suggest a return to this lifestyle, but he does favor a stripping away of some of the niceties of modern civilization in order to return to a more emotional, intuitive lifestyle. Philosophers who spend time thinking about life instead of living it are despised for destroying the earlier mystery religions. In *The Long Week-End*, Graves implies that the church had been in decline since the fifteenth century astronomer Copernicus advanced his heliocentric model and proved that the earth circled the sun. The acceptance of the Copernican system destroyed man's mystical appreciation of the universe and undermined the maxim "as above, so below", which had helped man connect the microcosm and macrocosm. The Copernican model damaged poetic mysteries as well by effectively killing various Hermetic and cabalistic views it drew from. The implication seems to be that Graves favors a return to earlier fifteenth century mysticism to rid man of the "crouching feeling of insignificance" imposed after Copernicus (Graves, Hodge 97).

Because of the ruinous effects of patriarchal invaders and classical philosophers, the mythic language Graves favors endured in only a few places. Eleusis, Corinth, and Samothrace all supported pagan mystery religions that taught this mythic language. After the early Christian emperors prohibited these cults, the same beliefs and language survived in druidic, and later bardic, colleges of Wales and Ireland. It also lasted in the witch covens of Europe. Outside of these sources, most early matriarchal mythology and the poetic language it inspired was lost in a sea of overwhelming iconotropy.

While Graves's theory of iconotropy does contain some valid points, it's weakened by his underlying assumptions. The idea that mythology has been corrupted, sometimes intentionally, by outsiders is valid. The belief that the "pure" state of mythology derives from a worldwide, prehistoric, matriarchal culture is not. Historians had already abandoned this theory by the 1940's and our usual suspects had fallen out of favor with the academic world. Their works remained popular with the general public mainly because of the delay between academic acceptance of a new model and the public's acceptance of the same idea.

In all fairness to Graves, there is much evidence that goddess worship predates other forms of paganism in many cultures. Despite his faults, Frazer did manage to prove that a large number of goddess related concepts have survived in many European cultures. The problem lies in trying to use this evidence to support the more untenable possibility of prehistoric matriarchies. Goddess worship and political matriarchies do not necessarily go hand in hand. Either can easily exist without the other.

Additionally, many supporters of matriarchal theories are not content with proving the existence of small, localized prehistoric matriarchies. Instead, they speculate on worldwide matriarchies, which unite far flung civilizations which never directly contacted each other. These theories quickly come to resemble the mythic golden age of peace and world unity under a single political and religious system. If the advancement of mankind as a whole in any way resembles the growth of the individual human, then this is the legend of mankind's infancy in which all people were cared for and lived under the rule of a single Great Mother. In supporting this theory, Graves is guilty of iconotropy just as much as the patriarchal religions he attacks. Depending upon worldwide matriarchal paganism to explain similarities between distant pagan cultures is akin to those biblical historians such as Davies who used the lost tribes of Israel to explain similarities between pagan worship and Old Testament religion.

To understand this we must grasp the two-fold nature of iconotropy. First, there is the criteria Graves uses to decide which myths suffer from iconotropy and which do not. Secondly, there is Graves's explanation of how iconotropy influenced those myths, which he claims it has corrupted. What we discover is that Graves decides which myths suffer from iconotropy and then decides exactly how they suffer. Basically, Graves creates his own criteria, applies it to the myths he wishes to debunk, and finally explains how this myth could have been twisted. Put bluntly, Graves decides how he would like to change a myth to better support his theory and then postulates why the myth doesn't already resemble his desired version.

According to this logic, certain types of myths are considered more pure than others and those passing the test are those expressing elements of goddess worship or female power. Those, which deny female divinity, are labeled as corrupt and resolved. For example, the birth of Athena fully grown from the head of Zeus could never be considered a pure myth because it implied that men could reproduce without female intervention and that the goddess of wisdom sprouted from male intellect. Graves calls this version of the myth "monstrous" (Graves 1993, 231). Conversely, the myth of Demeter and Core is exactly the sort that Graves considers pure. It depicts an earth goddess traversing the underworld to rescue her daughter and bring back fertility in a way that is associated with the passing of the seasons and it involves Core, Demeter, and Hecate as the three aspects of the triple goddess.

A strong feminist theme also motivated Graves to reinterpret the myth of Tereus and Procne in chapter twenty-four. This example, like the biblical example of iconotropy Graves cites in chapter eighteen, depends on the alleged existence of not a single image, but an entire series. This series of supposedly lost images became the foundation to the myth of Tereus, who raped and mutilated his sister-in-law Philamela.

The traditional myth claims that Tereus, son of Ares, had married Procne but secretly desired her younger sister Philamela. Tereus then invited Philamela back to his own home, where she could be reunited with her sister. On the voyage home, Tereus created a story of the death of Procne. Philamela, believing her sister dead, was easily pressured into marriage with Tereus as a substitute for her dead sister. Tereus ravished Philamela to his content then cut out her tongue and imprisoned her in a tower. Upon returning home, he informed Procne that her sister had died on the journey. While locked in the tower, Philamela secretly wove a tapestry, which brutally depicted her rape and mutilation by Tereus. She then sent the tapestry to Procne, who immediately understood the truth.

Procne slipped Philamela out of the tower and home with herself. Together they plotted revenge on Tereus. They killed his son Itys, cooked him, and Procne served him to Tereus for dinner. After he had finished the meal, Procne told him the truth and both she and her sister fled their home; Tereus pursuing with an ax. In the traditional (and nonsensical) ending, they were all changed into birds by the gods. Procne became the nightingale, who sings a sad song. Philamela became the swallow, who can hardly sing at all. Tereus supposedly became a hawk but Graves draws on another tradition, which claims he became a hoopoe, a bird often confused with the lapwing.

Graves argues that the entire myth is based on a series of icons, which the Phoenician Greeks misunderstood. This series, which Graves claims was lost, supposedly depicted various methods of divination used by the Pelasgians. Most of the methods described by Graves relate to other aspects of *The White Goddess* but only two deserve our attention.

First is the chewing of laurel leaves in much the same way Graves believes the Bassarids chewed ivy to induce trance. Graves first suggests the Bassarids possibly chewed ivy for its intoxicating effect in the last half of chapter ten. While Graves suggests that the Bassarids *may* have chewed ivy, Frazer leaves no doubt that they did (Frazer 109). Graves's hesitation to attribute ivy chewing to the Bassarids is one of the few instances where he shies away from Frazer's conclusions. However, based on the same Frazer passage Graves agrees that pagan priestesses also chewed laurel.

The second interesting divination method is the casting of sticks onto a white cloth as Tacitus claims the Germani had done and Herodotus credits to the Scythians. The I Ching is a similar system, with which Graves had experimented, and this probably explains his desire to include a similar method into his catalog of early divination methods.

Graves's subtle techniques of iconotropy appear again in his interpretation of the Paleolithic painting from Cogul, found in *The God of the Witches*. Murray claims this image depicts a male leading a group of female dancers. The male has unusual protrusions from his lower legs, which Murray claims are some sort of garter or strings to signify his rank in the cult. This interpretation is questionable but Graves carries it to the breaking point. Pushing farther than Murray would have dared, Graves claims that the central male figure is

Dionysus standing amid his female worshipers What Murray labeled as only garters or strings, Graves now claims as boots laced to the knee. The triangular shape of the female heads entices him to say that the women are wearing pointed witch hats and what appear to be sagging breasts on the leftmost females suggest to Graves three elderly crones. When viewing the original image the unbiased reader has difficulty justifying Graves's fantastic description.

Closely allied to Graves's treatment of the Cogul painting is his interpretation of the 1639 pamphlet *Robin Goodfellow, his mad pranks and merry gests*, where an ithyphallic Robin is depicted as part man, part goat. Robin holds a broom over one should and eleven dancers circle him. The total number of attendants is thirteen when we count Robin himself and a nearby musician. Like the cave painting of Cogul, Graves may have first discovered this image in *The God Of The Witches*. Murray implies that this version of Robin is a more recent expression of the ancient horned god of Cogul. Graves, following her lead, agrees completely.

Murray's treatment of this image is entirely unfair. She compares the image of Robin Goodfellow and his friends to the dancers of the Cogul painting and implies a direct continuation of ritual circle dancing held around an anthropomorphic male. She ignores that this pamphlet is a work of light comedy and its depiction of the witches sabbat and Robin Goodfellow are based upon popular misconceptions of the time. The title page clearly declares the pamphlet to be "full of honest mirth, and is a fit medicine for melancholy". The pamphlet is one of the countless broadsheets and broadsides containing humorous poems and ballads, which Graves believes contributed to the death of bardism.

How did Graves arrive at his theory of iconotropy? As we've already seen, he didn't create his argument or supporting evidence out of thin air. Everything needed to arrive at the theory of iconotropy was already existent before 1948 and as early as 1786, Richard Knight had suggested a similar process had corrupted the myths of Apollo. Perhaps what is surprising is the underlying assumption that there is a single correct way to read myth to begin with.

Ultimately, iconotropy is a variation upon earlier theories of syncretism or the constant reinterpretation of religious beliefs by outsiders, and the definition of religious syncretism strikes very close to Graves's definition of iconotropy. This syncretism applies to the treatments given to myth, ritual, and artwork and therefore includes Graves's definition of "deliberate misinterpretation of an ancient set of ritual icons". Iconotropy could be considered a specific subdivision of religious syncretism. When this syncretism corrupts artwork (rather than ritual or myth) it becomes iconotropy. Viewed in this light we see that iconotropy has existed for centuries and even the complaints of Richard Knight and Edward Davies were late by comparison. Caesar is guilty of exactly this sort of religious syncretism when he reinterprets Celtic deities in light of his own Roman beliefs.

Why did Graves believe that each myth only has a single correct interpretation? A look at his sources provides some clues. Davies's *Celtic Researches* complains that Greek and Roman poets have left us a mass of confusing material written in a highly figurative language and mixed with allegory and fable. Davies laments that our under-standing of their works will be forever distorted by innumerable interpretations. Likewise, *Lambspring* is written in extreme allegories, which Graves felt driven to refute. Other allegorical poems of the same era, which probably inspired the development of Graves's theory, include Langland's *Piers Ploughman* (highly recom-mended by Graves) and *Pearl*. *Piers* is highly allegorical and occasionally its readability suffers for the sake of religious allegory. The author frequently personifies non-tangible traits and then, by forcing these characters to socialize, he examines their relationships. Translator J. F. Goodridge mentions that Langland utilized allegory as "a dynamic way of thinking or "making out" the truth in pictorial and dramatic form, by intuition as well as by observation and logical argument" (Goodridge 14). This statement could equally apply to

The White Goddess.

Other sources such as A.B. Cook's *Zeus* and Harrison's *Prolegomena* provide numerous examples of their own unique interpretations. Both books are profusely illustrated with images of classical mythology and theater to support their sometimes unorthodox conclusions. Their overwhelming evidence easily convinces lay readers of the accuracy of their arguments. It becomes evident, even to the novice that Cook and Harrison have a firm understanding of classical Greek art and the deductions they draw from their examples are usually correct. The implication is that there is a single correct method to interpreting classical Greek art and a firm set of rules can usually be applied. In reality, there are exceptions to this method but readers of either Cook or Harrison can't be blamed for assuming an inflexible set of rules for interpretation. In all fairness, such generalizations are usually correct and as Greek art progressed, later artists enforced these rules with increasing vigor. As early as 1868, Skene complains that a similar process had reduced Celtic mythology to a symbolic shape, which veiled their factual foundations.

In the majority of their examples Cook and Harrison read Greek artistic images as icons with a single correct meaning and then scour ancient and classical literature for supporting evidence. Graves simply takes the method a step farther, but in doing so crosses the line between artistic interpretation and sheer guesswork. While Cook and Harrison believe in a single correct way to read Greek art, Graves believes in a single correct way to read those stories, which this artwork depicts. Cook and Harrison depend on ancient and classical mythology to support their interpretations of Greek art. Graves, using Greek art as a key, treats mythology as a series of icons to be decoded into their true meanings. In a sense, Graves is simply skipping a step and applying their icon method directly to the texts.

Harrison's influence on Graves is most evident in his explanation of the Gorgon mask. He claims that there never was a real Gorgon but only the ritual mask of the Gorgon. Such masks were placed on Greek ovens for protection, an idea also found in *The Greek Myths*. Both ideas come from Harrison: "The primitive Greek knew that there was in his ritual a horrid thing called a Gorgoneion, a grinning mask with glaring eyes and protruding beast-like tusks and pendent tongue. How did this Gorgoneion come to be? A hero had slain a beast called a Gorgon, and this was its head. Though many other associations gathered round it, the basis for the Gorgoneion is a cultus object, a ritual mask misunderstood. The ritual object comes first; then the monster is begotten to account for it; then the hero is supplied to account for the slaying of the monster" (Harrison 187).

Although it's never clearly stated it's probable that Harrison's account of the gorgon mask was inspired by Pausanias. He mentions a mask of Demeter stored in a sacred hollow stone at the temple of Delphi. We do not need an in depth analysis to see the influence of Pausanias or Harrison upon Graves's theory of iconotropy. Ritual masks stored within temples are a feature of *Hercules, King Jesus,* and *White Goddess*. By the time he wrote *The Greek Myths,* Graves viewed the gorgon mask as symbolic of protection of any sort of secret.

Harrison and Graves both wrote under the influence of not only Frazer but also Max Muller. Muller had theorized that mythology was the result of early abstract stories being taken too literally by later generations. Primitive tales used to explain such events as the sunrise or lunar phases were, by necessity, tales of personification. Later generations, upon hearing these early stories, took them literally and mythology developed.

Yet, Graves didn't adopt Harrison or Muller's techniques wholesale. While Graves is no historian, Harrison is no poet. No less than five times in *Prolegomena* does Harrison use the phrase "poets and philosophers" or "philosophers and poets", lumping together two professions which Graves considered incompatible. Harrison implies that these two classes together set the artistic standard in religion and myth with their poems and musings. Graves violently disagrees. To Graves, philosophers were the destroyers of myth and one wonders how he reacted to Harrison's combining of the two classes.

Cook and Harrison's methods merge in Graves's treatment of the crane, the crane bag, and the crane dance. According to the myth, Mercury is given a magic bag to hide his sacred symbols and this bag compares to the magic crane bag created by the Irish figure Manannan to conceal the treasures of the sea. By claiming that these treasures are the characters of yet another secret alphabet, Graves strengthens this connection. Furthermore, the crane is a symbol of the Irish god Mider, who posted three talking cranes outside his castle to warn away visitors. This use of cranes as warning devices leads Graves to believe that the sacred symbols and secret alphabets of Perseus, Mercury, and Manannan were stored in bags of crane skin for its magically protective qualities. In later works, Graves hedges his crane bag theory and insist that the bag was merely a metaphor for protective powers (Graves 1969, 5)

The protective powers of the crane bag then become linked to similar protective powers of the Gorgon mask, leading Graves to believe that the crane bag itself was either decorated with gorgon faces or was sealed by a gorgon clasp. This suggestion is strengthened by the fact that Perseus stored the Medusa head in a magic bag and the Medusa head was simply a gorgon mask. Graves claims that confusion between what was depicted on the bag and what was actually inside the bag lead to this misunderstanding. The outcome of these combined crane meanings is that the crane becomes a symbol of literacy because, as Hyginus wrote, they "make letters as they fly".

To the superstitious, the shape of the crane's flight implies that cranes can read. This fact amazed ancient pagans in much the same way that Graves was amazed when, as a child, he watched a heron neatly laying out caught fish in a spoked wheel pattern. These combined facts contributed to the crane's mythic associations to Apollo, Theseus, Mercury, Manannan, Mider, and others. In pagan Aegean civilization, these aspects of the crane contributed to the creation of the crane dance mentioned by Plutarch, Virgil, and Graves in his *Hercules* (Graves 1945, 225).

This crane dance is also known as "Troy town" and is sometimes linked to tales of the Trojan War. Similar Troy town dances are still seen in Britain today where the name Troy has obscured their more local origins. Modern dancers believe the dance celebrates aspects of the legendary founding of Britain by Trojan ancestors mentioned by Geoffrey of Monmouth. However, as one of Graves's sources observes, Geoffrey's works "cannot be treated as serious history" (Rhys, Brynmor-Jones 124). The British Troy town dances were probably danced on turf or rock cut mazes such as Miz-Maze at Leigh, Dorset. These mazes predate Geoffrey and may even predate the fall of Troy itself. Cook claims that the distribution of the Troy town mazes corresponds to the distribution of megalithic structures, implying that the same people built both (Cook 1: 490). Graves makes nearly the same remark near the end of chapter six when he writes that the dance entered Britain from the Mediterranean via Stone Age invaders.

The dance is performed by a group of dancers moving single file in a spiral shape. The dance itself is sometimes referred to as the "spiral dance" and in order for it to be the true Troy town, or crane dance, it must include the spiral movements, which Frazer believed to symbolize the sun's yearly path. Such dances were popular in medieval times and this led to accusations that it was danced at witch sabbats. The artificial connection between Troy town and witches served to obliterate earlier memories of its true pagan origin. This same connection was later used by Murray as evidence that medieval witches were consciously practicing paganism.

Classical Greeks believed the dance celebrated Theseus's defeat of the Minotaur within the labyrinth at Crete. Cretan coins still depicted the labyrinth in 500 BC, proving the popularity of the myth. Virgil clearly links the dance to the Cretan labyrinth and Plutarch claimed it was performed on the Greek island of Delos as well. Sir Arthur Evans's discovery of a complex and meandering palace at

Knossos reinforced this idea for a time, but later researchers denied this palace was the mythical labyrinth. Instead, it was suggested that there was no labyrinth and the myth was created to account for the complex spiral dance whose real origins were already forgotten.

Evidence of this was found in the complex maze-like patterns painted on a floor within the palace. Here was the true origin of the labyrinth. Following these painted lines, even an unskilled dancer could reconstruct the spiral dance much as European dancers followed their turf mazes. There was no Minotaur, no labyrinth, and no sacrifice of young men at Knossos. There was only a complex floor painting to help pagan Greeks dance their traditional spiral dance, whose meaning was already forgotten.

The true meaning of the Troy town dance is long forgotten but anthropologists can't be far from the truth when they suggest it had solar significance. Frazer considered it to assist the sun's yearly path across the sky and it was probably danced at the solstice and equinox. Graves knew of the Troy town dance but intentionally avoided these logical explanations. Instead he strived to link this dance to another practiced by his hypothetical bird cult and mentions the dance in connection to the crane dance of Delos. Yet, Graves never mentions the painted pattern on the dance floor found within Cook's *Zeus*. Once again, Graves follows his favorite sources up to a certain point and then turns their evidence to support a conclusion which they would have denied.

The widespread usage of the crane dance and crane symbolism allows Graves's pagan model to span several thousand miles and connect Celtic, Greek, and Hebrew cultures. To further this connection Graves offers a table revealing commonalties between the Greek, Hebrew, and Irish alphabets. By uniting these diverse cultures, Graves claims that a Cretan alphabet was used in the Peloponnese sometime before the twelfth century BC. Upon reaching the port of Pharos, it was modified by Phoenicians who carried it back to Greece after the patriarchal Dorians had overthrown Mycenaean civilization. Here it was refitted to correspond to the Cadmean alphabet. Lastly it was modified by Simonides.

We've clearly moved beyond *The White Goddess* as a poetic metaphor and have entered into a complex discussion of ancient literacy. In this discussion, Graves reconstructs lost pagan cultures, trade routes, and secret alphabets in a way that leaves readers bewildered. If this argument is metaphorical, we can only guess at the metaphor's meaning. Surely, if Graves was speaking metaphorically he would have chosen an easier metaphor. Considering his larger model of pagan Europe and the spread of ogham, we are forced to believe that Graves is writing literally.

Graves's theory of iconotropy developed in three stages. He was originally content to reinterpret existing artwork and then claim that his interpretation was the original meaning. He does this in chapter eighteen when discussing an Etruscan wine jar. Graves's interpretation of the jar's paintings roughly corresponds to popular opinion, but we suspect that the seven armed men do not depict seven winter months as Graves claims. Similar examples include Graves's interpretation of a Hittite seal within *King Jesus* and an ivory relief of the fourteenth century BC (Graves 1993, 331, 425). Incidentally, *The White Goddess* contains no illustrations of any of the artwork discussed and we are left to draw our conclusions based solely on Graves's interpretations.

Next, Graves takes iconotropy a step farther and describes hypothetical artwork that he suggests may have once existed. After theorizing about the possible existence of these hypothetical works, he then interprets their meaning in view of his theories of iconotropy. Numerous examples of such hypothetical images are cited within *The White Goddess*. Typical examples include the images of Dionysus and the pirates in chapter twenty-five and Graves's reinterpretation of the *Book of Jonah* and *Book of Judith* (Graves 1993, 287, 317, 467, 480).

At the final stage, Graves not only theorizes on the existence of hypothetical artwork which was misunderstood but recreates this artwork without admitting that the image he offers is a recreation draw specifically to fit his theory. Our best example of this stage is found in chapter thirteen where he examines the myth of Perseus. Graves creates a connection between Perseus, Mercury, Hermes, and other mythic heroes allowing him to combine their elements to produce his final version. In doing so, he refers to the cover art of the first edition of *The White Goddess*. This artwork depicts three females offering a male an eye-like emblem. Based on the description Graves offers, we would assume it to be something Graves found on an authentic Greek vase and which he interpreted in light of his own opinions.

However, this is not the case. Rather, the image described in this passage and depicted on the book's cover was actually drawn by Karl Gay, Graves's personal assistant and secretary. Graves admits in a letter to T.S. Eliot that the cover art was drawn by Gay under Graves's supervision (O'Prey 40). This cover art is no less than a misleading forgery. Although Graves never claims the artwork is an actual Greek vase, his careful wording easily leads unknowing readers to assume such a vase existed. Yet, the vase does not exist and this image was specifically tailored to his specifications.

Graves's method of interpretation demanded that certain concepts could only be depicted by specific images and where those images didn't exist Graves speculates on their possible existence and later loss. This method restricted Graves's arguments, but it's unlikely that he felt hindered by such restrictions. Despite its flaws, Graves truly supported his interpretation methods and it's likely he wholeheartedly believed that artwork like that which he describes, had actually been lost at some point. Repeatedly in *The White Goddess*, *King Jesus*, *Hercules*, and *The Greek Myths* Graves suggests that he had found the one proper way to interpret mythology. However, other schools of thought did exist and, far from being unaware of them, Graves drew pieces from each of them.

The interpretation of mythology is probably as old as mythology itself. It's unlikely that primitive humans told tales of magical adventure simply to pass time. There was a guiding logic for each myth despite the fact that we may not be able to discover that logic today. Different theories attempt to rationalize the creation of mythology in various ways and historians and anthropologists have several schools of thought regarding the problem.

Some claim myths developed around actual events, which became exaggerated over time and often use the Trojan War as an example. Another school suggests that myths are projections of the human psyche's attempts to express spiritual ideas. Others claim that myths symbolize seasonal or astronomical changes such as the progress of the solar year or the Pleiades. Harrison favored the idea that myths were dramatic fictions based on older rituals whose meanings have been forgotten. Yet, this theory implies the existence of an earlier ritual, which in turn implies the existence of an even earlier myth. It becomes the proverbial chicken and egg question. Does myth develop before ritual, does ritual develop before myth, or do they develop simultaneously?

It's probably best to subscribe to no particular school of thought and simply conclude that each school holds a portion of the truth. It's unlikely that all mythology can be attributed to a single theory. The problem isn't how to make all myths comply to one theory, but knowing which theory applies to which myths, and why. This multi-faceted approach is surely the most advanced but is also more susceptible to abuse. Graves uses this multifaceted approach and at times, he seems to adopt whichever of the above schools suits his needs.

Graves needs a mythological system that supports his model of prehistoric Europe. He needs this mythological support just as much as he needs historical support. For his historical support, Graves drew from our usual suspects. For his mythological support, he was required to reinvent some aspects of the Greek, Roman, and Celtic mythos. He found it easiest to reinvent these myths if he subscribed to no one school but instead shifted between schools as needed. In the end, this allows him to closely fuse mythology to his own poetic symbolism.

Clearly, Graves's definition of poetry goes beyond the common man's and differs even from most other poets. Graves regards poetry as mystical, magical, sometimes even occult, and always spiritual. He held this view as early as 1922, when he wrote that poetry was a faith rather than a science and was closely related to primitive magic (Graves 1922, 50, 19). He introduces this view in *The White Goddess* by his reference to "the altogether different nature of poetry" (Graves 1993, 17). Put simply, Graves believes that poetry is magic and its purpose is to examine spiritual concepts.

Despite his attacks on the supernatural and occult, Graves was a firm believer in magic. However, his definition of magic wasn't the sleight of hand tricks done on stage; nor was it the ritualistic rites performed by the pagans he influenced. Graves's magic was more akin to what we now call altered states of consciousness. It was a merger between consciousness, dream state, and mythic symbolism. This was his analeptic state and he argues that it's a valid method for researching the past or even predicting the future. In this state, history and science become subjective instruments susceptible to change as needed. History is interpreted emotionally and this leads to many historic inaccuracies and criticisms of the analeptic method.

Graves argues that poetry is magic because it tries to express universal or spiritual concepts, much as myth does. Poetry, like myth, tries to define the divine. It's an expression of the sort of truths that can't be proven in and of themselves, but must be proven by example. The use of allegory and metaphor become the verbal equivalent of sympathetic magic and what is expressed in poetry often cannot be rendered into prose.

Poetry's magic comes partly from this fact and also the fact that all words are in a sense mystic because no two people have the same definition for any given word. Language is a set of symbols, which are vaguely agreed upon but under closer investigation, we find that most definitions are highly interpretive and personal. *Love, hate, fear,* and *fascination* are words we use daily despite the fact that no two people define them in the same way. Other words are loaded terms that affect separate people differently or have a different meaning depending on their context. *Ass* carries a different definition for the farmer than it does for the prostitute and racial slurs carry a different reaction depending on the race of the listener and speaker. Poetry is magic because it plays on words and therefore alters our ability to experience and express reality. A skilled poet is a word master who can shape our perceptions of reality by limiting or liberating our vocabulary. It's no coincidence that ancient Celts considered poets as magicians able to bring fortune or disaster by mere words.

This explains why Graves believes philosophers are a threat to poetry and myth: philosophers seek to express ultimate truth in exactly defined words. In order to express their thoughts philosophers create an exact body of terminology; thus denying the mystic power of words and the art of interpretation. As evidence of this, witness the use of the highly symbolic and abstract language of logic used to express philosophical concepts. Poetry suggests that there is no ultimate reality or at least that we may not be able to express it because of the mystic power of words. Since ultimate reality is either impossible, or at best inexpressible, reality is ultimately defined by the individual, hence the statement that we make our own reality.

This places poetry in direct confrontation with Christianity, exactly as Graves proclaims. Ever shifting poetic expressions blur the line between the symbolic and the literal, making the supernatural possible. Mainstream Christianity denies this ability of the poet and therefore most poetry falls outside of traditional Christian approval. This forces many Christians to interpret the Bible literally instead of as metaphor or allegory.

Graves complains that this poetic expression of reality has disappeared now that there are no longer poetic schools and no standard to measure poetry by. At one time, such schools and standards existed and poetry had rules. These rules taught pagan religion to the initiated, while concealing the true meaning from the uninitiated who were unable to interpret poetry. Now these rules are lost and "true poetry" is rare among modern poets who fail to understand its spiritual significance. *The White Goddess* examines the function of true poetry in ancient Celtic society and shows its links to pagan religious concepts.

Graves isn't the first writer to claim that Celtic poetry had a hidden religious side concealing pagan doctrine. During the Celtic Renaissance of the nineteenth and twentieth centuries, there was massive support for the idea that traditional Celtic poetry contained genuine druidic beliefs. Earlier writers such as Davies, Morganwg, and Nash were still being read despite the fact that much of their research was faulty. Newer poets such as Yeats and George William Russell reworked these ideas into newer forms within their own material. Druidic groups also existed at the time, playing on stock images of druidism and adding their own views to the pool of Celtic literature. Books like *Myvyrian Archaiology* allowed the public to study sixth century Celtic poets and search for traces of hidden druidism.

Davies expressed this attitude in a comment remarkably similar to Graves's later assertions: "the bards of that age [the sixth century], used all the means in their power, to conceal their secrets from the knowledge of the populace, to guard them from the persecution of Christian princes and ministers, and at the same time, to transmit them safe and unblemished, to future ages" (Davies 1809, 481-482). Davies and Morganwg weren't alone in believing that traditional Celtic poetry contained concealed druidism. Edward Jones believed that Taliesin had personal knowledge of druidic beliefs, which he communicated in his poetry.

Other experts disagreed. In 1914, T. Gwynn Jones stated that "Welsh bardism, in the earliest records we have of it, is an eminently Christian organization" (Jones 1915, 286). Not only did Jones deny the pagan content of bardic poetry, he also denied connections between medieval bards and their ancient ancestors; claiming instead that so much bardism had been lost and recreated that the bards of the Middle Ages had little connection with their more druidic forefathers. Instead, medieval bardism was based on contemporary poetics and popular misconceptions of earlier bardism. He concludes that "there is no evidence whatever, so far is now known, that the bardic organization of the twelfth century was a survival of the druidic system of religion and philosophy" and believes that bardism was entirely Christian by the tenth century (Jones 1915, 226, 297).

D.W. Nash also sees through the unfounded claims of Davies and the forgeries of Morganwg. In *Taliesin* he writes:

> There is hardly a piece in the collection of the *Myvyrian Archaiology* which does not bear direct testimony to the fact of the writer having been a Christian, and that the persons to whom these poems were addressed were Christians also. Such arguments, however, are of little weight in the opinions of those who maintain that the Druidical doctrines to be found in these poems were cherished in secret, as esoteric, and carefully hidden from the eye of the people at large, though known to and acknowledged by the select initiated among the higher classes. (Nash 65-66)

It seems that Jones and Nash are speaking directly to Davies and Morganwg, and perhaps to Robert Graves himself. Yet, Graves cites all four authors and therefore must realize their opinions. We must wonder how he felt when he began developing his own theory of hidden druidism in Celtic poetry and then encountered the above passage in a book so essential to his argument. Nor were Nash and Jones the only Celtic experts to dismiss the idea of druidic survivals in Celtic literature. Kenneth Jackson expressed similar opinions on alleged Celtic mysticism and suggested that supernatural episodes were sometimes introduced into Celtic literature for the sake of humor and irreverence (Jackson 20, 28). More recently, in a 1997 article, Peter Ellis fulminates against faux Celtic mysticism surrounding ogham and places blame squarely on Robert Graves and Roderic O'Flaherty.

If we anticipate Graves's argument, we can learn just what he means by "true poetry". We've already seen that Graves believes true poetry is magical or spiritual and this is one way to discriminate between a true poet and what he calls a "mere versifier". Now he narrows the definition even further by explaining that all true poetry must deal with the single theme of the cycle of life and death, or as poet Alun Lewis put it, "the single poetic theme of Life and Death...the question of what survives of the beloved" (Graves 1993, 21). These are the only valid themes and the only acceptable variations are those which render the plot more easily understood within any given culture or era. To Graves, this is the only story worth telling, the comparison of the personal love affair to the rise and fall of a seasonal god whose consort is the threefold nature goddess.

This goddess is the triple goddess of Celtic myth and the myths of several other cultures. She is the divine female principle and her three forms of maiden, mother, and crone symbolize youth, adulthood, and old age. She is seasonal, symbolic of the wheel of the year, and rebirth. She's the goddess of Wicca, the inspiration of poets, and the white goddess for whom Graves's book is named. Put simply, she is the Muse personified. Graves believes that all true poets record their experiences of her, all poetry invokes her, and acknowledges female divinity. The best description of her comes from chapter one where Graves describes her as a thin, attractive woman with light skin, red lips, blue eyes, and blonde hair.

Although Graves throws new light onto it, the myth of the dying god is no new story. It may be the oldest story of all and underlies many mythic cycles; entire religions are based upon it. A.B. Cook outlines the main plot as the story of a divine child who rapidly grows to adulthood and finds a divine consort, only to be killed by dark powers seeking his position. After a magical resurrection, the hero defeats the envious evil ones and resumes his former glory. Cook finds these elements in most Mediterranean paganism (Cook 1: 695). Graves himself sums it up succinctly as "the antique story, which falls into thirteen chapters and an epilogue, of the birth, life, death, and resurrection of the God of the Waxing Year" (Graves 1993, 24). Neither Graves, Joseph Campbell, nor Cook are the first to explain the myth of the dying god. It's also central to the works of Frazer and Murray. Greek, Roman, Egyptian, and Celtic mythologies all contain examples of this ancient motif and Odysseus, Odin, Lugh, Merlin, and Jesus fit the pattern.

When exploring this pattern in chapter nine, Graves associates Jesus with Belin, Apollo, and Arthur. Each were cult heroes who descended to the other world and returned for the good of man. By further linking Jesus to the biblical David and Adam, Graves is also able to place Jesus into his interpretation of *Hanes Taliesin*. This triple figure of Adam-David-Jesus allegedly visited and returned from Arianrhod's castle, a euphemism for the underworld. In chapter sixteen, Graves link Jesus to Thoth, Hermes, and Mercury on similar grounds. The idea of Jesus as the most recent incarnation of such a hero is nothing new. Frazer made comparisons between Jesus and Adonis, which threw doubt onto Jesus' existence. Murray, in her haste to defend witches, took this approach a step farther and compared the divine story of Jesus to the very human story of witch persecution.

Graves goes further still and uses the theme of the dying god as a definition of true poetry. To him, all poetry must address an aspect of this myth. While it's true that much memorable poetry does employ this myth, there is no reason to believe this is the only valid subject. Graves builds a case in favor of mythic poetry and against non-mythic poetry even before entering the debate. He stacks the cards in his favor by declaring what is and isn't valid poetry even before presenting his evidence.

Graves gives three qualifying tests of poetry to support his defin-ition. First, he mentions Housman's test of making the hairs on your chin bristle if you recite the poem while shaving. Several poets have used a similar test, asking if it makes the hairs on the back of the neck or arm stand up. The second test is also from Housman, who says that true poetry should remind one of Keats's "everything that reminds me of her goes through me like a spear" (Graves 1993, 24). The last test is from Graves himself and is implied rather than explicitly stated. He mentions that classical poetry seldom makes the heart leap or the hairs raise. Here he implies that true poetry should invoke the reactions of raised hairs and leaping heart.

Again, we must note Graves's bias. Having established what true poetry is, he now explains how we should react to it. The proper reaction is one of intense delight, horror, ecstasy, or shock. He wants us to believe this even before entering the argument. Graves sets the grounds for reader reactions to poems he cites and sets limits to the sort of evidence acceptable in proving his thesis. We can already assume that anyone who disagrees with these qualifiers will be dismissed as a mere versifier. This reaction of delight or horror is a double-edged sword in his mind. Not only should we react this way to true mythic poetry but he also implies that any poem that invokes this reaction is true poetry. This allows him to declare that a poem is "pure" even if it doesn't deal directly with mythic images.

We see Graves's bias in action, in *The White Goddess* and elsewhere, as he attacks fellow poets for misunderstanding the one true theme. Some of his favorite targets were Auden, Yeats, Housman, and Pound. The exact reasons for the attacks varied but all revolved around Graves's belief that his contemporaries didn't understand the true nature of poetry. Housman was homosexual and therefore couldn't understand the goddess. Homosexuals were unable to grasp a poet's relationship to the Muse because they aren't part of the reproductive cycle. At least this is what Graves's theory suggests. However, the fact that Graves seemed to agree with Housman's tests of poetry implies that he was uncomfortable with his own theory on homosexual poets.

CHAPTER VI

CELTIC RELIGION AND OGHAM

In order to document the survival of ancient poetic ideas in various pagan practices and witchcraft Graves delves deep into pre-Christian Celtic religion and archeology. Readers unfamiliar with commonly accepted aspects of Celtic paganism are at a disadvantage. A brief outline of this religion illustrates where Graves departs from commonly known facts and popular opinion. The available material on Celtic religion is immense and the following outline is not intended as a substitute for the more detailed sources referred to in the bibliography.

Like most ancient pagans, the Celts followed a belief system, which we could roughly label "nature worship". This religion is comparable to the beliefs of the Native Americans and comparisons between early Celts and Native Americans are common. It would be wrong to over simplify this comparison, or to stick too firmly to Frazer's views of primitive religion. Yet, many of Frazer's basic ideas are found within Celtic religion.

Celtic religion was organized by an authoritative body of specialists called *druids*. The druids were not a priesthood per se with a strictly defined hierarchy similar to that of the Catholic church. Nor were they considered a caste, or separate social class, as the Brahmins of India. Perhaps it's best to consider the druids as the intellectual class of the ancient Celts. They were better educated than the masses and received higher respect because of this, yet they were found within all levels of society and often earned livings in secular positions. Those druids, which were not part of the chief's entourage, earned their living as farmers, herders, traders, or any number of typical jobs; yet they remained druids nonetheless and retained their social standing. Collectively, the druids acted as custodians to Celtic paganism by supervising religious functions and public education. The predominance of the druids within Celtic paganism has led many historians to apply the term *druidism* when speaking of ancient Celtic beliefs.

To call Celtic religion druidism is our first mistake. Although the druids served as the organizers of Celtic religion, that religion was not named after them and they were not its sole participants or representatives. Labeling Celtic religion as druidism simply because it was organized by druids is akin to calling Christianity *priestism* simply because it's organized by priests. In reality, the Celts had no single label for their religion. There was no need for such a label. When speaking of religion the Celts simply spoke of *the religion*, their own. As far as they were concerned, there was no other religion to speak of. All Celts followed this Celtic religion and what the non-Celtic world thought or believed was no concern to the ancient Celts. Like most primitive people, the Celts regarded their own tribes as the only authentic people with the only authentic religion. When they encountered foreigners through trade or warfare, the Celts simply dismissed their beliefs as insubstantial in the same way that Greeks disregarded non-Greeks as barbarians. An ancient Celt who was asked to name his religion would probably indignantly reply, "*the* religion" or "the religion of *my* people". More than likely, he would consider us idiots for asking. For our purposes, we are content to use the term druidism so long as we remember that the term refers explicitly to pre-Christian Celtic paganism.

The refusal to name their religion and the flexible role of the druids has led to many misunderstandings regarding Celtic paganism. The inability to pinpoint a hierarchical priesthood or a standardized set of rituals has led many historians to conclude that early Celts had no religion at all. Even the Irish historian Patrick Joyce declares that Irish Celts lacked a supreme god, standardized worship, temples, or prayers. In short, he concludes they had "no well-defined connected system of religion" (Joyce 1:219). Later historians come closer to the truth when they note similarities between druidism and Native American religions or the Roman worship of *lares* and *penates*. Like early Roman paganism, Celtic religion took many private forms rather than a rigid public liturgy. An infinite array of rituals, prayers, and deities were allowed so long as they conformed to the wider Celtic culture in which they occurred. Druids did not guide public worship or dictate the details of ritual or sacrifice. They merely taught the spiritual framework from which pagan Celts must operate and ensured that both public and private worship conformed to this wider Celtic context.

The first century historian Strabo wrote that the Gauls venerated three classes of religious dignitaries: bards, ovates, and druids. Strabo saw the bards as poets and chanters of spells, the ovates as priests overseeing rituals, and the druids as moral philosophers. Later historians have assumed that all three classes were distinct and successive. Thus, druidic students became first a bard, then an ovate, and finally a true druid. Accordingly, a druid could serve as an ovate or bard when needed but the two lower classes couldn't assume the role of druid because they hadn't yet finished their druidic training. Modern historians have come to question this assumed structure. A more critical reading of Celtic culture reveals that this three-leveled system is an illusion. There's no evidence that all bards attempted to become druids. More significantly, the term *ovate* apparently signified mastery of any skill and was not limited to religious functions. In Ireland, the term was equivalent to our modern *doctor*. Irish poets could become an ovate of poetry but, by the same token, a man could become an ovate of medicine or any other field. Perhaps there were more poetic ovates than any other type but the term itself carried no explicitly religious connotation.

Because the ancient Celts left behind no substantial writing, all early records of druidism descend from non-Celtic sources. These second hand accounts were mostly written by Greek and Roman historians attempting to understand a foreign religion. To compound the problem, many of these authors had never even met a druid and couldn't speak a Celtic language. Their accounts are mainly drawn, second hand, from those merchants and soldiers who had encountered Celts at the fringe of the Roman Empire. These accounts tended to focus on the unique aspects of druidism rather than on its commonalties with Greek, Roman, or other Indo-European religions. Like any travelers, ancient Greeks and Romans enjoyed recounting the unusual habits of foreigners and those aspects of druidism, which are best recorded, are those that place it apart from the wider Indo-European framework it developed from. The result is that druidism appears to be a freak development devoid of any connections with its more civilized neighbors.

In reality, druidism simply reflects an earlier stage of Indo-European paganism hidden beneath a veneer of Celtic culture. The Celts were at the fringe of the Indo-European expansion and therefore received few of the newer developments, which were occurring at the heart of the population explosion. As population pressure increased, it drove the Celts farther and farther from the Indo-European homeland and they carried its earliest form of religion with them as they moved. With fewer outside forces to shape their lifestyle, the Celts began to emerge as a distinct people, separate from the earlier Indo-European population from which they descended. Being pushed to the fringe of population expansion early in their development caused the Celts to develop a culture, and religion, which preserved archaic features alongside their own unique developments.

Our best account of druidism is Julius Caesar's eyewitness descriptions of the Celts during his invasion of Gaul in the first century BC. Caesar was one of the few Romans to have actually met with and spoken to authentic druids and he could list a number of druids as personal friends (and personal enemies). Yet Caesar's account is flawed. Although Caesar wrote more about the druids than any other eye witness, his account is still tantalizingly short and vague. Throughout his entire conquest of Gaul Caesar only writes two or three really interesting accounts of druidism and even these are shallow and biased. Caesar's writings were addressed to the Romans back home, especially the Roman senate. He knew that by depicting the Celts as savage barbarians who threatened the Roman Empire, he could secure approval (and funding) for his war, and war is exactly what Caesar needed to increase his popularity.

Caesar depicts the druids as a highly respected and feared class apart from the masses whom they controlled. Druids, he said, were one of only two groups able to rise above the low social ranking of the Celtic masses. It was the druids who kept order in Celtic society and because of this they were exempt from both taxes and military service and were respected by all Celtic tribes. These incentives lured a great many young Celts into the druid order and Caesar claims these students spent up to twenty years mastering druidism in a strictly oral curriculum. The Celts, Caesar claims, used Greek characters for simple record keeping but their religious beliefs were never written down. Caesar's claim that the druids refused to record their beliefs and did not possess their own form of writing has lead some historians to believe pagan Celts were completely illiterate. The question of ancient Celtic literacy and the alphabets they may have used becomes a main point of contention in *The White Goddess*.

Overall, Caesar's comments offer very little outside of the stereotypical image of the shaman or Rousseau's noble savage. According to Caesar the druids shunned writing, taught secret beliefs orally, demanded high respect, human sacrifice, and claimed access to all worldly knowledge. When pressed to explain exactly what sort of knowledge the druids possessed Caesar simply mentions philosophy and astrology without going into details and we are left with the impression that Caesar placed no great importance on druidic teachings. Possibly Caesar had a deeper knowledge of druidism but didn't feel it was worth recording, but it may be that he was intentionally vague because he wasn't really sure what the druids believed. It has even been suggested that Caesar was drawing on earlier written accounts of druidism instead of firsthand knowledge. Either way, he saw no need to elaborate on the details of a barbarian people whom he considered inferior and hostile to

Rome.

To Caesar, druids were bloodthirsty savages demanding frequent human sacrifice. These sacrifices were drawn from prisoners of war and Celtic criminals. If prisoners and criminals failed to fill the quota, Caesar claimed that innocent Celtic civilians were also sacrificed. Caesar never explains why human sacrifice was required or the names of the deities sacrificed to. From his refusal to name a single Celtic deity, it seems that Caesar was unfamiliar with the Celtic pantheon. Instead, he makes comparisons and substitutes the names of Roman deities for Celtic ones when he finds a roughly corresponding pair. Thus, Caesar explains that the Celts worshiped Apollo, Mars, Jupiter, and Mercury when in reality he means that they worshiped native Celtic deities who roughly corresponded to these Roman gods. Exactly how well the Celtic deities corresponded to the Roman pantheon is questionable. Later historians would develop a better understanding of the Celtic pantheon and question Caesar's comparisons.

Additionally, we must remember that what Caesar describes was not typical Celtic society. It was a society under unusual strain, under attack, and threatened by Caesar himself. Caesar's assault on Gaul was itself putting pressure on Celtic religion; changing the degree of Celtic devotion. It's unlikely that Caesar witnessed human sacrifices but rumors of sacrifice certainly reached him. Caesar mentions enemy Celts sacrificing victims before and after battle, yet surely this is something that enemy tribes wouldn't allow Caesar to witness first hand. More likely, rumors of such sacrifices were reaching him with increasing regularity as he defeated more and more of Gaul and the remaining Celts became increasingly desperate in their attempts to stop him. Caesar depicts the druids as rousing Celtic troops before battle, casting curses against Roman armies, and promising to sacrifice prisoners after the battle. Surely, this was not typical Celtic religion but instead was a fanatical reaction to Rome's invasion.

Later Greek and Roman authors depict the druids in the same

savage light, but most of these authors were drawing from Caesar's account and had no personal knowledge of Celtic culture. Many of these same authors struggled to correlate Caesar's vicious depiction of the druids and their own desire to develop the romantic image of the Celts. Even before Caesar, the stoic philosopher Posidonius had mentioned the druids, contributing to this savage and romantic image. Indeed, the combination of savagery and elegance often attributed to ancient Celts is itself a trait of the noble savage stereotype. Even as early as the second century BC, the druids carried an air of mysticism in the more civilized world.

This desire to whitewash druidism extends to sources beyond Caesar and Posidonius. In chapter twenty-two of *White Goddess*, Graves attempts to whitewash one of the unpleasant observations upon Celtic religion made by Giraldus Cambrensis. Cambrensis reveals that twelfth century Irish kings retained the most savage aspects of paganism. During their coronation, Irish kings were supposedly required to enact certain prurient pagan rituals — with a horse. Graves quickly glosses over the exact content of this ritual by claiming that the king played the role of the horse's foal in a ritual rebirth (Graves 1993, 384). However, most historians agree that the king was imitating the stud rather than the foal and that his duty was not to ritually nurse from the mare, but to ritually mate with it. The mare symbolized sovereignty and it was the king's duty to demonstrate his right to rule by his ability to mate with sovereignty. In defense of the Irish, it should be noted that Cambrensis never actually witnessed this ritual himself but is merely repeating rumors. Graves refuses to interpret Cambrensis's statement as ritual bestiality but takes the alternate stance because he wishes to imply the rebirth of the king though the goddess, symbolized by the horse.

Second only to Caesar's account of druidism is Pliny the Elder who lived in the first century AD. Pliny drew most of his material from earlier written sources but may have also had some slight first hand contact with druidism. The two memorable features of Pliny's account are the ritual cutting of the mistletoe and the creation of the *glain*, or druid's egg. Both of these items are subjects of endless debate among historians and modern druidic groups.

Pliny claims that the druids refused to build temples, or images of their deities, but instead worshiped in wooded groves where they showed particular reverence to certain plants. The two most venerated plants were the oak tree and the mistletoe and to the druids nothing was more sacred than finding mistletoe growing on an oak tree. Such mistletoe was cut with a golden sickle during an elaborate ritual in which white bulls were sacrificed. After the cutting ritual, the sacred mistletoe would serve as a magic charm or be used for its medicinal powers. Modern historians are critical of Pliny's mistletoe story and question his sources for the description of the elaborate bull sacrifice. However, they can't deny that Pliny was correct in claiming the Celts venerated mistletoe or that they realized its medicinal powers. Mistletoe is found repeatedly in the wider family of European religions and although its mention in Celtic sources are few, it played a strong role in the Germanic and Nordic paganism neighboring the Celtic territories. The fact that mistletoe is underrepresented in Celtic mythology may depend either on its accidental omission over time or on the possibility that druids placed less importance on the plant than Pliny believed. The fact that mistletoe is not native to Ireland further complicates the issue.

Graves mentions druids cutting mistletoe from oak trees with a golden sickle and rightly observes that the legendary golden sickle would be inconvenient for cutting anything. Gold is far too soft to hold an effective edge and Graves, like many before and after him, suggests that the sickle was actually bronze. Considering the wide distribution of Pliny's story, it's pointless to wonder where Graves first read it. However, it's significant that Frazer mentions the same ritual in *Golden Bough* (Frazer 764).

Pliny's belief that the Celts refused to make images of their deities is completely unfounded. Celtic deities in wood, stone, and metal are numerous and archaeological manuals abound with examples. Better known examples include the Irish Cromm Cruaich, a carved monolith, which may have once been gilded in gold, and the deities depicted on the Gundestrup cauldron. Possibly, the belief that the Celts refused to portray their gods derives from the fact that Pythagoras detested graven images and, according to popular legend, the Celtic religion reflected Pythagorean philosophy. Pliny, who relied heavily on hearsay and second hand accounts, may have accepted this erroneous association.

Pliny's other item of interest, the glain, must be taken with equal caution. Supposedly, the glain, serpent's egg, or druid's egg, was a magical amulet venerated by the Celts. It was described as a spongy and pockmarked sphere formed by the drying spittle of mating serpents. Anyone wishing to capture the glain must steal it from mating serpents while they were in the act. Anyone accomplishing this received the magical benefits of the glain, which included super- natural knowledge without study and all around good luck in general. Pliny wrote that the druids wore the glain as a pendant on a necklace and he claimed to have seen one first hand.

Obviously, the story of the glain's origin is false. Mating serpents do not produce any ball of spittle and Pliny was probably lied to by someone ignorant of the truth or protecting the true origins of the glain. Pliny did see something, which he believed to be the magically congealed spittle of serpents but Pliny was gullible at times and also believed in unicorns and werewolves. Nor was he the only Roman to believe in the glain's power. He claims that a Celtic chief was killed for bringing a glain to Roman court in an attempt to magically influence the trial.

The exact identity of the glain remains a mystery but certain suggestions can be made. Graves suggests that the glain may have been a fossil of a sea urchin and mentions that such fossils have been found in Iron Age burials. MacCulloch made a similar suggestion as early as 1911 but critics rightly observe that Pliny should have recog- nized such a fossil for what it was. Others suggest that the glain was an egg shaped golden amulet but Pliny wouldn't have mistaken a manmade object for a natural one; nor have any such golden amulets survived. Pliny's ability to differentiate between a natural object and a man made amulet also rules out the small glass beads sometimes found in Welsh graves. MacCulloch and Davies mentions that such beads were commonly called *glain naidr*, or "serpent's glass", but this may be a late label in a conscious attempt to link such beads to the mysterious glain (Davies 1809, 210).

Other possibilities include the cluster of empty eggshells of the Whelk. This seems the most likely alternative and would also account for an unexplained passage in the *Auraicept* which mentions "a certain animal lair that dwells on the seashore [in litore] named Molossus, and whoever sees the lair of that animal, to him is revealed knowledge without study" (Calder 137). "Knowledge without study" is exactly what the glain was believed to bestow and such a talisman would be popular with druidic students who spent twenty years memorizing druidic lore.

The White Goddess compares the glain to the symbol of the "world-egg" used by the Greek Orphic religion. Graves wasn't the first to make this comparison. The writers of the Celtic Revival of the late eighteenth and early nineteenth centuries also sought to link the glain with the Orphic egg. Such associations are questionable since the two eggs are quite different in purpose. The Orphic egg was merely a symbol, maybe even a metaphor, which was seldom if ever represented by an actual replica. It was a local variation of a worldwide concept also found in Africa, China, India, and Japan. Although it may have also existed in Celtic mythology, there are no outstanding references to eggs in Celtic myth or art. Conversely, the glain was an actual egg, or at least something like an egg. Thus, it either actually existed or was at least represented by replicas. The Orphic egg was a mythic metaphor while the glain was a ritual item supposedly containing magic power.

It's difficult to place an exact date on the demise of druidism and the question of druidic survival is crucial to *The White Goddess*. Caesar's invasion of Gaul infringed on druidism there but did little to eliminate the religion. It's been suggested that Gallic nobility abandoned druidism in their haste to adopt Roman culture but, even if this were true, the Celtic masses retained their native faith; much to the annoyance of Rome. Rome persecuted druids when they could but the opportunity seldom arose. Celtic disdain of urban life meant that druids were thinly spread over wide areas. Placing garrisons upon major villages was one solution to both druidism and Celtic revolt but because druids often served as laymen, they may have been difficult to distinguish from the average Celt. Despite modern romantic images, there is little evidence that druids could be distinguished by appearance. They certainly did not drape themselves in white robes, flowing beards, and magical staff and their fellow Celts would be loath to assist the Romans in identifying them. Furthermore, the existence of Belgic tribes on both sides of the English Channel suggests the possibility that druids fleeing Gaul were welcomed in Great Britain.

When Rome extended its realm to the British islands druidism there was supposedly driven underground, pushed beyond the Roman wall, or relocated to Ireland. The Roman's destruction of the druid community at Anglesey in 61 AD has often been considered the deathblow to British druidism but modern historians now question this scenario. It seems that ancient historians overstated the importance of the Anglesey community and its destruction was not the deathblow to druidism, which Rome intended. The nonhierarchical nature of druidism meant that it couldn't be eliminated by the simple destruction of its buildings or groves. Oral education and private tutoring allowed druidism to survive even after losing its temples and groves and druidism lingered on in Britain until at least the second century. Possibly, Rome's prohibition against Celtic religion was undermined by Irish druidic influence.

The absence of Roman occupation allowed Ireland's druidism to thrive unchecked until the arrival of Christianity and druids could still be found in Ireland during the fourth century. Patrick preached to druids and was surprised by the strength of their arguments;

implying that druidism was still a coherent religion during his lifetime. It's commonly believed that druidic religion underlies the Pelagian heresy of the fourth century and later deviant traditions of the Irish Culdees. Druidism in Ireland eventually crumbled not from Roman persecution but by slow erosion from Christian missionaries.

Druidism continued as a secret tradition well into the so-called Dark Ages and exactly when it died out is unknown. Several rituals, superstitions, and observances thrived well into the Middle Ages and beyond. Frazer catalogs numerous obscure Celtic rituals, which probably descend from druidism. May day celebrations, fire leaping, animal sacrifice, well worship, and bobbing for apples were all practiced throughout the Middle Ages and are commonly believed to have druidic origins. Were these medieval rituals performed with authentic understanding or were they simple folk traditions divorced from their theology? Most historians favor the latter theory and deny the survival of any true Celtic paganism. The confused state of medieval bardic literature reinforces this view. It's commonly accepted that even the secretly taught druidism of the post-Roman era had died before Taliesin ever set pen to paper in the sixth century.

The accounts of Caesar and Pliny are the most important of all classical writings upon druidism. Their works dominate the next several centuries of druidic writing as later authors fall into idle speculation and wishful thinking. It would be generations before better scholarship refuted these wild theories. Today's archeology enhances our understanding of druidism and reveals the works of Edward Davies and Iolo Morganwg for the absurdities they are. However, we have little need to summarize Celtic archaeological finds in order to understand Graves's argument. Most of the major advancements in Celtic archeology occurred only after 1948 and Graves was unable to use them during his writing. The only major discovery of Celtic archeology to have significant impact on *The White Goddess* is the rediscovery of the ogham alphabet.

Graves's theories on the creation and use of ogham are so radical that attempting to define exactly what ogham is would itself contradict Graves's claim. Graves argues that ogham was: "a religious calendar, a fortune-telling device, a mathematical system ... a means of signaling in a deaf-and-dumb language, and the base of a hundred and fifty ogham speech-ciphers" (Graves 1969, 5). He believed this secret alphabet was used by goddess worshiping pagans to record secret religious tenets. Furthermore, ogham served as a mnemonic aid for druidic students and provided a framework upon which most of druidic religion depended. Each ogham letter was assigned a symbolic tree and various other seasonal associations, which allowed ogham to serve as an alphabet and calendar. At the risk of oversimplification, each letter represented a single lunar month and each month was symbolized by a tree, which bloomed or thrived within that month. Much of *The White Goddess* involves Graves's reconstruction of this system and the significance of the tree symbolism. Unfortunately for Graves, most of his ideas contradict commonly accepted theories of ogham's history.

Most modern Celtic historians agree that ogham cannot possibly date to the remote period that Graves suggests. Instead, they produce overwhelming evidence suggesting that ogham dates to the fifth century AD and was created mainly as an inscriptional alphabet to be used on gravestones and boundary markers. The simple and straight form of ogham letters suggests that it was developed for stone cutting rather than paper. The earliest ogham examples are a collection of standing stones, which were probably inscribed in the fifth century AD. Nearly all known examples of ogham are either gravestones or boundary markers and there is little evidence for the use of ogham outside of inscriptional purposes. These inscriptions may have been added later to stones erected at an earlier date, but the date of the inscriptions themselves indicates a fifth century origin.

There are roughly 370 known ogham inscriptions, most of them in Ireland but others occur in Wales, Scotland, England, and the Isle of Man. Based on their distribution, the occurrences of proper names, and their mention in Irish mythology it's commonly accepted that ogham is an Irish invention of the late fourth or early fifth century. Ogham is also claimed as an Irish invention in later Irish manuscripts such as the fourteenth century *Book of Ballymote*. The ninth century *Cormac's Glossary* mentions ogham and ogham may have appeared in Irish manuscripts as early as the eighth century.

However, the earliest existing Irish manuscripts are ambiguous regarding the history and use of ogham. The *Auraicept's* account of ogham's creation may contain a grain of truth but this truth is hidden beneath layers of mythological corruption and perhaps even intention deception. Additionally, scribal errors within the *Book of Ballymote* suggest that the scribe drew from multiple sources which themselves may have been corrupt. It seems that later scribes were less familiar with ogham than the fifth century engravers of Irish gravestones. The body of knowledge surrounding ogham may have already been in decline when the script was first put on paper. This explains the vague mythical origins attributed to ogham, the scribal errors, and the scribe's obsession with simple cyphers derived from authentic ogham. Overall, later medieval manuscripts may represent an attempt by later authors to record fading memories of ogham and revive an obsolete tradition. Such manuscripts may contain hints of authentic fifth century ogham traditions but we must remain critical. In the end, these manuscripts can only be regarded as records of their own era.

From this point forward, the ogham alphabet becomes a keystone of Graves's work and he attempts to prove that its use can be found in both *Cad Goddeu* and *Hanes Taliesin*. Graves's theory that ogham was the secret alphabet of pagan Europe goes against the above evidence and places ogham's existence before Caesar's invasion of Gaul in the first century BC; well before the commonly accepted fifth century origin. Throughout *The White Goddess* Graves argues that ogham is at least as old as the Bronze age and its origin is on the continent rather than Ireland. Graves's matriarchal pagans had supposedly already established ogham throughout Europe before the battle of *Cad Goddeu* instituted a change in ogham's already existing structure. In order to prove this Graves must eradicate any evidence showing that ogham was inspired by any preexisting scripts.

The possibility that ogham predates Caesar's invasion is slim but can't be easily discredited. Caesar clearly states that the Celts used the Greek alphabet for what little writing they did do and that the druids prohibited religious records of any sort. Thus, if druids used ogham it has been kept secret not only from Caesar but from all historians to date. Some historians speculate that the druids had their own secret script but this is considered an unorthodox theory and only the most radical researchers have suggested that this script was ogham. Most supporters of this theory have only voiced their opinion after the publication of *White Goddess* and we can conclude that Graves inspired them. Significantly, there are no known examples of ogham in Gaul or Spain and this weakens any claim that ogham originated from the mainland.

As Graves says, the *Book of Ballymote* claims that ogham was invented by the Irish god Ogma, a typical warrior-poet deity. Ogma's British counterpart was Ogmia. In Gaul, he was Ogmios and the second century writer Lucian described him as a Celtic Heracles. Graves also mentions this Lucian story, but notice that in doing so he creates confusion between Ogma and Ogmios. Graves claims that Lucian was describing the Irish Ogma instead of the Gallic Ogmios. It's a slight change but it helps Graves present a more unified image of the Celtic pantheon. Presenting such a unified pantheon where perhaps none existed aids Graves in concealing local variations of Celtic culture that clash with his theories on ogham's development. Graves implies that because Ogma was credited with the invention of ogham in Ireland then Ogmios must have been credited with its invention in Gaul. In Graves's defense, we should note that both Rhys and MacCulloch favor this idea of Ogma or Ogmios as a pan-

Celtic god and it's likely that Graves developed his theory after reading these authors. Like Graves, both authors use the Lucian story of Ogma to define the Gallic Ogmios and regard both deities as gods of knowledge.

Considering the arguments of Rhys and MacCulloch, it seems fair to equate the Irish Ogma and Gallic Ogmios as Graves has done. However, with no surviving examples of ogham in Gaul this comparison can't be used to support the suggestion that the Gallic Ogmios was credited with the invention of ogham. MacCulloch himself realized this and although he supported the idea of Ogma as a pan-Celtic deity he described Ogma's connection to ogham as "mere folk-etymology" (MacCulloch 75). Incidentally, Graves never claims ogham was found in Gaul but by overlooking the differences between Ogma and Ogmios he's slowly setting the stage for assuming its existence there despite the evidence of sources like Patrick Joyce who claimed ogham was unique to the Irish (Joyce 1:78).

In chapter seven, Graves provides examples of ogham from Rhys and Macalister and cites Macalister's belief that ogham resembles a fifth century BC Greek script called Formello-Cervetri. Macalister believed that Formello-Cervetri is the Greek script that the druids used at the time of Caesar. Graves agrees on both points. Both authors ignore or belittle the fact that there is a 500-year span between the fifth century BC, when Formello-Cervetri was used in Italy, and Caesar's invasion of Gaul.

In his search for ogham's origins, Graves claims that all of the trees commonly linked to the ogham are native to the British Isles, with the exception of the vine, which was imported in Roman times. Based on this botanical evidence, Graves searches for the origins of ogham along the southern coast of the Black Sea. This strengthens his claim that European paganism spread northwest from ancient Greece.

This use of botanical evidence to date the ogham is creative and has inspired others to follow suit. Unfortunately, such botanical evidence is weak and can't be made to support the argument which most of these authors advance. Critics suggest that the association between the ogham characters and the trees is a later creation and can be dated to roughly the eleventh century and may have been taken from even earlier sources. Regrettably, this still leaves a span of centuries between the fifth century inscriptions and the tenth or eleventh century manuscripts, which establish this tree connection. If ogham was created before Formello-Cervetri then this time frame is nearly doubled. Thus, although the vine was imported it was still imported early enough to have found its way into later manuscripts such as the *Auraicept*. Bede reveals that the vine was cultivated in both Britain and Ireland in the eighth century and therefore predates the earliest surviving copies of all known manuscripts.

By arguing that ogham predates Formello-Cervetri Graves pushes ogham's existence back to a point before the first Belgic invasion of Britain and therefore contemporary with the battle of *Cad Goddeu*. If Graves is right, ogham would be at least 2400 years old. This predates all known ogham inscriptions by several centuries. It's more likely that ogham is a later invention and had other origins or was an artificial creation.

The possibility remains that ogham does date to before the fifth century BC but the likelihood is questionable. If this is so, ogham would have been kept secret from the fifth century BC to the fifth century AD, when ogham inscriptions began appearing publicly. This is exactly what Graves suggests. Some readers agree and attribute the lack of earlier inscriptions to two factors: the druids were successful in keeping their secret and any ogham inscriptions would have been made on wood, parchment, or other non-durable material that has since decomposed.

This coincides with the belief that druids wrote on sticks and staffs. Such sticks are sometimes mentioned in Celtic myth, but none have survived. Joyce mentions that a number of such staves existed in the seventeenth century but he fails to speculate on their age. Another mention of such staves occurred in 1020 but these staves were destroyed and their origins remain a mystery. Probably these staves were a late invention rather than actual relics of the fifth century. Joyce reveals that such writing on staves must post date Roman contact because their Irish name derives from the Latin language (Joyce 1:482-486).

Those who believe the druids wrote on such staves claim that any examples would have decomposed long ago leaving no trace and Macalister himself claimed that damp soil conditions in Ireland contributes to the quick decay of wooden artifacts. Yet, if this stick theory were true, it seems at least one example should have survived. Celtic bogs have preserved such an assortment of artifacts that it's difficult to believe all traces of earlier ogham inscriptions have vanished. Wooden offerings, such as those found at the source of the River Seine and Les Roches, have been discovered but they lack ogham inscriptions (Piggott 80). Such figures date to the late Bronze Age and no wooden pre-Roman images are known to exist. Other Celtic wooden artifacts also survive, but there are no ogham inscriptions among them.

Lastly, if druids did use ogham they possibly kept a library of some sort. References to such libraries do exist in Celtic literature, especially in Ireland, but no libraries survive. Joyce mentions the alleged existence of an entire book written in ogham but, like his staves mentioned earlier, he fails to produce them (Joyce 1:397). Ogham appears in the *Voyage of Bran*, an eighth century AD manuscript that has pre-Christian origins. It also appears in the *Tain Bo Cooley* and the stories *Midir the Proud* and *Baile Mac Buain*. The *Book of Leinster* also makes references to druidic writings preserved on carved sticks called *Tech Screpta*. Yet, no tech screpta have surfaced. Supporters of this druidic library theory claim that such libraries have either decomposed or were burned by Romans, Christian missionaries, or the Vikings. This argument may carry some weight.

Irish legend attests that St. Patrick burned over 180 pagan books in Ireland. If this story is true it's evidence that druids did at least possess books which have not survived. The *Yellow Book of Lecan* states that Patricks's burning inspired other fires and eventually destroyed the druidic religion. It has been argued that these "books" weren't books at all but were actually the tech screpta.

Edward Davies claims that druids were literate before the Roman era and favors the idea of these druidic libraries. His claim is the most extravagant of any who support this theory. He credits the pre-Roman druids with recording their "sacred history, and rituals of the Druids, together with the rules of divination, and most mysterious doctrines of the ancient priesthood" (Davies 1809, 511). From this statement, we conclude that Davies considers these druidic texts to be fairly numerous. Davies doesn't connect this druidic writing with ogham but does conclude that this writing utilized reeds and the points and shoots of trees. Additionally, he credits the druids with divination by casting wooden lots and believes these wooden pieces are depicted upon early British coins. The exact details of druidic writing are never explained but the connection between writing and tree symbolism is reinforced.

Later authors, such as Patrick Joyce, refused to carry the argument as far. Joyce believes that ogham was pre-Christian and came from Ireland. He attempts to date ogham's creation by comparing its linguistic forms to fifth century Gaulish inscriptions and remarks that ogham's letters are not arranged upon the Latin model (Joyce 1:398, 400). He cites earlier historians, such as Zeuss, who also believed ogham was invented before Latin reached Ireland. Joyce also mentions the possibility that ogham was inscribed on yew sticks but refuses to speculate as far as Davies. He admits that the *Book of Ballymote* refers to divination by lot casting but doesn't connect this to ogham (Joyce 1:303).

A final bit of evidence that Ireland had its own writing, independent of Greek, comes from the statement made by Aethicus of Istria. In his *Cosmography of the World*, written in the third or fourth century AD, Aethicus boasts that he visited Ireland and was allowed to read some of their books. As Ellis says, "Aethicus calls these books *ideomochos*, implying that the literature was particular to Ireland and quite new and strange to him" (Ellis 166). Could Aethicus have been reading books written in ogham? Perhaps he was even reading from the tech screpta themselves.

Ultimately, we see that Irish pagans did have some form of writing which may have been kept on wooden rods. This alone doesn't prove that they used ogham, although the implication is obvious. Yet this Irish evidence doesn't support the existence of ogham in Gaul. Graves must prove that ogham was in Gaul before c.400 BC but he can only prove ogham as being no older than the fifth century AD and that Ireland may have used it slightly sooner. Graves's depiction of ogham as an ancient secret of mainland Europe is central to *The White Goddess* and his challenging of popular opinion becomes a stumbling block for the book's entire argument.

Graves mentions that the ogham supposedly corresponds to a "deaf-and-dumb finger-language" referred to in the *Book of Ballymote* (Graves 1993, 113). Macalister explored this possibility years earlier in both his *Ancient Ireland* and *Secret Languages* and suggests that this sign language was a simple matter of extending the proper amount of fingers in the right direction for each character. Thus, B was one finger pointed down, C was three fingers pointed up, Z was four fingers slanted and so on. Although Macalister compares this sign language to modern sign language, the comparison is inadequate.

To begin with, American Sign Language (ASL) has many signs for complete words. Anyone speaking in ASL who wishes to say *family* could simply use the sign for the word. Anyone wanting to say *family* in ogham would have to finger spell, displaying the letters f-a-m-i-l-y successively. Ogham users would have to finger spell every word they used, without exception. Graves rightfully says this would be a tiresome and clumsy method and Macalister calls the entire ogham system "childishly impractical" (Macalister 1976, 20). It would exhaust the wrist after a few minutes of steady conversation and slow the conversation to a crawl as entire sentences were spelled out letter by letter.

Graves instead advances what he calls a "key-board" system. In his method, letter values are attributed to different parts of the hand and signaling may be conveyed quickly and discretely by touching the right places on either your own hand, or the hand of the receiver when working in close quarters. Just how Graves developed this key-board and why he placed certain letters at certain points of the hand is questionable. While there is limited evidence that ogham was used for signaling, there is no evidence that such signaling took the form of the key-board Graves suggests and Graves may instead be borrowing an obscure cabalistic method which attributes Hebrew letters to the fingers in much the same way. Later Graves addresses some of the reasoning behind his key-board and uses various poetic associations to justify his creation. However, there is another possibility.

What Graves doesn't admit is that this isn't his first encounter with a signaling system and perhaps his earlier encounter influenced his recreation of the ogham method he offers. As a child of eight Graves had examined the book *Life of Sir William Rowan Hamilton* and discovered a method of signaling which he memorized and practiced with his sister (R.P. Graves 1986, 52). It's possible that Graves created his key-board idea from memories of this book. A cursory glance at Hamilton's method reveals that it's nothing like Graves's creation, yet the vowels are grouped together as those of Graves's key-board (R.P. Graves 1975, 88).

That Hamilton's works impressed Graves is beyond doubt. Graves mentions him in *The White Goddess* when discussing the coincidences which made the book possible. Hamilton, Graves claims, thought in the same nonlinear way as many poets (Graves 1993, 342). In his *Crane Bag*, Graves states that Hamilton experienced "visionary flashes" (Graves 1969, 65). Graves later claims that all the best poets, mathematicians, and scientists worked in this trance state and balanced their poetic and scientific sides. Hamilton's private letters reveal that he struggled to balance this poetic flair with his scientific personality and often feared that any imbalance impaired his ability as a scientist. In one letter, Hamilton concludes that he cannot be a poet and a scientist simultaneously; yet, he later complains against those scientists who aren't religious but see the universe as merely controlled by scientific law (R.P. Graves 1975 1:314-15, 2:272).

Graves's ogham theory is impractical and historically unsound but it serves a function. It lends order to the otherwise confused material found in various Celtic manuscripts, particularly the *Book of Ballymote* and the *Auraicept* contained within it. By bending both history and mythology, Graves can force these manuscripts to support his own matriarchal theories and utilize the ogham as he desires. Graves repeatedly places a seasonal interpretation on ogham's letter order and then strives to place various other attributes upon ogham in order to support this seasonal view. In his hands, ogham becomes an alphabet, calendar, a sign language, and the key to several secret cyphers or codes. In his haste to recreate ogham, Graves neglects the one aspect of ogham, which appears most obvious and practical: a memory system.

To understand the mnemonic significance of ogham we must understand that ogham is not a true alphabet in the same sense that our "A, B, C" is an alphabet. An alphabet is simply a set of written symbols representing a syllabary or the collected sounds of a language. Seldom are the alphabetic symbols ordered or designed with any logic; it's equally rare to find a modern syllabary with a logical ordering. In other words, there's little reasoning behind the shapes of our letters and the only reason our alphabet it written in ABC order is because our syllabary is spoken in that order. The reason our English syllabary is spoken in this order is equally illogical. The order of our spoken syllabary, the order of the letters, and the shapes of those letters are all illogical and are the end result of centuries of corruption and revision. This is the natural course taken as a spoken and written language evolves.

Ogham is different and reveals an underlying logic in both the order of the sounds and the shape of the letters. This, more than anything, reveals ogham to be an artificial creation: the invention of a single mind or a small group of people. Ogham sprung fully formed from the head of an intellectual, like Athena from the head of Zeus. Apart from common spelling errors, ogham inscriptions contain little stylistic variation, which suggests that its limited usage prohibited the development of local variations. Ogham suddenly appeared and quickly vanished before it could evolve. Thus, it had a short life span and, if most ogham inscriptions date to the fifth century AD, this life must have been within that era.

The shape of the ogham letters, or *fews*, reveal a subtle logic, which most other alphabets lack. The inelegant lines of ogham were not designed for beauty or ease of writing. Instead, they suggest, at a glance, the location of the relevant sound within the syllabary used. If we look at the English letter A, we find no indication that this is the first letter of our alphabet; looking at the first ogham few, however, reveals something different. The first ogham few contains a single line stroke away from the center line, the second few contains two strokes, the third contains three and so on until reaching five strokes. Then, the number of stokes is repeated on the opposite side of the line. For the next five fews, those same lines are again repeated, this time at a slant. Finally, the same five lines are repeated for the final five letters as straight lines, which cross the central line. Thus, ogham fews not only relate the proper sound within the Irish syllabary but also indicate the numerical order of those sounds. The ogham few for *Beth* isn't merely an illogical symbol equivalent to our English A, it's a numerical notation revealing that Beth is the first letter of the Irish syllabary. If the reader knows the four variations used upon the central line, then he can recognize the numerical order of the Irish syllabary with a simple glance at any ogham inscription.

This means that ogham could, theoretically, be applied to any spoken syllabary. The ogham few for the Irish *Coll* doesn't truly mean Coll. It simply indicates the ninth sound of the syllabary. If ogham was applied to another syllabary the shapes of the letters wouldn't change but the sounds would. Thus, ogham could be applied to English and the character now known as Coll would still indicate the ninth sound of the syllabary, but in our new English example, this ninth sound would be *I* instead. Ogham is less of a typical alphabet and more akin to a simple numbering of the spoken sounds used. Function was more important than elegance and the ogham characters were designed to clearly indicate the numerical order of the sounds with as few written symbols as possible. In light of this understanding labeling ogham as cumbersome and childish is unfair. It's actually the most efficient form of notation once the true objective is understood.

Only the forfeda depart from this logic. Their shapes reveal no indication of their numerical order and are difficult to engrave on stone. From this, we may conclude that they are a late addition created by authors who failed to understand the importance of ogham's numerical basis. The fact that the forfeda seldom occur in inscriptions but are common within later manuscripts supports this theory. Nearly all historians, even those (such as Graves) who fail to understand the numerical importance of ogham's characters, have concluded that the forfeda is a late addition.

Readers wishing a better understanding of this numerical ordering and its relationship to the shape of ogham characters may find an interesting analogy in the works of J.R.R. Tolkien. Tolkien was a medieval scholar and the Merton Professor of English at Oxford as well as a fantasy author and he based his imaginary *tengwar* script upon the same principles as ogham. Tengwar contains thirty-six letters; twenty-four standard letters and twelve additional letters added later. Like ogham, Tolkien's tengwar is based upon a central line and the six letter groups each derive from standardized variations upon this line. Instead of a simple line branching from the central line, Tolkien prefers to use "bows" or curved extensions. The first column of tengwar extends its bows to the right while the second column extends to the left and so on. Tengwar is also divided into rows and each row also contains a underlying logic. The first row places its bows in the top half of the central line, the second row places two bows in the top half, the third row uses the bottom half of the center line, the fourth row uses double bows on the lower half and so on (Tolkien 396-397). Tolkien could have devised tengwar without previous knowledge of other alphabets but his knowledge of ogham and runes certainly helped. Likewise, the creator of ogham could have been completely ignorant of other alphabets. Memorization of the intended syllabary was the only requirement.

A careful reading of the *Auraicept* suggests that fourteenth-century Irish poets were attempting to use ogham as a memory system. By the fourteenth century, bardism was slipping into error, even in Ireland, and Irish poets (*fili*) were eager to create or revise any system of mental training, which could streamline their traditions. The recent influx of non-Celtic texts gave them the raw material needed. The result is that Irish authors, under the influence of Greek, Roman, and biblical sources, attempted to place themselves in a worldwide intellectual tradition. One of the results of this movement was the expansion of ogham's role. The crude alphabet preserved on eroding gravestones already carried an air of mysticism and was commonly believed to possess druidic magic. Now, it would be organized into a mnemonic aid. The authors of the *Auraicept* weren't recording authentic ogham beliefs of the fifth century. They were merely streamlining the attempts of the last two or three generations, which depicted ogham as the holy secret of the Gaelic language in much the same way Jews placed mystical value on Hebrew. In short, ogham was the cabala of the Irish and the *Auraicept*'s history and structure was based on earlier cabalistic, Hermetic, and Greco-Roman astrological traditions, which may have reached Ireland in the fifth or sixth centuries.

Many authors, including Graves and Macalister, have inverted ogham's relationship to memory training. The long lists of cryptic ogham associations within the *Auraicept* have often been used to support the idea that ogham was a secret language communicated by complex lists of letter associations. The *Auraicept* mentions a wide range of ogham variations in which each letter is named after objects following a common theme. Examples include "Fortress Ogham" which names each ogham letter after a fortress beginning with the relevant letter. Other examples include "Bird Ogham" and "Church Ogham" in which ogham letters take the names of various birds and churches respectively. By way of example, it may be best to construct an analogous cypher based on the English alphabet. If we imagine a "Vegetable alphabet" in which *A* equals asparagus, *B* equals broccoli and, *C* equals cauliflower we come closer to understanding these ogham variations.

Graves, Macalister, and many other historians believe that ogham was secretly transmitted between druids by referring to the correct letters by their cypher names. These cypher names could then be included in Celtic poetry to secretly encode druidic messages. Graves illustrates the method in chapter sixteen of *White Goddess* when spelling out the word *tomorrow*. This method seems unrealistic, slow, and clumsy. More likely, Graves and Macalister have reversed the *Auraicept*'s true intention. The real point of these lists was not to secretly communicate druidic messages but to become a mnemonic aid allowing the user to memorize long lists of important names, places, or events. In its most basic form, this memory system needed no religious or poetic value at all. However, poets could draw upon these mental lists when needed and such ogham listings could supply a needed word when the poet either suffered writers block or recited impromptu poetry. A poet needing a word that started with B could mentally scour the various ogham listings for a fortress, church, bird, or other object to flesh out his composition.

Evidence suggests that this is exactly what the *fili* did. Graves mentions the Irish pagan practice of *Dichetal do Chennaib* ("recital from the finger-ends") in which the practitioner recites an impromptu poem by consulting his finger tips. *Cormac's Glossary* states that *Dichetal do Chennaib* allowed the poet to create a poem instantly and without study. This is because the poet is counting off the ogham on his fingertips and reciting the rhyming letter attributes derived from the ogham cyphers. There is nothing mystical, or even religious, in this method. A poet reciting a poem upon the Irish character Balor could quickly count off on his fingers and rhyme Balor to a relevant fortress, church, and bird from his memorized list of ogham variations. The result wouldn't be a deeply esoteric poem of druidic mysticism as Graves believes. It would instead be a piece of hack poetry based on commonly known ogham associations. Only those who were unfamiliar with the ogham cyphers would be impressed and this is additional evidence that the *fili* kept such ogham cyphers secret. Learning these lists would be a cumbersome task central to *fili* training and this reveals why the *Auraicept* demands a three-year study of one hundred and fifth ogham listings before any other poetic training. The fact that ogham associations are scarce in bardic poetry doesn't disprove this method; it merely reveals that little of our surviving poetry depended upon this ogham filler. *Dichetal do Chennaib's* non-religious purpose is proven by the fact that St. Patrick allowed its practice even after the introduction of Christianity.

Patrick had been confronted with three methods of poetic prophecy: *Imbas Forasnai*, *Teinm Laegda*, and *Dichetal do Chennaib*. *Imbas* involved overtly pagan elements: prayers were offered to pagan deities and the prophet ate bull flesh, drank bull broth, and finally slept with his hands placed against his face. The prayers, feast, and laying on of hands supposedly induced a visionary dream. *Teinm Laegda* was a similar ritual differing only in the spoken prayers and the desired vision. *Dichetal do Chennaib*, as we have seen, contained no pagan elements but was a simple mnemonic trick. Patrick prohibited *Imbas* and *Teinm* but allowed *Dichetal* to continue. Apparently, Patrick realized the non-religious origins of the last method and considered it non-threatening to his missionary aims.

Graves's refusal to acknowledge the mnemonic purpose of

ogham reveals his desire to mystify the alphabet to suit his pagan framework. He was fully aware of the possibility of *Dichetal do Chennaib*'s mundane origins. Chapter eleven of *White Goddess* discusses this prophetic method and quotes Patrick Joyce's definition within his *Social History of Ireland*: "the utterance of an extempore prophecy or poem that seems to have been accomplished with the aid of mnemonic contrivance of some sort in which the fingers played a principle part" (Graves 1993, 198; Joyce 1:243). Joyce also mentions that "the fingers were used as a mnemonic aid in the pagan *Dichetal do Chennaib*" (Joyce 1:453). While building his own definition of *Dichetal do Chennaib,* Graves also cites the same passage of *Cormac's Glossary,* which Joyce quotes (Graves 1993, 198; Joyce 1:244). In short, Joyce provided Graves with sufficient evidence to disprove his mystical interpretation of this simple mnemonic trick.

Now we begin to understand the vague references within the *Book of Ballymote,* which imply ogham hand signaling between the *fili. Dichetal do Chennaib* involved "recital from the finger tips" in which the poet consulted his fingertips to compose an impromptu poem. Undoubtedly, this is a reference to the habit of counting on the fingers as the *fili* mentally cycles through his memorized ogham lists. A *fili* mentally consulting the ogham while reciting may very well count upon his fingers during recital. A fellow poet who observes him could very easily reconstruct his thoughts because he also knew the relevant ogham lists. Thus, one poet watching another count off his fingers could simultaneously arrive at the same rhyming word. If he blurted it out before his partner, it would appear to the ignorant observer that the two men had secretly communicated the word from one to the other. To see this method in action we may stand in a crowd and count upon our fingers while reciting "thirty days hath September". Inevitably, someone will join the rhyme and this would appear to be the result of secret communication to any observers unfamiliar with the poem.

A poem cited in *Barddas* suggests that Wales had an identical system: "A didactic bard...on the fingers it is necessary to question him". The Welsh hero Hu supposedly wrote the first Welsh mnemonic poem and his follower, Tydain, made such mnemonic poetry the primary method of record keeping. However, there's no direct evidence that ogham was incorporated into this Welsh system. Welsh bards may have counted on their fingers during recital and may have possessed a formalized system of memory based on such counting, but the lack of ogham within Welsh legends and manuscripts suggests that their memory system used other methods.

This finger counting method destroys the assertion that druids and later *fili* could conduct two different conversations at once, one verbally and another via signaling. Macalister suggests that such methods were possible and that the *fili* could verbally say one thing while secretly conveying a contradictory meaning to a fellow poet via signaling. This was unlikely. If the poet said anything during his finger counting it was most likely a muttered recital of the ogham listings he was reviewing. The ability to count off ogham listings while simultaneously speaking on an entirely different subject is unrealistic. The *fili* could no more review their ogham listings during conversation than a modern English speaker could find the fifteenth letter of the alphabet without muttering the entire alphabet under the breath and counting his fingers.

If this theory is correct, why does the *Auraicept* mention "shin ogham", "nose ogham" and other ogham signaling performed against various straight, flat surfaces? Is it possible that these methods were used as subtle prompts to reciting *fili* from an observing colleague? Impromptu recitals were part of the *fili*'s final testing and demonstrated his mastery of the 150 ogham listings. Possibly a floundering *fili* received assistance from a colleague during his testing. Likewise, this signaling could be used during critical public recitals, thereby protecting the integrity of the *fili* order as a whole. This silent coaching was a far cry from the blatant signals flashed between coaches and players in modern baseball and is more akin to the modern practice of lawyers secretly prompting their clients during court testimony or the subtle cues used between celebrities and talk show hosts to ensure a smooth dialog during live performance.

CHAPTER VII

BARDS V. MINSTRELS

Early in his work, Graves distinguishes between proper Welsh bards of the thirteenth century and their lesser cousins, which he refers to as "wandering minstrels". This distinction is central to much of the forthcoming argument. In short, court bards had a canon of memorized poems taken from a highly valued oral tradition. Their high education removed their poetry from the hands of the common man and led them to write mainly for their patrons and each other. Graves claims they "seldom met without a lively exchange of poetic wit"; a paraphrase of Joyce's claim that Irish poets met with "a playful contest of wit" (Graves 1993, 23; Joyce 1:459). Originality among court bards was discouraged as a break from the traditional poetic forms, which were most demanded within the courts they served. After the court bards converted to Christianity, their subject matter became limited to Christian themes, the prince of the court in which the bard served, and heroes of the past. Pagan myths and symbolism were discouraged. Thus, they eventually forgot their own roots and became bombastic puppets of the church and state.

The wandering minstrels were the larger of the two groups. They were bards without courts to serve and were therefore less restricted in form and subject matter. Likewise, they often held a lower poetic standard than the court bards. With no courts to support and nobody to enforce a standard, wandering minstrels were free to write or recite as they pleased. This also served as a lure to lesser poets who couldn't master the difficult regulations of bardic poetry. Thus, the body of wandering minstrels quickly came to comprise not only of master poets who had no courts but a large number of entertainers who could be considered as poetic dropouts of varying degrees of training. Nash suggests that most of these minstrels were illiterate.

These wandering minstrels retained pre-cymric, pagan myths which fell outside the official bardic canon and which were more creative, colorful, and more pagan than the court bards. They took temporary work where they could find it and maintained a close contact to the common men of Wales rather than the royalty.

This division of Welsh poets into two schools is not simply a creation by Graves. There is ample evidence to show that his summary is fairly correct. The primary source for Graves's depiction is the article entitled "Bardism and Romance", by T. Gwynn Jones, found within the 1915 edition of the *Transactions of the Honourable Society of the Cymmrodorion*. Jones divides Welsh literature into a vibrant tradition of romances and legends and a sterile and difficult tradition of later court poetry, which rarely acknowledged these romances. He repeatedly asserts that the court bards shunned the common romances, thereby creating this division. Jones further argues that the romantic tradition is older and, although it is less educated, it retains better characterization, action, and romance. He believes these tales originated with the Goidelic speaking people and were later repressed by the Brythonic invaders who became the ruling class. Then, with the arrival of the Norman families, the older romances found an audience again. This argument is virtually identical with Graves's depiction of the struggle between bards and minstrels. Graves combines this concept with Murray's statement that Norman invaders were a Christian nobility ruling over the pagan masses to arrive at his final theory.

Davies also divides Welsh bards into two groups and claims that Taliesin's poems revealed conflict between the two. Davies, however, insisted that this conflict originated over misunderstandings of the Arkite religion. More realistically, Nash cites Archdeacon Williams as believing that as early as the fifth century there were two schools of bardism. He maintains that two distinct styles can be found in the later manuscripts of the medieval period and concludes that the older poems are often easier to understand than those written between the twelfth and fourteenth centuries.

These older poems were the product of simpler times and predated the rise of complex meter, alliteration, and rhythm.

The tenth century laws of king Howel ranked the Welsh bard tenth in court. Ranking just before him was the Queen's chaplain and just under him was the court crier. This indicates the declining importance of bardism in the face of Christianity. What once had been a position ranked in esteem and linked to druidism had become secondary to the Queen's chaplain and ranked just above the court's messenger boy. Graves himself observed that the ranking of Welsh bards was considerably lower than that of their Irish brothers. Yet, even in Ireland, poets were divided into two classes, the *fili* (master poet) and the common bard.

By the thirteenth century, Welsh bardism was in decline. Although it still existed as an art form and as a career, there were fewer positions available than in the past. The consolidation (and eventual destruction) of Welsh nobility and the shift towards Christianity reduced the need for a large number of professional poets. In later works, Graves also blames the decline in patronage upon the War of the Roses. In time, court supported bards became fewer and competed harder to earn and retain their honored place at court. This resulted in more unemployed bards, who became wandering minstrels. These poets lived nomadically, constantly moving from home to home telling stories in exchange for cash, meals, or a bed for the night. They tended to follow the seasonal festivals and great numbers of them could be found performing at any public gathering.

The fact that Welsh society supported such a high number of these wandering minstrels indicates the mentality of the common Welsh of the time. While the courts were turning out more bards onto the streets, the layman was more than willing to employ them on a temporary basis. It was probably a matter of pride for a common working family to be able to support a wandering minstrel for a week, a weekend, or even a single night. Many common families would like to boast that they had housed an ex-court bard and been entertained by the same poet who had once entertained royalty. By traveling a wide circuit, a wandering minstrel could easily find work year round.

This lured others into the profession. The nomadic lifestyle appealed to the dishonest members of society and the lack of credentials made it easy to claim bardic status. Working on a temporary basis and nomadic living made it easy to conceal income, evade taxes, and commit other crimes before moving to the next town. Vagrants and scam artists claimed to be wandering minstrels by simply adding a few well known poems or stories to their careers of petty theft and deception.

By the twelfth century, these minstrels were a strain on Welsh society. Their status was comparable to that of the gypsy in other European countries. They drifted randomly, finding temporary work as poets, storytellers, and entertainers. Those who supplemented their income with petty theft created a negative image for the entire profession. Langland's *Piers Ploughman* makes multiple attacks on exactly this sort of minstrel and likely contributed to Graves's divisions of wandering minstrels and court bards. The authorities were showing an interest in culling the minstrels, and by the late eleventh or early twelfth century, the laws regarding bards and minstrels had been revised by Grufudd ab Cynan.

Cynan's legal changes are insignificant but serve as a prelude to further changes implemented by his grandson, David. David had married Emma, sister of Henry II, and under her influence, he merged aspects of Norman and Welsh laws. The marriage of David and Emma is exactly what Graves is referring to when he mentions that itinerant poets were gaining access to royal courts through the mixing of Welsh and Norman families; a fact he gleaned from Jones.

Legal changes in the twelfth and thirteenth centuries were again implemented to limit the power of traveling minstrels, who were starting to take positions away from court bards, cutting into their income, and creating tension in royal courts. *Piers Ploughman* reveals that by the fourteenth century some of these minstrels were no longer itinerant but were permanently attached to certain courts. Court bards suddenly feared losing their *cadair*, or bardic chair, to a less trained minstrel. The cadair was more than a metaphorical term for the position of royal court bard, it was a literal chair. Among the privileges of being the official court bard was the possession of a special chair in the presence of the king. Lesser ranked court officials were made to stand in the king's presence. The bard sat at his own throne during formal occasions and ate with the royal family. Loss of this position was considered disgraceful, especially if lost to a minstrel with no formal training. To avoid such tensions traveling minstrels were given a circuit, which they could only travel once every three years.

Later attempts to organize minstrels into an actual school failed and in 1402 Henry IV passed a law discouraging the Welsh from supporting traveling entertainers (Graves 1993, 146). By 1403, traveling minstrels were all but illegal. As Graves observes in his later works, the last handful of traveling minstrels vanished in the Elizabethan age with the arrival of ballad sellers who peddled printed poetry instead of reciting it. Court bards were naturally pleased by this, but their enjoyment of the bardic chair was darkened by the realization that their entire profession was slowly dying. By the sixteenth century, Welsh bardism was writing its own elegy. Their Irish brothers lasted a century more but their institutions eventually collapsed in the face seventeenth-century turmoil. In Scotland, bardism struggled on slightly longer only to die in the first half of the eighteenth century.

Several factors contributed to the death of bardism. Major causes included the decreasing number of royal families, complex rules and laws limiting bardic subject matter and style, and increased production of manuscripts in the fourteenth century. This abundance of manuscripts and the invention of the printing press in the mid-fifteenth century reduced the need for oral education and exhaustive memory training. Overall, there were fewer Welsh families willing to employ bards on a permanent basis and printed poetry books destroyed the intimate teacher-student relationship inherent to bardism. The invention of the printing press was nearly the deathblow to both bardism and the hand written copying of Welsh manuscripts.

Graves cites a particular conflict between one Phylip Brydydd, a court bard, and a lesser trained poet whom Phylip calls Bleiddri. Phylip supposedly lived c.1200-c.1250 and six of his poems survive in the *Myvyrian Archaiology*, including the ones in question. Davies provides a partial translation of one such poem in his *Mythology and Rites* but fails to relate the entire tale and Graves is instead forced to cite T. Gwynn Jones's *Transactions*. Bleiddri's identity isn't clear but he may be identical to Bledri, a poet who was known to translate Welsh tales into French during the same time period.

Phylip and Bleiddri competed for the privilege to recite first on Christmas day in the court of Prince Rhys Ieuanc, a known Norman supporter. From Phylip's poems we learn that he lost this privilege to the lesser trained Bleiddri. Phylip's poem complains that Bleiddri's poems are nontraditional and not worth hearing. Davies translates his complaint as: "The chair of the great Maelgwn was publicly prepared for bards, and not to poetasters was it given". This is clearly an example of an old style Celtic bard losing his chair to a wandering minstrel who found favor with the less traditional Norman court. Prince Ieuanc was a Norman supporter and his court therefore supported the minstrels over the bards. The conflict between Phylip and Bleiddri is trivial but proves Graves's point that this conflict between bard and minstrel was very real and not simply a speculation based on historical reconstruction. These were real men fighting over a real position and its benefits. Similar poetic battles were happening at other courts and Davies cites other examples.

Despite his impassioned outcry, we shouldn't feel too much sympathy for Phylip. Superficially, the conflict between Phylip and Bleiddri appears to have damaged poetic tradition. After all, a traditional Celtic bard has been usurped by an uneducated drifter. Yet, it was time for a change. Phylip supported the old school, which had grown bloated with pride and tradition, yet had contributed nothing new to poetry for generations. They hid behind alliteration, metaphor, hyperbole, and meter but behind these was the same formulas packaged in cultural expressions that had grown worn and boring. Jones rightfully accuses them of being "intentionally archaic".

Bleiddri represented the new school. He hadn't attended bardic college. There was no need. All the best parts of bardism had been repeated endlessly for generations. Even the lowest ranked field laborer knew the best tales. The *Mabinogion*, the tales of Taliesin, and all the rest had leaked from the courts into the streets long ago. The only thing the bards had kept secret was their various complex meters and Bleiddri didn't want those. Instead, he wanted to translate the best of Celtic mythology into French for the benefit of the new nobility, who had never heard the tales. It's here, in the low class, uneducated poets that Graves argues the most pagan aspects of Celtic poetry survived. Those pagan beliefs were inherent in the theme of the stories, not in their form or meter.

These conflicts between pompous court bards and humble minstrels is typified by Sion Kent (1367-1430). Kent was both a priest of Kenchurch and a humble poet. Although he wasn't a wandering minstrel his poetry favors that of the common man rather than the Welsh courts. He often ridicules the vanity of court bards and argues that true sincerity lay in the common man; a typical attitude for a fifteenth century poet-priest. His reputation for attacking bardic vanity, satire, and the many legends of his supernatural power reveal that he represents those wandering minstrels whom Graves believes were popularly accredited with magic power.

The victory of Bleiddri over Phylip only reiterates the fact that the best Celtic poets recognized poetic themes and retained high standing in their culture. In earlier times, the king answered to the poet and not vice versa. These earlier bards carried even more power, often becoming priests and judges besides poets. They were the last representatives of an even earlier system in which bards were considered akin to druids. Such bards weren't simply entertainers but law givers and magicians able to curse or kill by poetic satire. Mythic examples of satire's powers appear in the *Mabinogion* and the story of *Deirdre*. Real life examples occur in Calder's introduction to the *Auraicept*, Spenser's *View of the Present State of Ireland*, and Joyce's *History of Ireland*. Graves himself cites Spenser's passage and remarked in one interview that satire's power is destructive and left handed (Kersnowski 165).

By comparison, Graves says, English poets have had only limited encounters with this discipline. The English language descends mainly from the Anglo-Saxon of Germanic invaders and retains few Celtic traits. This Anglo-Saxon language is generally regarded as less developed and less poetic than the Celtic tongues it replaced. English poetry didn't flourish until much later and when it did it had few roots to build on. Even some of the best Old English poetry, such as *Beowulf*, was written in a mixed dialect differing from contemporary spoken language. English poets received a diluted poetic tradition rather than drinking first hand from the well of inspiration. Graves claims this tradition has swung from stuffy bombast to literary anarchy ever since and that modern English poets are once again looking to stabilize their tradition. He calls for a rediscovery of "true poetry", whose only valid theme is life and death and *The White Goddess* is his attempt to provide this missing English tradition by drawing from Old English, Celtic, Greek, and Roman mythology and placing it all on the framework of ogham.

Respect for poets still exists in remote parts of Wales and Ireland because although the Anglo-Saxons destroyed the British chiefs they didn't kill off the peasants. This allowed pagan themes to survive among the lower class and rural inhabitants. Eventually, these people reintroduced pagan poetics back into the courts, just as Bleiddri had done. In making this claim, Graves is modeling his views of the medieval poetic tradition upon Murray's ideas of the witch-cult. Graves claims that the poetic tradition survived in exactly the same places, which Murray claims to have been the last strongholds of paganism and both claim the lower class preserved these ideas despite changes in the nobility. Graves equates his poetic tradition to paganism and believes native peasants under Anglo-Saxon rule continued their British paganism, retained the poetic theme of life and death, and remained loyal to the goddess.

By way of comparison, it's interesting to place Welsh poetic tradition beside the Irish and see how vigorous Celtic paganism could be retained when unchecked by invasion. Ireland's poets were also divided into two classes: ecclesiastical and lay poets. Professionally trained Irish poets were called *fili*, meaning a seer; in Welsh, they were *derwydd*, meaning *oak-seer*, which some historians believe to be the origin of the word *druid*. Both the Irish *fili* and Welsh *derwydd*, were considered sacrosanct but the *fili* was the more respected within medieval times. A master *fili* was termed an *ollave*. This term is probably connected to *ovate*, the Celtic term of mastery encountered earlier. Ovate supposedly meant "one skilled or versed in anything, a teacher or leader" and his duty was to "improve and multiply knowledge". Rhys claims an etymological connection between ovate and the Celtic deity Ogma and implies that Ogma was the ovate's god of knowledge (Rhys 1888, 16). According to the *Auraicept*, an *ollave* had finished at least seven years of a twelve-year course and was granted up to a dozen personal attendants. These attendants were probably drawn from the ranks of lesser-trained *fili* and the *ollave* was their instructor as well as their master.

Such poets were held apart from common entertainers in Celtic courts. Common entertainers could be heckled and abused if they performed poorly, but nobody insulted a Welsh bard or Irish *fili*. They could supposedly work magic by their poetry and were to be respected. Lesser entertainers had no magic power and if they were offended, their only option was to sue the offender as any common man would. Graves mentions that such low class performers could be pelted with beef bones, an image he had used in an early poem titled *The Bards*.

In Ireland, the term bard was reserved for inferior poets rather than the professionally trained *fili*. An Irish bard was "one without lawful learning but his own intellect", a quote from a seventh century Irish law tract which Graves found in Joyce's works (Graves 1993, 22; Joyce 1:448). In Wales, bard meant master poet. Yet by medieval times, even the informal Irish bards were better trained than the highest ranked of their Welsh brothers and held a higher position within the courts. Where the Welsh bard had fallen to a position below that of the priest, the Irish bard ranked directly under the king and queen and sat beside them at feasts.

Although they were expected to memorize over three hundred tales, the Irish *fili* studied more than mere poetry. They alone were responsible for the education of the royalty and the general public. The difference in education between the nobility and the lower class was quantitative, not qualitative. The bards simply spent more time instructing the nobility than they did the lower class and the teacher-student relationship often continued for life. The bard or druid who was instructor to the young nobleman became court bard and advisor to the same man when he became king or general. This system prevailed on both sides of the Irish Sea. In Ireland, the eighth century king, Aed Ordnidhe promoted his childhood tutor to a court advisor (Joyce 1:460). The best-known example of this system is Merlin, who educated the young Arthur and later became his advisor at Camelot. St. Columba was also reputed to have been educated by druids in his youth.

The few schools that did exist in ancient and medieval Ireland were run by druids and (later) *ollaves*. Youths who couldn't attend such schools were often fostered onto other druids or bards who served as private tutors. This explains how an *ollave* could acquire a dozen personal attendants by his seventh year. This tradition of fosterage reinforced political and family unity in ancient time and continued well into the nineteenth century (Carmichael 166). Originally, it was the druids who controlled Celtic society by educating and advising kings and drafting their brightest students for positions of power such as kings, generals, or druids themselves. By medieval times, institutionalized druidism had collapsed, but bards retained respect as the Celtic intellectual class.

Graves claims poetic integrity has been declining since druidism's collapse. When the druids proper died out, the bards carried on in a degenerate tradition. From them it passed to the traveling minstrels and finally even they were made obsolete by the rise of Christianity. Western poetry has suffered to precisely the same degree that Western paganism has suffered.

Graves makes no detailed attempt to document this downfall but simply cites those causes already mentioned. Economic hardships, warrior tribes, patriarchal attitudes, and Christianity are leading causes. As proof, Graves cites several instances where mythology has become corrupt over time. Some of these examples are factual while others seem to emanate more from Graves's personal opinion. Yet, either way, Graves provides few examples of actual poetry in decline. We would expect him to cite various famous poems from each of the literary eras and dissect them in an attempt to show the progression of corruption; as he does in other works. However, *The White Goddess* is not a standard book of literary criticism and Graves satisfies himself with simple accusations against a handful of poets and sweeping generalizations regarding certain literary eras.

Graves's favorite targets include the classical Greek period and he had been attacking it for years. Classical poets wrote vividly but were failures because they didn't understand the single poetic theme. Philosophy was to blame but other factors played roles. Anti-feminism was not the least of these. Graves believes that classical poets often had a low opinion of females. The rise of patriarchal attitudes meant that men turned to other men as their visions of both spiritual and physical perfection. Graves explicitly ties this idea to the classical Greek acceptance of homosexuality (Graves 1993, 12). Men reveled in their own intellect as well as their own bodies to such an extent that homosexuality was preferable to heterosexuality. When a man wanted love, understanding, or sexual pleasure he turned to his equal, another man. When he wanted children, a menial servant, hot meals, and clean clothes, he turned to a woman. Eventually he married one; for these reasons alone. Once the female was secured in his life, he again turned his attention to his male friends at the bathhouse, theater, gymnasium, or wherever he preferred to loiter and discuss the finer points of philosophy.

This view of classical Greece clashes with popular opinion but Graves obstinately clings to it despite contradictory evidence. Greek mythology is full of goddesses and strong willed, well-educated women. Graves resolves the conflict by claiming these myths predate the classical Olympic mythos and are the underlying traces of the old matriarchal system he supports. The myths of goddesses and dominant females are the true myths and the rise of Zeus's patriarchal system is a late corruption. Now, we understand exactly how Graves calls iconotropy in to his service and utilizes different schools of mythic interpretation for support.

The romantic poets were no better. Romantic poets helped popularize female spirituality, but they weren't true poets. Graves's description of the typical nineteenth-century romantic poet was that of a manic-depressive drug addict who only honored the death aspect of the goddess. He only accepted her in the sense that he was hopelessly doomed to inadequately serve her until driven to madness or death. Edgar Allen Poe comes easily to mind and this same attitude exists today in hordes of adolescent gothic poets who churn out "dark poetry" or hack verse about their own miserable lives. Predictably, many of these same youths consider the romantic poets their role models and share many of their vices and disorders. Graves had been attacking exactly this sort of introverted literary poseur since 1922 (Graves 1922, 38).

Graves is undoubtedly correct in his criticism of both the classical and romantic periods, but he's slanting the facts. He glosses over entire literary eras in a few words and draws on negative stereotypes to uphold his own negative views. Granted, homosexuality was common in classical Greece, just as drug addiction was common to the romantics, but this doesn't invalidate the literature of either era. Graves himself draws on both eras freely to support his own poetic style.

Sappho, one of the most famous Greek poets, was a female of the classical tradition and has long been suspected of being lesbian. Graves cleverly avoids the question of homosexuality and equates her with Caridwen, whom he considers to be the Celtic Muse personified. In doing so, he argues that she somehow stands outside of the usual classical tradition and relates the humorous story regarding his Oxford tutor who seemed disturbed by Sappho's poetic expertise. Graves uses the story to imply that Sappho was somehow outside of the classical tradition. Why else would a classical Oxford scholar dislike her?

Contradicting Graves's stereotype of the romantic era is equally easy and again our evidence is found within *The White Goddess*. As already noted, Graves cites a test of true poetry which indirectly draws from John Keats, one of the most accomplished romantic poets. Graves uses the Keats line "everything that reminds me of her goes through me like a spear" as a standard which all other poetry should be compared against; nor is this the end of Graves's involvement with Keats. In chapter twenty-four, Graves devotes nearly seven pages to him, reproduces *La Belle Dame Sans Merci* in its entirety, and then proceeds to show Keats's adherence to pagan themes. Graves reveals that Keats honored the single poetic theme and drew predominantly from Celtic and Arthurian sources. In his desire to link Keats to the pagan poetic tradition, Graves finally concludes, "He was not a Christian" (Graves 1993, 433).

In his 1922, *On English Poetry* Graves covers many of the same points regarding Keats's poem and *The White Goddess* even contains direct quotes taken from Graves's earlier book. Both books also contain the vivid image of Keats closing his brother's eyes for the last time, the handshake between Keats and Coleridge, and the relationship between *La Belle Dame Sans Merci* and *Thomas the Rhymer*. Significantly, *On English Poetry* refers to Frazer's *Golden*

Bough in the same chapter in which he studies *La Belle Dame Sans Merci*. In all, *The White Goddess* reproduces the earlier Keats material of *On English Poetry* with little change and we can assume that Graves repeats himself because he felt the relationship between Keats and Fanny Brawne, typifies the relationship between poet and Muse.

Graves's portrait of Keats places him in a difficult position. On one hand, Graves wishes to typify romantic poets as manic-depressive drug addicts with no understanding of poetry. Yet, simultaneously, he upholds the most famous poet of the romantic era as the embodiment of his own pagan idealism. Graves would be better to acknowledge the fact that nineteenth century concepts of Greek paganism and Neoplatonic philosophy were major influences driving the romantic movement. While it's true that the spirit of melancholy predominated, this mood was explicitly linked to misconceptions of paganism and the concept of divine imminence of nature. Keats was no exception to the romantic era: he was its high priest. Graves's statement that "He was not a Christian" is correct.

Romantic poets such as Keats and Shelley glorified the paganism of Greece and Rome, giving it an acceptable image and inspiring authors such as Frazer to undertake serious studies of pagan religion. Keats, Shelley, and other romantics dedicated poems to Greek gods and Shelley had gone so far as to build an altar to Pan; nor was he alone. Painter Edward Calvert soon followed Shelley's example and built a similar altar (Hutton 25). Keats had used the imagery of a moon goddess as early as 1818 and by his third volume of poetry, he was combining images of Greek, Roman, and Celtic paganism. It was a common trait of the romantic authors to whitewash pagan deities and favor them over the silent and invisible Nobodaddy, which Blake had ridiculed. Even bona fide historians occasionally fell for this method; Joyce's *Social History of Ireland* continually attempts to purge the cruder aspects of Irish paganism. This romantic concept of melancholy paganism lingered well into the early twentieth century and exerted its power over even the minor authors of hack poetry. H.P. Lovecraft relished this macabre atmosphere and confessed that he too had built altars not only to Pan, but Apollo and Athena as well.

The fifteenth century poet Sion Kent receives similar ambiguous treatment within *White Goddess*. In chapter nine Graves criticizes Kent for his attack on Hu Gardarn and pagan superstition. Graves takes issue with Kent's position as a priest of Kenchurch and theorizes that Kent may have been jealous of the poetic ability of the more pagan poets surrounding him. Later, in chapter fourteen, Graves champions Kent as a true pagan poet who had enough sense to "sip an apple", overcome the conflict between heaven and hell, and gain "poetic immortality". These opinions contradict each other so strongly that understanding Graves's attitude towards Kent becomes impossible.

History suggests that the truth lies between these two extremes. As already seen, Kent's poetry is often humble, leans towards that of the minstrel variety, and rejects the flattery of court poetry. However, Kent's position as priest indicates that he isn't one of the quasi-pagan poets. If anything, Kent's reserved attitude and his attacks on the vain and proud nobility reveal him to be a staunch priest of the common people. Kent is both a sincere poet and a devoted priest; falling outside of the two categories Graves utilizes to classify poets of the Middle Ages.

CHAPTER VIII

LEGENDS OF TALIESIN

If one name stands above all other poets within *The White Goddess*, it's not any classical or romantic author, but Taliesin. We have already briefly encountered Taliesin. We know that Graves consults a poem titled *Hanes Taliesin* and that one of his major sources is Nash's *Taliesin*. Due to the commercialization of Celtic culture and faux Celtic fantasy novels, the general public is already familiar with the name Taliesin. Those who aren't can piece together enough relevant information from *The White Goddess* to follow the thread of Graves's argument. Yet, neither modern fantasy novels nor *The White Goddess* do justice to the most famous of Welsh poets. An in depth analysis of Taliesin's history, legends, and poetry isn't required for our study but the reader may gain better insight into Graves's argument if the high points of Taliesin's fame are mentioned.

Proving the existence of a historical Taliesin is a problem that Celtic historians have pondered for centuries without resolution. The question is bound up with various non-historical complexities. History, language, and Celtic pride all converge into the issue. In many ways, the reputation of Taliesin reflects that of Homer and his existence is equally difficult to confirm. Both were poets who embodied the myths of their age and became national symbols. They represented the high points of their culture's oral traditions but left us no works in their own hands. Later (inferior) works foisted onto them confused the matter and, unfortunately, little historical evidence supporting their existence remains.

At least three threads are woven into the character of Taliesin. First, is the limited evidence for the existence of an authentic Welsh bard who was either named Taliesin, or whom at least wrote under that name, in the sixth century AD. Second, the body of myth, legend, and forgeries attributed to Taliesin within the Middle Ages. Lastly, are the various interpretations, which modern researchers have placed on this Taliesin material in their attempts to uphold their own pet theories. *The White Goddess* uses each of these threads but uses them differently than other studies.

Apparently, Taliesin was a real sixth century bard who worked within oral tradition and left behind few authentic works of his own. He was eventually regarded as the best bard of Wales and perhaps even enjoyed this reputation within his lifetime. The exact dates of his birth and death are unknown and even estimates of where he might have lived or what courts employed him are hotly debated. In later tales, various courts attempted to claim him as their own until he eventually entered Arthurian legend and became, in some tales, a bard to Arthur. This led to occasional confusion between Taliesin and Merlin, who may also have been a real person. Perhaps it's best to limit ourselves to the most basic facts, the bare minimum required for understanding Graves's argument. In a nutshell: Taliesin was a real sixth century Welsh bard and none of his original works survives intact. Few, if any, early Welsh poems can be confidently attributed to him and even those, which suggest his reality, exist only in corrupt copies. Like Homer, nothing survives from his own hand and we are left with only a name and assumptions of what he might have written. This is everything we need to know about the factual Taliesin. The factual Taliesin plays an insignificant role in *The White Goddess*.

The legendary Taliesin is another story altogether and much more important to Graves. Due to his fame, Taliesin became the subject of many legends, which mention his poetic and magical abilities. As the memory of the authentic Taliesin faded, it was inevitable that these legends appeared. Nor should we overlook the possibility that Taliesin may have perpetuated such legends himself. Taliesin was much closer to the druidic origins of bardism than Phylip Brydydd and Bleiddri and may have performed for a court, which had only recently turned from paganism to Christianity. It's completely plausible that a Welsh bard of the time would create his own air of mysticism. If a thirteenth-century bard could command magical awe from his listeners, how much would a sixth-century bard have gained by intentionally cultivating such an image?

Indeed, if Taliesin was the most respected bard of Wales, it seems likely that he performed for the most pagan court, where respect for bardic training remained strongest. Incidentally, popular tradition claims that Taliesin visited the court of Maelgwn, the sixth century king of Gwynedd. Maelgwn was a quasi-Christian king who still upheld many pagan traditions. Towards the middle of the sixth century, the Christian historian Gildas wrote that Maelgwn was the most powerful, and most sinful, of five Welsh kings who still retained pagan affections. Among the charges Gildas leveled at him, was the crime of retaining pagan bards. Unlike the bards of the Christian courts, Maelgwn's bards sung not to the glory of God, but directly to the divinity of Maelgwn. By the ninth century Taliesin, the most powerful bard of the sixth century, was popularly linked with Maelgwn, the most pagan Welsh king of his lifetime.

The legend of Taliesin visiting Maelgwn appears in Guest's *Mabinogion*. Guest translated material from the *Myvyrian Archaiology*, and drew from documents in the collection of Iolo Morganwg. The *Myvyrian Archaiology* versions of these stories drew from authentic medieval manuscripts, most importantly, from the medieval *Book of Taliesin*, itself part of a larger manuscript titled *The Red Book of Hergist*. Conversely, the documents from Morganwg may have been late forgeries. The most important of these suspicious documents was *Anthony Powel of Llwydarth's Manuscript*, which Morganwg claims to have translated. Guest drew from the translations and may never have seen an original document. This manuscript is the most suspicious of Morganwg's contributions to Guest's *Mabinogion*.

The story begins with a magical family who live on a island in lake Tegid, or perhaps even live within the lake itself. Caridwen wishes to brew a magic potion to make her son, Morvran, all knowing. She spends a year gathering magical herbs and during her absence, she forces a little boy, Gwion Bach, to continually stir the magic cauldron. Before the potion can be given to Caridwen's son three drops splash out onto Gwion's fingers and burn him. Gwion instinctively shoves his fingers into his mouth and accidentally inherits the magical power meant for Morvran. Endowed with supernatural intelligence Gwion now realizes that Caridwen intends to kill him when his task is finished. He flees and she pursues him. Gwion uses his new powers to change into a hare, fish, and bird. Finally, he tries to hide as a grain of wheat in a barn, but Caridwen finds and eats him. Nine months later, she gives birth to a handsome baby boy of supernatural powers. Gwion Bach had been reborn as Taliesin. However, Caridwen places him in a leather bag, which she throws into the sea.

The bag floats to Cardigan Bay and snags in a weir belonging to a man named Gwyddno. Gwyddno's son, Elphin, discovers the bag while fishing and brings Taliesin home to raise as his own. Elphin discovers that Taliesin is no average baby. He can already talk, sing, and recite poetry. He's more intelligent than Elphin and he grows at a rate double that of an average child. Elphin raises Taliesin for a few years and gains significant fame and pleasure from housing the supernatural bard. Finally, at one of King Maelgwn's drunken parties, Elphin brags that Taliesin is wiser than all of Maelgwn's bards combined. Maelgwn is offended, imprisons Elphin, and insists that he shall remain imprisoned until Taliesin can prove his superiority.

Taliesin is not disturbed by Maelgwn's threats. He heads directly to the king and uses his magic to make fools of Maelgwn's bards and demand the release of Elphin. Taliesin cleverly enchants Maelgwn's bards so that they stutter and stumble during their recitations. The king is enraged and accuses the bards of drunkenness. When Taliesin is given his turn to recite, he displays the stereotypical bardic eloquence that real world bards idealize. Maelgwn is amazed but remains defiant until little Taliesin turns his poetry to vicious satire of increasing intensity. The climax of the poem is also the climax of the entire legend. Taliesin's poem reaches a fevered pitch and at its peak, the sheer force of his recitation shakes the entire castle. Maelgwn orders Elphin to be brought forth and when he appears the chains magically fall from his body. Maelgwn finally acknowledges Taliesin's supernatural knowledge and questions him on various subjects. Taliesin answers in poetry edged with egotism and satire and at one point, he recites *Cad Goddeu*. Unfortunately, the story breaks off in mid conversation and we are left hanging on Taliesin's broken dialog. Although Guest's translation lacks an ending it's commonly assumed that Maelgwn dismisses his worthless bards and hires Taliesin instead; much as Vortigern supposedly employed the child Merlin after witnessing his prophetic powers.

The above three paragraphs summarize the entire Taliesin legend but do not serve as a substitute. Readers wishing to fully grasp the tale are referred to *The White Goddess* and Lady Guest's translation with the accompanying notes. However, despite her masterly telling and extensive notes Guest fails to provide *Cad Goddeu* in her translation. Possibly, she was unsure of the poem's relationship to the rest of the story. Many poems attributed to Taliesin are collected in the legend with no clear indication of their relationship and Guest may have felt it was best to avoid the entire issue and provide only that part of the tale with which she was confident. Nor is this the only point of interest in relationship to Graves's book and current pagan ideas.

First, there is no concrete evidence that Caridwen is a Celtic goddess. This view was advanced by Owen and repeated by Davies and Guest. None of these sources is able to support Caridwen's divinity. There are no surviving pre-Taliesin sources to compare against and by the time of the Taliesin legend Caridwen is an established witch figure of the sixteenth century. She and her family live alone on an island in the middle of a lake and it's possible that at some earlier point she was regarded as actually living under the waters of the lake. If so then she may equate to the character named Cymidei Cymeinfoll of *Branwen*, the second branch of the *Mabinogion*. Cymidei Cymeinfoll and her husband appeared from the bottom of an Irish lake carrying a magic cauldron and were eventually driven to Wales.

Caridwen's entire family seems to be magically enchanted. She possesses magical powers, her daughter is irresistibly beautiful, and her son is horribly ugly and stupid. Caridwen intends to remedy her son's trouble with her own magic power and therefore adopts typical witchcraft behavior and boils a magic potion in a cauldron. The story says this potion requires a year and a day to prepare and that Caridwen must add "all charm bearing herbs" gathered in their correct "planetary hours" (Guest 263). The author was familiar with the image of witches tossing magical herbs into boiling cauldrons roughly a century before Shakespeare's *Macbeth*. He was also familiar with the astrological concept of "planetary hours", those magical times when herbs are believed to be most effective. Additionally, both Davies and Guest reveal that Caridwen found her magic recipe in "the books of the Fferyllt" and gathered her herbs "according to the books of the astronomers" (Davies 1809, 213; Guest 263). In all, the author was at least superficially familiar with occult concepts of the time.

It's not surprising that Welsh poets of the era recognized the witch stereotype. By the sixteenth century, the witchcraft trials had firmly established the image of the witch with her black hat, broomstick, and cauldron. The term "wicked witch" had been used as early as 1475 and as early as the fourth-century writers such as John Chrysostom claimed that "drunken and silly old women" used magic cures for healing (Kieckhefer 39). Thus, Caridwen's description can't be taken as part of an authentic Celtic tradition. More likely, the cauldron, herbs, planetary hours, and magic books were late additions to the story in an attempt to modernize Caridwen's evil image.

It would be interesting to know exactly what Caridwen's image was before this modernization. It's possible that the late witch image was superimposed over an earlier description, which contained aspects of genuine Celtic paganism. Graves, citing MacCulloch, derives Caridwen from Celtic root words meaning *white* and *inspired arts* and implies that she was regarded as a Celtic Muse of poetry. Other sources state that Caridwen means "fair and loved" and implies that she was at one time regarded favorably. Later researchers have suggested that *Caridwen* was originally *Cyrridfen* ("bent woman") (Bromwich 308). Cyrridfen may be a more suitable name but if this was her original name, we have no explanation of why this bent old witch eventually became Caridwen the fair and loved. Most likely, it wasn't Caridwen's name, which was changed, but her image.

Nash argues that Caridwen derives from *Cecidwen* ("white necked") and was a term applied by bards to females of their affections (Nash 187). In light of this, we must conclude that Caridwen was once considered a beautiful woman, both "fair and loved" and "white necked". Undoubtedly, she was believed to conform to typical ideas of Celtic beauty; white skin, red lips, and black hair. Possibly, this image of Caridwen was forgotten by the thirteenth century and later bards fleshed out her character with stereotypical witch images. The beautiful maiden who dispensed inspiration from her cauldron became the evil witch and her magic brew could only be acquired by theft or accident. Such misunderstandings became increasingly common as bardism declined from the thirteenth century onward.

The "books of the Fferyllt" and "books of the astronomers" were magical spell books. These terms are used generically and it's unlikely that any specific books are intended. Exotic *grimoires*, or spell books such as *Death of the Soul* and the works of Henry Agrippa, had appeared among medieval occultists long before *Cad Goddeu* reached it final state. Most likely, the mention of such books in the Taliesin legend is a bit of literary posturing by a scribe wishing to appear well read in the taboo subjects of his time. It's unlikely that the author was intimately familiar with authentic occult works; more likely, he was simply aware that such books were circulated among the nobility.

The "books of the Fferyllt" have become problematic in Celtic paganism and their mention in Guest's *Mabinogion* deserves attention. Long before Guest, Davies utilized the variant *Pheryllt* in his translation of the Taliesin story and reveals that the pheryllt operated an "establishment" at Oxford before the founding of the current University of Oxford (Davies 1809, 213, 215). He equates the pheryllt with chemists and metallurgists and declares them to be priests of the Arkite religion who produced coins and talismans (Davies 1809, 610). Lastly, he mentions that the term was also applied to Virgil at one point. Guest, following Davies, derives the term from *Feryll*, meaning "a worker in metal" and suggests that *fferyllt* (or *pheryllt*) were a body of metal smiths believed to possess occult powers (Guest 402). Such magical powers are commonly credited to metalworkers in early societies and one of the supposed powers of the *Tuatha De Danaan* was the magic of metal working. Likewise, Brigit was the Celtic patron goddess of poets, magicians, and metalworkers. St. Patrick knew of the connection between metalworkers and magic; his prayer asks for protection from women, druids, and metal workers as if all three possessed dangerous occult powers. Both Graves and Briffault observed the connection between metalworkers and magicians but neither specifically cited the Welsh fferyllt as examples.

The belief that metalworkers were magicians led to the belief that they possessed magical books detailing their arts and the claim that the fferyllt possessed such books may have grown from the popularity of those occult books already mentioned. These books popularized cabalism and Neoplatonism among the upper class, who could afford to posses such works. Although the book of the fferyllt never existed, it lent Taliesin's legend an air of authenticity by citing an obscure magical tome similar to those with which the bard's listeners were probably familiar. Referencing a fictional book to lend support to another fictional tale is a common technique. More recent examples include H. P. Lovecraft's fictional *Necronomicon*, which is still occasionally taken seriously by the uneducated.

The ritual gathering of herbs predates both *Cad Goddeu* and the medieval grimoires and may be one of the oldest magical practices known. Early herbal manuals contained an assortment of magical charms and spells and served as the basis for these later medieval grimoires. Pliny's *Natural History* contains many examples and the often quoted ritual of tricking a dog to pull up a mandrake in order to avert its evil powers was known by the twelfth century (Kieckhefer 14). Accordingly, the inclusion of magical herbs in the Taliesin story shouldn't surprise us.

Caridwen's mistake of making Gwion Bach stir the cauldron instead of supervising it herself is a typical fairy tale motif and reminds us that the *Romance of Taliesin* is closer to Grimm's fairy tales than any true Celtic mythology. Forcing a child to perform an important task is a common device in such tales. Similar examples include the Irish tale of Fionn burning his thumb while cooking the Salmon of Knowledge. Fionn puts the burnt thumb in his mouth and suddenly becomes all-knowing. The fourteenth century Germanic *Volsungasaga* includes a parallel tale in which Sigurd burns his fingers while cooking the magic heart of a dragon. When he places his fingers in his mouth, he tastes the dragon's blood and gains supernatural knowledge. Possibly, the Irish, Welsh, and Germanic versions all derive from a common source.

Gwion's attempted escape from Caridwen is central to Graves's theory that the story conceals a seasonal calendar. Graves argues that Gwion's animal shapes are symbolic of the seasons and cites several similar legends to support the view. However, many of these legends give his theory no better support that the Taliesin story itself and he is forced to reorder the animals in the sequence much as he reorders the trees of *Cad Goddeu*. While Graves's theory is faulty, he is correct in claiming that such escape sequences are common to both mythology and later fairy tales. Shape shifting pursuits are so common that Joseph Campbell has termed them "transformation flight".

Those tales Graves mentions, include the transformations of Proteus in *The Odyssey* and the ballad *The Coal Black Smith*. Several other transformation sequences are referenced but, oddly, Graves neglects to mention two of the most interesting transformation sequences from his sources. Cook's *Zeus* mentions a battle between two magicians in which they become a lion, serpent, bird, and flame and the myth of Zeus's transformational escape from the Titans (Cook 1: 174, 647). For whatever reason, Graves ignores both tales.

The next interesting feature of Taliesin's story is his placement into the leather bag, which is thrown into the sea. Lady Guest insists that Taliesin was placed into a leather bag; Ford translates it as "a coracle or hide-covered basket" (Ford 164). The *Anthony Powel of Llwydarth's Manuscript* deviates considerably from the standard Guest version but clearly states Taliesin was found in a coracle (Guest 425). Each of these versions is reminiscent of another fairy tale motif involving an abandoned infant. The same motifs occur in the birth and discovery of Moses. Likewise, Greek mythology abounds with instances of abandoned children being discovered by humans, gods, or animals. While this is a world-wide concept we shouldn't forget that it isn't an entirely literary invention. Exposure of unwanted children had long been a crude method of birth control and survived in Europe well into the Middle Ages.

Taliesin's landing near Aberystwyth on Cardigan Bay is evidence that the story is neither true nor ancient. Aberystwyth developed around a thirteenth-century Norman castle between the mouth of the Ystwyth and Rheidol rivers and Taliesin was credited with having landed there only sometime after the town became an important cultural center of Wales. Most likely, the story was placed at Aberystwyth in order to boost Welsh nationalism and because the author wished to imply that the Norman castle was Maelgwn's fortress.

Gwyddno Garanhir, the weir's owner, is mentioned in the Welsh

Triads as a king who lost his lands when his embankments against the sea were washed away. His kingdom had originally been the land west of Aberystwyth but the sea submerged his kingdom in a single night and Gwyddno spent his wealth to assist the victims. Reduced to poverty he lived near Aberystwyth and sustained himself and his son by fishing from his single weir. He also possessed a magical basket, which could produce food for a hundred men. Possibly, this basket was the same one Taliesin was supposedly found in. Gwyddno is surely an early variation of the fisher king whose lands suffer while he is reduced to a life of fishing, despite the fact that he possesses the vessel of infinite life.

Taliesin's rate of growth is double that of an average child and again we shouldn't be surprised. This trick is often used to advance the action of myths and fairy tales. Other examples within Celtic myth include Llew and Cuchulainn. Such heroes have interesting births and maybe an interesting incident or two as children but most of their adventures happen only after they grow up. Therefore, their childhood years are quickly passed over. The ability to grow quickly also allows the hero to grow up before the parents get too old to accompany them in the adventure. Even Jesus fits this pattern of interesting birth, years of obscurity, and a sudden reappearance as an adult.

The final interesting point of the tale is Elphin's liberation. After being fetched from Maelgwn's dungeon, the prisoner is brought before both the king and Taliesin. Taliesin recites another magic poem and the shackles fall from Elphin's legs. It's a powerful scene, but by the time the *Book of Taliesin* was written it was already cliché. Bede had used the same trick in the eighth century. In Bede's story, a prisoner being held by a nobleman of king Ethelred is magically freed from his chains when his brother recites the Mass. Bede recounts this tale as fact and offers it as evidence of the power of Christian prayer. Possibly, his motive was to place Christian prayer on equal footing with pagan poetry and refute the superiority of pagan magic. A similar story occurs in the *Life of St. Cadoc*, proving that this incident was a literary device common to both pagans and Christians.

It's noteworthy that Davies provides only a fragmentary account of the Taliesin story within his *Mythology and Rites*. Davies dedicates no less than sixty six pages to the story but only mentions about half of the interesting points; mainly those which support his Arkite theory. Davies sees *Hanes Taliesin* as a "mythological allegory, upon the subject of initiation into the mystical rites of Ceridwen" (Davies 1809, 186). His examination of the Taliesin legend is padded in the typical overblown style of an early nineteenth century historian and, ultimately, Graves finds little use for the Davies translation.

So far, we've examined important aspects of both the historical Taliesin and the Taliesin of legend. The last thread to be woven into Taliesin's composite character is the more recent interpretations of his legends. As already mentioned, Morganwg, Davies, and Nash viciously debated the possibility that Taliesin's poetry contained druidic mysticism. Skene, meanwhile, sat on the sidelines occasionally offering historical commentary and avoiding the entire question of mysticism. Yet, Skene couldn't remain entirely neutral. His desire to avoid mysticism naturally inclined him towards Nash, who denied its existence entirely.

All of these authors shared one trait, which Graves lacks, an interest in the historical Taliesin and a desire to identify his authentic works. The issue of a historical Taliesin is secondary to Graves. Instead, he is primarily interested in the later forgeries and developing a theory of when and why these later poems were written. Graves is the first writer to disregard the history of Taliesin and focus on the history of the debate itself. Graves admits that Taliesin's two most famous poems *Hanes Taliesin* and *Cad Goddeu* are both late forgeries or, at best, corruptions of Taliesin's original works. Yet, this is exactly what sparks his interest in them. Where Davies claims that both poems were authentic works of Taliesin and contained druidic beliefs, Graves claims they are both late poems but still contain druidic beliefs. In this way, Graves can acknowledge the indisputable fact that both poems are late corruptions and simultaneously uphold his claim that druidism survived into the Middle Ages.

Early in chapter five Graves postulates that there are two Taliesins. The first Taliesin was the original sixth century poet whose alleged poems survive in the *Red Book* and who possibly served under Maelgwn. Graves believes the second Taliesin wrote sometime in the twelfth century and calls this Taliesin "Gwion" (the name of Taliesin before his transformation) to avoid confusion with the earlier Taliesin. This Gwion revised the ninth-century *Romance of Taliesin* to conceal pagan religious tenets, which he had discovered. Thus, Graves argues that Gwion stumbled onto pagan secrets hidden in the *Romance of Taliesin* and became enlightened to the nature of poetry. Taking the name Taliesin, he began to ridicule the court bards for their ignorance. His ridicule of court bards implies that he was not one of their ranks. Most likely, Gwion was a wandering minstrel and had become enlightened by the revival of reading which Graves mentions. Gwion is exactly the sort of minstrel which Phylip Brydydd complains against; a self-educated poet with pagan leanings. He, like Graves, is a heretical outcast among his fellow poets.

Gwion claimed descent from Bran and Graves questions why Gwion identifies himself with the losing side of the battle of *Cad Goddeu* over 1200 years after the battle. Graves believes the answer is obvious: Bran was the champion of the traditional paganism that Gwion supported. Rhys had also suggested this when he wrote that Taliesin belonged to a more pagan school of poetry which often attacked the more orthodox court bards (Rhys 1888, 547). Furthermore, by Gwion's time Bran was regarded as the patron of the bards and the owner of Caridwen's inspirational cauldron.

The theory of two Taliesins is dubious and Graves has little evidence to support it. Obviously, later hands tampered with earlier poems attributed to Taliesin but this doesn't prove the existence of secret paganism in the twelfth century. Rhys had even stated that who wrote the Taliesin material or how many authors were involved is irrelevant. Yet, this attitude implies the possibility that there were at least two authors writing as Taliesin. Other authors also suggested the possibility of two Taliesins and J. G. Evans anticipates Graves's theory when he states his belief that there was a sixth century Taliesin and a later author who "revamped" Taliesin's material in the twelfth century (Evans vi). However, Evans later demolished his own argument. Graves supports this theory because it's the only way he can support his preconceived ideas on Celtic paganism. For Graves's theories to work there must be two Taliesins and the later one must be secretly pagan in a medieval Christian world.

Graves is in good company when he suggests that medieval bards concealed druidism in works falsely attributed to Taliesin. Many earlier authors shared this view based on equally scanty evidence. MacCulloch had also suggested the existence of two Taliesins, as did Rees before him. Yet, this falls short of Graves's suggestion. The existence of two Taliesins, or a collection of medieval poems attacking the orthodox court bards, doesn't necessitate the existence of a secret druidic following. It merely reveals that a minority of medieval bards hid behind the name of Taliesin when attacking their hypocritical contemporaries. There is no reason to suppose these anonymous attackers were secretly pagan. More likely, they were the strictest of Christians and attacked the court bards for their laxity in the style of Sion Kent.

To support his theory of two Taliesins Graves offers a long excerpt from the *Anthony Powel of Llwydarth's Manuscript* already mentioned. This document is also quoted in Nash and differs from the main text of the Taliesin story that Guest offers. A summary of the manuscript's plot reveals interesting differences.

According to *Anthony Powel*, Taliesin is fishing in a coracle with Elphin when he is seized by pirates heading towards Ireland. Taliesin escapes in his coracle while the pirates are drunk and rowing with a shield, he eventually becomes snagged on a pole in the weir of Gwyddno. Coincidentally, Gwyddno also has a son named Elphin and Taliesin is asked to become his tutor. Taliesin agrees and thereby becomes the primary bard in two different courts. He freely moves between tutoring the original Elphin in the court of Urien Rheged and his new student, also named Elphin, in the court of Gwyddno. Later, Taliesin was invited to the court of Arthur where he became a celebrated bard.

While this story is clumsy, it does serve a purpose. Indeed, it serves its purpose so well that we can only suspect it's a forgery by Morganwg in an attempt to harmonize three conflicting traditions. This document cleverly removes all supernatural content from Taliesin's history and places it within the realm of the possible. These supernatural transformations were major obstacles for those claiming Taliesin was a real person. Their elimination from the tale is a major step away from legend and towards authentic history. Additionally, *Anthony Powel* explains how Taliesin could be the primary bard of Urien Rheged, Gwyddno, and Arthur simultaneously, a problem that had vexed researchers for years. Suddenly, thanks to a manuscript, which Morganwg alone possessed, Taliesin could again be viewed as a real person and his presence at three different courts was explained. Nash, on the other hand, claimed that the *Anthony Powel* document was forged to meet this need. Graves himself suspects the story to be an eighteenth century forgery but is willing to cite it because it upholds his own view that Gwion-Taliesin was more than one person.

Now that Graves has supported the belief that there were two Taliesins, the original and a later Gwion, he takes the argument a step farther by claiming there may have been more than one Gwion. To summarize, Graves suggests that a group of people hostile to the court bards discovered the pagan secret hidden in the *Romance of Taliesin*. This explains how Gwion-Taliesin was present at three different courts and yet frees Graves from having to depend on the clumsy *Anthony Powel MS*. Instead of claiming that the manuscript was authentic, he can now simply claim it was written by one of these people to explain their presence at different locations. Graves depends on the forged document just as Morganwg did, but Graves uses it in a new way to support a different argument.

While Rhys and Graves disagree on fine details, they do agree that a medieval school of poets, writing under the name of Taliesin, were hostile to Christian court bards. Graves believes this school was a secret pagan sect and connects them to the twelfth century Welsh prophets called the *Awenyddion*; mentioned by Giraldus Cambrensis and probably discovered by Graves in Jones's article (Jones 1915, 237). Giraldus wrote that the Awenyddion went into fits and became possessed as they gave their predictions. Graves argues that they may have feigned insanity or spirit possession when delivering their prophecies. If so then we have evidence of a secret druidic cult in the twelfth and thirteenth centuries and public soothsayers operating in full view of Christian bards and their courts. The later Gwion poems may be directly based on the rantings of Awenyddion visions and this may explain their confused imagery and broken narratives. Ifor Williams suggested similar conclusions in his *Lectures on Early Welsh Poetry*, as Graves observes.

The suggestion that these poems are the result of the ecstatic babbling of the Awenyddion supports the statements from the Forward of *White Goddess* and the opening paragraphs of chapter one, which claim that even modern European poetry results from comparable ranting of contemporary poets. Graves's assertion implies that modern European minds have been inclined against poetry ever since the industrial revolution taught men to think like machines. Since then poetry has only been written by those poets who revert to earlier symbolic language; often ranting it in a seething rejection of modern society's artificial values. This viewpoint contradicts his later assertion that true poets never lose their sense of awareness during trance and require no recovery time. In chapter twenty-four, he agrees with ancient Hebrews who believed such ecstatic babbling and thrashing signified a false prophet. These conflicting modes of inspiration have long been recognized and were examined by earlier occultists such as the philosopher, poet, and Hermetic student Giordano Bruno in the sixteenth century.

CHAPTER IX

THE BATTLE OF CAD GODDEU

Graves admits that he is unable to read *Cad Goddeu* in the original Welsh and instead depends on Nash's rough and outdated translation. Despite its inadequacies, this translation serves as our original because it's the translation that Graves favored and could be considered the pre-Gravesian version. We must keep this translation in mind as we work through *The White Goddess*. Graves constantly refers back to this poem and shows various interpretations of it by rearranging the lines to suit his needs.

Like earlier researchers, Graves believed *Cad Goddeu* was scrambled or mixed with other poems. This is distinctly possible. Other medieval Celtic poems were likewise confused due to the long history of scribes copying from earlier works. Davies believes the *Gododin* was likewise confused and Nash said the same of many of the poems of the *Myvyrian Archaiology* (Davies 1809, 320). Markale states his belief that *Cad Goddeu* was actually a combination of poems (Nash 72, 222; Markale 243). Yet, this does not necessarily mean that Graves is qualified to disentangle them as he desires.

After quoting Nash's translation of *Cad Goddeu*, Graves immediately begins a mind-boggling game with its contents until he arrives at his desired results. Like a three-card monte dealer, Graves shuffles lines and individual trees into a complex pattern, which guarantees his theory is upheld. To anticipate his results: Graves is trying to show that the trees mentioned in *Cad Goddeu* correspond to the trees associated with the ogham alphabet. Exactly how he "proves" this theory is a feat of questionable integrity. It's easy to become swept up in Graves's logic as he breaks down *Cad Goddeu* into various sub-poems and reorders the lines as he desires. Yet, when we return to the original, we realize just how tentative

Graves's method is.

First, he fails to account for all the plants mentioned in the poem. Graves is mainly concerned with trees and not the lesser plants. Yet, we can't assume the author had such a division in mind when writing. Even Graves questions exactly what constitutes a true tree when he disputes whether or not the reed was included. Knowing that he wishes to produce a list of trees matching those associated with the ogham, Graves cleverly discards nearly all mention of any plants not regarded as trees. These lesser plants become assigned to various sub-poems in his scheme. Among these sub-poems is the poem telling of the creation of Blodeuwedd from nine types of flower. It was Nash who first suggested that this flower poem was concealed within *Cad Goddeu* (Nash 231). Graves uses this sub-poem to discard several of the plants not needed for his ogham theory, including the bean, primrose, and broom. This helps him account for the mention of several plants not related to the ogham, yet still maintain his theory that the poem itself contains hidden references to the ogham. This reduces his list of plants to match the actual number of ogham letters. After all, a statistical examination of *Cad Goddeu* is detrimental to Graves's theory.

Examining Nash's translation of *Cad Goddeu* we find that there are a total of 31 plants, mentioned a total of 35 times. (Beech, cherry, oak, and privet appear twice.) The complete ogham, including the forfeda, contains twenty-five characters. Disregarding the five later characters of the forfeda gives us a total of twenty basic ogham characters. The math simply doesn't work. Graves needed to disregard at least six plants and, logically, he disregarded those not associated with ogham. These unneeded plants were discretely regulated to the sub-poems which Graves claims are concealed within *Cad Goddeu*. An alternate translation of the poem appears in Skene's *Four Ancient Books*, but its tally is no better. The Skene translation gives us 28 types of plants mentioned a total of 32 times. (Repeat offenders this time include privet, oak, birch, and pine.) A third source for Graves was the 1915 translation by J. G. Evans, which lists 27 trees with only a single repeat. None of these tallies match the number of letters contained in the ogham.

Yet, even disregarding those plants that were not linked to the ogham still doesn't leave us with a perfect list of corresponding trees. Examining the "tentative restoration" of *Cad Goddeu* Graves offers, produces a list, which is a closer match, yet the order is still incorrect. In his restoration, Graves has shortened the poem from Nash's 237 lines to a mere 52 lines. Only by disregarding over three-fourths of the poem, rearranging the remnants, and making substitutions, can Graves arrive at the needed letter sequence to "prove" that *Cad Goddeu* concealed the trees commonly associated with the ogham alphabet.

In explaining why this letter order was established he suggests that the vowels were not originally separated from the consonants but were intermixed between them as found in the Greek, Latin, and English alphabets. Here again Graves suggests a solution which contradicts established tradition and has no supporting evidence. The separation of ogham's vowels can be traced to the *Auraicept*. Granted, the existing copies of the *Auraicept* are later than most ogham inscriptions but they are still the most complete record of ogham's history and usage and there is no reason to believe that the position of the vowels has altered between the date of the earliest ogham inscriptions and the date of the *Auraicept*.

In reality, the separation of ogham's vowels indicate that it is an artificial alphabet in the sense that it did not evolve naturally to fulfill a literary need. Instead, ogham was probably created without any vowels at all and only the consonants were used in inscriptions. Few examples of ogham inscriptions reproduce the vowels and this implies that their characters were a late addition to an alphabet, which was meant to depict words whose pronunciations may have been disputed. Even today, standardized spelling of Irish mythological characters is erratic and we can only assume that in the fifth century the spelling were less certain. The inventors of ogham were wise to exclude the vowels and leave the pronunciation of personal names to the discretion of the reader. In doing so, they had adopted the same solution, which early Hebrews and others had arrived at.

Later scribes, writing on paper rather than stone, noticed the lack of vowels and filled the void. Thus, the vowels were conveniently appended to the end of the alphabet in an obviously intentional order; Rhys and Brynmor-Jones had observed as early as 1900 that ogham's vowels were ordered from "broad and slender" (Rhys, Brynmor-Jones 3). In 1935, Macalister likewise noted that the vowels were placed in phonetic order. This intentional ordering of the vowels allows them to be pronounced consecutively in a single smooth-flowing sound when read from A to I. This can hardly be accidental and implies that the author knew exactly what he was doing.

The separation of the vowels has often been used to suggest that the inventor was merely rearranging a preexisting alphabet. Exactly which alphabet he used is unknown and various historians, including Graves, have viciously debated the point. It's often assumed that ogham was developed from Latin but this idea has come under heavy fire from both Graves and more knowledgeable historians. Theoretically, ogham's creators need not have been familiar with any other alphabets at all. Separation of the vowels merely implies that the creator was able to identify the vowels of his native language.

Yet none of this deters Graves from his predetermined course. By ignoring this vowel ordering, Graves could uphold his theory of a seasonal calendar. He claims that ogham's vowels were once scatted between the consonants and he places them at intervals within the alphabet. His distribution retains the letter order of A, O, U, E and I, but he sprinkles them more or less evenly throughout the consonants. Graves bases this decision on the seasonal sequence he claims is concealed within the letter order. Lastly, he translates the letter names to their Greek equivalents to assist his search for hidden meanings.

Considering all of the twisting required to reach the desired end, we have to wonder why Graves was driven to search for the ogham alphabet within *Cad Goddeu* at all. As we've seen, Graves was under the influence of Davies, who believed that Celtic literature concealed druidic secrets. During his reconstruction of *Cad Goddeu* Graves cites Davies, who claimed that *Cad Goddeu* described not a literal battle but a battle of ideas. Both authors also note how trees sometimes symbolize letters in Celtic myth and that the Beth-Luis-Nion, took its name from trees. Graves may also have been thinking of the acrostic poem in Bede's *History*, which conceals the alphabet. Graves concludes that the battle of *Cad Goddeu* was a battle over literature or a battle for literacy. Taliesin is using tree symbolism to say that the church was killing poetic mysticism, but now that literacy was increasing, poetic mysteries were returning. With that popularity, claims Graves, came a revival of druidic teachings concealed in Celtic poetry.

Slowly we are drawing a detailed map of the tangled woods Graves has led us into and have made significant discoveries. Graves's belief that *Cad Goddeu* concealed the ogham was sparked by a reading of Davies, which inspired Graves to reread Guest's *Mabinogion*. With a renewed interest in Taliesin Graves turns to *Cad Goddeu* and begins speculating on the hidden ogham. The acrostics within Bede and *Piers Ploughman* convince him that he's on the right track. Based on the Nash translation (and possibly Skene) Graves rewrites the poem to support his theory. Our list of key sources is growing but there are at least three others to consider: Roman poet Ovid, John Skelton's *Garland of Laurel*, and Graves's own early poem *The Avengers*. Each of these is a possible source for Graves's inspiration if not his actual reconstruction of *Cad Goddeu*.

Ovid's contribution is significant only because his works are the prototype of John Skelton, who in turn influenced Robert Graves. Ovid's *Metamorphoses* is a study of transformational themes in myth and literature. If Graves wanted to compare Taliesin's transformations against a wider array of ancient examples, Ovid would have been the likely starting point. Additionally, *Metamorphoses* is the original source for the story of Orpheus and his dancing trees, which both Graves and Davies cite. Ovid's version mentions twenty-eight trees and therefore fails to match the number of letters in the ogham alphabet, although his tree listing inspired later imitations.

One of these imitators was fifteenth-century poet John Skelton; a favorite of Graves. Skelton's best-known work, *Garland of Laurel*, receives only one mention within *White Goddess* but its impact is inversely proportional to its mention. *Garland of Laurel* contains a montage of poetic styles in English, Latin, and French and suddenly, about forty lines from the end, it breaks into Latin hexameters. These hexameters continue for thirteen lines and contain a listing of twenty-eight trees in an intentional imitation of Ovid. *Garland's* tone is often playful and here Skelton is blatantly showing off in much the same way Ifor Williams accuses Taliesin of showing off. More importantly, at least one acrostic has been discovered in *Garland of Laurel*; possibly Graves believed there was another concealed in the tree listing. Other critics argue that mimicking the tree listings of the Latin poets was a standard poetic exercise of Skelton's time (Brownlow 206).

With all this in mind, we must now turn to Graves's own poem, *The Avengers*, written decades before *White Goddess*. In this poem, Graves depicts trees as battling soldiers and this suggests he may have been reading into *Cad Goddeu* more than the original author intended. A comparison between *The Avengers* and previous translations of *Cad Goddeu* is interesting. Vickery argues that the choice of trees given in *The Avengers* later influenced the choice of trees Graves associates to the ogham (Vickery 15). However, this is unlikely. Graves didn't invent the association between ogham characters and the trees. This connection dates to at least medieval times and associations between ogham characters and certain trees had already existed in several books, which Graves consulted, including the *Auraicept* and O'Flaherty's *Ogygia*. It's likely that Graves was familiar with ogham's tree associations as early as 1923, roughly when *The Avengers* was written. Certainly, he was already familiar with Ovid and Skelton by this point.

Although Graves's reconstruction of *Cad Goddeu* is based more on personal opinion than fact, it still has an important purpose. It becomes his personal system of poetry and mythology, and a framework from which all his past work can be linked, and all his future work based upon. Graves not only ties ogham symbolism into all of his own works but strives to fit nearly the entire Western poetic tradition into its mold. While this feat remains impossible, we can't help but be impressed by how well he succeeds in putting a square peg into a round hole. As far as historical truth is concerned, *The White Goddess* is nearly worthless. Yet as far as poetic truths are concerned, the book is an unparalleled masterpiece. Graves's biggest fault was his claim that the book was true in both senses. How he uses his poetic system is revealed in the methods and reasoning behind his reconstruction of *Cad Goddeu*. His reconstruction draws not only from his own earlier works but upon an impressive body of literature. His ability to bolster his argument with well-known literary sources lends his system an illusion of credibility while drawing on a handful of lesser-known works seems to confirm Graves's theory in even the smallest details. A few examples will suffice.

Graves mentions that yew trees are commonly planted near church entrances; where marriages are traditionally celebrated. This is one of two references Graves makes to yew trees growing in churchyards or graveyards. His other reference appears in chapter eleven where he mentions the folk belief that a yew planted in a graveyard will grow a root to the mouth of each corpse. Both of these references are reminiscent of Giraldus Cambrensis's claim that yew trees often grew near churches during the twelfth century. The same idea occurs in Gilbert White's *Natural History of Selborne* and earlier Irish poetry. While it can't be proven that Graves drew his yew tree symbolism from White we discover that Graves draws from this eighteenth-century naturalist for other reasons. Of course, White can't be drawn directly into the argument as someone who knowingly used ogham symbolism, but placing his works beside Giraldus Cambrensis's text and Celtic poetry implies that ogham symbolism is well founded both inside Celtic literature and beyond.

In chapter eleven Graves provides a list of trees protected under Irish Brehon Law and mentions the various fines for their unlawful felling. By citing Brehon Law, the *Triads of Ireland*, and other poems Graves shows the declining respect for trees in Celtic society as their culture became increasingly Romanized and eventually Christianized. Yet, respect for certain sacred trees never completely vanished in Celtic culture and Graves mentions that the term *Neimhead* (nobility) could still be applied to a sacred grove with more justification than it could be applied to Church dignitaries. Even in the medieval era, holiness could be ascribed to trees before it was ascribed to Christians. Graves delights in pointing out this fact and citing Brehon Law and the triads lends support to his tree scheme.

In the same manner, the quote from Venantius Fortunatus is cited as evidence that beech trees are symbolically linked with letters. Further evidence of Graves linking other authors into his ogham system can be found in his reference to "the ash from which sure-thrusting spears were made" (Graves 1993, 40). The *Book of Taliesin* contains a poem referencing "ashen spears" and Davies uses the same phrase in his translation of the *Gododdin*. The *Auraicept* contains a similar reference (Calder 91). Graves was aware of at least one of these references and this influenced his decision to cite the term "ashen spears" as evidence as he reconstructed *Cad Goddeu*. By linking the "ashen spears" to his own "restless reed" Graves implies that he is fully aware of the Celtic poetic tradition he draws on and is qualified to make the claims he does to support his argument. In a roundabout way, Graves is claiming that his poetic system corresponds to the symbolism used in the *Book of Taliesin*, *Gododdin*, and the *Auraicept*.

Nor is this the only time Graves uses his own works to validate his ogham symbolism or pagan ideas. In dealing with the bean plant Graves mentions the Greek and Roman defense against ghosts was to spit beans at them. This is a fact he also used in *Hercules* (Graves 1945, 98). Like his use of the "restless reed", Graves's use of the bean spitting theory is evidence that he believed he had a firm grasp on the poetic symbolism, which inspired ancient pagans and contributed to ogham's creation.

While the reconstruction of *Cad Goddeu* on such thin evidence is questionable, Graves becomes more questionable still in his attempt to link mistletoe into the poem. Based on almost no evidence, he claims that the speaker of *Cad Goddeu* may be identified with the mistletoe. Although there is no internal evidence for this, and despite the fact that mistletoe plays no part in the ogham, Graves knew that it was an important plant in druidism and therefore had to somehow be linked into his poetic system if he was going to make any claim to Celtic paganism.

The famous connection between druidism and mistletoe had been established by Pliny and Graves couldn't afford to ignore it. Nor could he ignore the Norse story of Balder's deathblow, delivered by a dart of mistletoe. Additionally, there was the ancient Scandinavian custom of swearing loyalty, and kissing, under mistletoe. Collectively, these factors implied the importance of mistletoe within much of European paganism. Graves was obligated to include this plant in order to claim the wide range usage of his ogham system.

Repeatedly Graves cites Celtic literature, and other authors, to uphold a system that is actually his own creation. Nor does he limit his associations to the trees of the ogham. Two examples which best illustrate his methods are not used to support any of the trees of the ogham but to support one of the plants which he discarded into the flower poem, the primrose. Graves argues that the primrose symbolizes wantonness and quotes both Shakespeare's *Hamlet* and Brathwait's *Golden Fleece* to support this.

The conclusion is that Graves has rewritten *Cad Goddeu* to suit his aims and then retroactively gone back and found evidence within literature to support his new version of the poem. The few examples of this which appear in chapter two, can be compared against the multiple examples found in chapter ten, where Graves examines the symbolic meaning of each tree, tying it into poetic tradition.

Graves's poetic style is founded on ogham symbolism, which in turn is linked to *Cad Goddeu* by a series of arguments he claims are historically valid. What should be a mythic system becomes real history to Graves. Thus, to drive a wedge between ogham and *Cad Goddeu* would weaken the entire system. We have already driven several smaller wedges into the argument, but a larger fault in his defenses is awaiting an even larger wedge. That fault is the Nash translation itself.

The original Welsh version of *Cad Goddeu* contains eight lines, which Nash couldn't translate and therefore are not included in *The White Goddess*. Graves admits that these lines could either be part of the original *Cad Goddeu* or a late corruption. This makes Nash's "unreliable" translation even less reliable. The conclusions that Graves draws from it, and especially the variations of the poem which he draws from Nash, are even more suspect.

More importantly, Graves is intentionally suppressing the lines in question. Although Nash doesn't translate these lines, they have been translated by Skene. It's ironic that Nash repeatedly claims that medieval Welsh poetry is not nearly as obscure as Davies and Morganwg claimed, yet Nash himself doesn't attempt to translate the eight lines which Skene was able to translate. Why Graves refused to use Skene's translation is unknown but he likely knew of its existence.

Perhaps he saw Skene's translation as inferior to the Nash version, despite the missing lines. In all fairness, we've already seen that Graves declares the Nash translation to be "unreliable" (Graves 1993, 30). To the layman, each translation is equally unreadable, yet Skene's version gives a stronger implication that *Cad Goddeu* was a mental battle fought with intellectual powers. Why this aspect of Skene's translation didn't appeal to Graves is unknown but is probably related to the fact that Skene places the actual battle of the poem in the fifth century. This undermines Graves's later claim that the battle took place sometime between the first and second Belgic invasions of Britain, nearly a thousand years earlier.

After this, Graves gives his own "restored" version of *Battle of the Trees*. This restored version is so near a complete rewrite that it hardly merits consideration in our argument. Instead, it should be seen as an original poem by Robert Graves, which was only inspired by *Cad Goddeu*. A comparison of this poem with the Nash translation is revealing. What began as a 237-line poem in the Nash translation has become a 96-line poem by Graves. More significantly, the order of the trees in Graves's final version still do not reflect the order of the ogham alphabet. After all the trouble Graves goes through to establish the fact that the ogham is concealed within *Cad Goddeu*, he doesn't bother to use the letter sequence in his own finished version. Surely, this was no accident and we must question why he felt the need to deviate from the order, which he himself wished to establish.

The idea of trees doing battle was familiar to Graves. He had already read the description of armed Highlanders appearing from the woods, found in a passage of Sir Walter Scott's *Lady of the Lake*:

> From shingles gray their lances start,
> The bracken bush sends forth the dart,
> The rushes and the willow wand
> Are bristling into axe and brand,
> And every tuft of broom gives life
> To plaided warrior armed for strife.

Notice that Scott has no qualms regarding the comparison of Celtic warriors to trees and rushes, willow, and broom are specifically mentioned. Scott knew that each of these trees played a role in Celtic mythology. Murray quotes the same passage and connects it to her idea that the members of the witch-cult were masters of concealment (Murray 1970, 56). Its appearance in Murray's works likely contributed to Graves's *Cad Goddeu* ideas.

Of the various sub-poems that Graves breaks *Cad Goddeu* into, perhaps the most interesting is the one he creates from lines 29-32, 36-37 and 234-237. Here Graves joins various descriptive lines to create a toad-like monster with a hundred heads and claws. Graves links this creature to Ladon, the dragon or serpent who protected the golden apples of Hesperides, and the jeweled toad mentioned by Duke Senior in Shakespeare's *As You Like It*.

In his explanation of *Cad Goddeu* Graves reveals the motive of the battle by citing the following passage:

These are the Englyns [epigrammatic verses] that were sung at the *Cad Goddeu*, or, as others call it, the Battle of Achren, which was on account of a white roebuck and a whelp; and they came from Annwn [the Underworld], and Amathaon ap Don brought them. And therefore Amathaon ap Don, and Arawn, king of Annwn, fought. And there was a man in that battle, unless his name were known he could not be overcome; and there was on the other side a woman called Achren ['Trees'], and unless her name were known her party could not be overcome. And Gwydion ap Don guessed the name of the man, and sang the two Englyns following:

Sure-hoofed is my steed impelled by the spur;
The high sprigs of alder are on thy shield;
Bran art thou called, of the glittering branches.

Sure-hoofed is my steed in the day of battle:
The high sprigs of alder are in thy hand:
Bran thou art, by the branch thou bearest—
Amathaon the Good has prevailed.'

Graves claims that this quote comes from the *Myvyrian Archaiology* but it does not. The *Myvyrian Archaiology* reproduces these lines in

their original Welsh. Graves was forced to consult an English translation and the true source of the above passage is either Guest or
Nash. Both authors cite this passage verbatim (Guest 324; Nash 222).
Incidentally, this exact passage is also quoted by Skene and this
could imply that Graves had read Skene as well (Skene 205).

This passage reveals that the battle of *Cad Goddeu* was fought by
the brothers Amathon ap Don and Gwydion ap Don under the
service of a female named Achren. They fought against Bran, the
commander of the enemy forces. Bran served under Arawn, king of
Annwn, and couldn't be defeated unless his name was guessed. The
battle ended when Gwydion guessed Bran's name and sang it in a
poem. We must understand that *Cad Goddeu* was not the poem
Gwydion sang. The poem Gwydion sang is the two stanzas quoted
above. The *Cad Goddeu* is a later poem celebrating the entire battle
and was supposedly written by Taliesin in the sixth century.

Amathon and Gwydion were sons of the god Beli and the
goddess Don. Beli was a pan-Celtic god also worshiped as Bel,
Belinos, Belenus, and Bile. Don was a Welsh goddess, which Graves
links to the Irish Danu. This makes Amathon and Gwydion
members of the *Tuatha Dé Danaan*, "the sons of Danu", a magical
race in Irish mythology. Graves believes Amathon and Gwydion
represented tribes of the Tuatha Dé Danaan who fought together at
Cad Goddeu against Arawn, king of Annwn. He further identifies
Annwn with the British underworld and a British national
necropolis, which he claims is Avebury. As evidence of the link
between Annwn and the British underworld Graves cites the
Mabinogion's first branch, *Pwyll Prince of Dyved*, where Annwn is
represented as a magical other world bordering our own.

Much of Graves's supporting evidence is correct, but the conclu-
sions he draws from it are questionable. It's true that Amathon and
Gwydion were mythic brothers, and sons of Beli and Don. It's also
commonly accepted that the Welsh goddess Don equates to the Irish
Danu. Lastly, it's true that *Pwyll Prince of Dyved*, depicts Annwn as a
Welsh underworld. However, there is no evidence that Amathon

and Gwydion were personifications of actual tribes; nor is it likely that Annwn represents Avebury or any other national necropolis. Lastly, as we've already seen from the conflict between Davies and Nash, there is confusion as to whether or not *Cad Goddeu* was a literal battle.

The distinction between these interpretations is critical to Graves's theory, yet even he seems to be unsure of which stance to take. At times, he speaks of *Cad Goddeu* as an actual battle of the first Belgic invasion involving a union of Danaan tribes. At other times, he speaks of it as a battle of ideas expressed in medieval Celtic poetry as druidic teachings begin to resurface in the wake of public literacy. It's probably best to assume Graves sees it both ways and that *Cad Goddeu* tells of a revival of druidic beliefs through an allusion to an earlier battle, which established one pagan view over another in pre-Christian Britain.

The name of the female heading Gwydion's forces is Achren, another term for the Welsh other world. This is further evidence that *Cad Goddeu* wasn't a real battle but rather a mythological conflict involving armies of otherworldly creatures. Note that Achren fought *against* Arawn and Bran. We would expect someone whose name means both *trees* and *other world* to fight on their side rather than against them. The fact that she doesn't implies that maybe both sides of the battle represented otherworldly forces or that *Cad Goddeu* was a battle between two interpretations of the other world. It could be considered a struggle between conflicting religious ideas, as Graves claims.

It may also be significant that Achren can mean both *trees* and *other world* in the Welsh language. This implies a strong association between the two words in Celtic religion. Clearly, there was a popular symbolic link between the other world and trees within Celtic mythology, although the exact relationship is impossible to grasp from this poem alone.

Exactly when did this battle take place and what evidence does Graves have to date it? Graves dates the poem to the thirteenth century and in chapter five, he speculates on even earlier versions. However, he puts the actual battle of *Cad Goddeu* in the fourth century BC, a full 1600 years before the poem was written. Even assuming Taliesin actually did write *Cad Goddeu* this only places us in the late sixth century AD, still roughly 1000 years after Graves's proposed battle. This is further evidence that the poem should be regarded as referring to two battles; the original battle and the later revival of druidism through medieval literacy.

As for the actual battle, Graves claims that the Danaan tribes overthrew the Bran cult in Britain before reaching Ireland. He argues that the Danaan tribes, which eventually became the Irish Tuatha Dé Danaan, originally came from Greece and were identical with the Danaan tribes Homer mentions in the *Illiad*. At the time of *Cad Goddeu* the Danaans lived in Britain with the Bran cult and may have lived there for centuries before supplanting them. The Amathon tribe was a Danaan tribe already established in Britain from an earlier wave of invasions and the Gwydion tribe represented more recent invaders who helped them achieve victory.

Graves says that the Danaans were a matriarchal tribal confederacy who invaded Ireland from Britain in the early Bronze Age. The goddess Danu was eventually masculinized to Don and considered the male ancestor of the tribe. In *Math Son of Mathonwy* she is sister to king Math of Gwynedd and Gwydion and Amathon are her sons. Graves reinforces the connection between Welsh and Irish myth by claiming Gwydion and Amathon were tribal gods of the Tuatha Dé Danaan. The *Book of Invasions* claims that the Tuatha Dé Danaan were originally driven from Greece by invading Syrians. They eventually reached Ireland via Denmark and North Britain. Graves says there is some archaeological evidence for this, but fails to cite this evidence in his argument.

Put simply, Graves is attempting to portray the Danaan Amathon worshipers as a people who settled in Britain after an earlier invasion, which predated the invasion that inspired *Cad Goddeu*. These Amathon worshipers lived peacefully with the Bran cult until the arrival of the next wave of Danaans; worshipers of Gwydion. Graves has modeled this theory on two successive British invasions: the early struggle between Brythonic and Goidelic Celts and the later Belgic invasion. He contends that these later invading Belgae were supported in their conquest by earlier Danaan tribes and their combined forces overpowered the older Bran cult. Graves's association between these two invasions and pagan cults dedicated to Amathon and Gwydion is a novel twist on an already accepted British invasion theory.

The *Book of Invasions* claims that the Tuatha Dé Danaan reached Britain in 1472 BC and Graves leans towards roughly the same era. He supports his claim by citing Herodotus who mentions a Phoenician invasion, which captured the temple of Io at Argos. Supposedly, this is the same invasion. Graves places this Phoenician invasion before the destruction of Knossos in 1400 BC. Ironically, by supporting Herodotus and the Irish *Book of Invasions* Graves is undercutting his own theory.

Graves wants us to believe that the invasion Herodotus mentions was the earlier phase of the same invasion, which reached Britain and resulted in the battle of *Cad Goddeu* before finally reaching Ireland. Clearly, Graves is trying to consolidate two separate traditions and in doing so only confuses his argument. Later, Graves claims that the battle of *Cad Goddeu* occurred in c. 400 BC. This would be a more realistic date if Herodotus's invasion was linked to *Cad Goddeu*, but this would invalidate the *Book Of Invasions*'s own claim that the Tuatha Dé Danaan were already in Ireland by that time. Either way, Graves conflicts with the recorded dates within Herodotus's account or the *Book of Invasions*. The unrealistic time frame, which Graves favors, gives indirect support to his contention that a fast moving wave of patriarchal nomads overran earlier goddess worshipers.

Graves also believes another invasion of Ireland happened 200 years after the Tuatha Dé Danaan invasion. Traces of this second wave also occur in the *Book of Invasions* and in Bede's *History*. In this invasion, a wave of Picts originated near Thrace, moved through the Mediterranean, and finally reached the Atlantic. They eventually reached Ireland and fought the Tuatha De Danaan who convinced them to go to North Britain, then called Albany. This invasion plays little part in *The White Goddess* and Graves's mention of it in the middle of his explanation of *Cad Goddeu* only confuses matters.

To uphold the *Book of Invasions*'s Greek origin of the Tuatha De Danaan Graves suggests that they were originally a tribe of the Aegean sea goddess Amathaounta. This theory holds that the tribe of Amathaounta went from Crete to Amathus, in Cyprus, near the end of the second millennium BC. However, both the *Book of Invasions* and Graves's theory are questionable.

Graves ties this invasion to the Belgic invasion of Britain and from this point forward, Graves's Belgic invasion theory plays a large role in *The White Goddess*. The basic theory is that a confederation of Belgic tribes invaded Britain from Gaul at about 400 BC. They held new religious ideas that led to conflicts between the Bran and Beli cults that had lived peaceably together until that time. They also brought their tribal god Gwydion to Britain and as these Belgic tribes became accepted by the Beli tribes, Gwydion was made brother of Amathon and son of Beli and Danu.

Admittedly, there is some evidence for this theory. While it can't be proven that the Belgic invasion of Britain was the same invasion that brought the Tuatha Dé Danaan to Ireland, there is ample evidence that Belgic tribes did invade Britain in the first century BC. Caesar claimed the aboriginal people of Britain lived inland and the coast was populated by Belgic tribes who settled after earlier campaigns of looting and warfare. Caesar also encountered Belgic tribal names in Britain once he arrived. Further evidence that Caesar was aware of the Belgic element in Britain is the fact that when he made his first British assault, he tried to force the Belgic chief Dumnorix to accompany him. Caesar wanted to wrench from him any useful information about the Belgic tribes of Britain.

Caesar's mention of these earlier looting expeditions is the only account of this Belgic invasion, but archeology supports Caesar's claim. Evidence proves that the Belgae had executed British raids sometime around the first century BC. These raids may not constitute an invasion, but resulted in Belgic settlement in Britain and British acculturation by trade and intermarriage sometime before Caesar's arrival. Early twentieth-century historians often allowed Caesar's comments to outweigh archaeological evidence and Caesar's claim of an all out invasion lasted well into the 1900's. Some historians believed the Belgic invasion was the last of three Celtic invasions into Britain and that it occurred in the first half of the second century BC (Hubert 1988, 212, 216). This places the invasion in the early La Tene period, about the same time that iron was introduced to Britain. Other experts label this invasion more of a migration but agree with popular dating placing it at the early part of the first century BC and claim it was the last phase of Celtic colonization before the Roman conquest in Britain (Powell 10, 49-50, 54). Markale, like Graves, favors an earlier date and suggests a similar Belgic wave of Celtic farmers in the fifth century BC who brought iron tools and weapons with them (Markale 106). All of these experts favor Murray's claim that the Iron Age entered Britain via invasion of a hostile tribe with superior iron weapons and tools.

Logically enough these Belgae settlements were mainly along the Southern coast and focused around Kent. Historians contend that these settlements were located between the Isle of Wright and Firth of Forth and penetrated as far as Staffordshire (Rhys, Brynmor-Jones 7). Caesar reported that these Belgic tribes had gone to Britain to plunder but had eventually settled down peacefully. Here archaeological evidence supports Caesar again. Examining the hill-forts of the area we can distinguish two styles. One is the more comfortable type that appears more like a fortified town or community, possibly built by defenders protecting their establishment. The other is more offensive in style, possibly built by invaders as a foothold in the new land.

This so called Belgic invasion was actually little more than the usual Celtic tradition of cattle raids, practiced on the mainland as well as the islands. Raids upon neighboring tribes were common in the Celtic world and the English Channel was no deterrent. Raiding across a large body of water presented them with no difficulties but instead opened up new possibilities in choice of targets, landing points, and the ability to approach in almost total silence.

Archaeological evidence reveals that these raids eventually ended in peace and Rhys depicts the later Belgic invasion as inspiring unity between the older Brythons and Goidels rather than reviving old rivalries (Rhys, Brynmor-Jones 12). Additionally, Strabo reported that the Belgic tribe of the Veneti feared that Caesar would cross from Brittany and sever their trade links with Britain. His statement implies that peaceful trading existed between Belgic tribes on each side of the Channel and there is evidence that entire families moved into Britain, bringing with them women, children, and common non-warlike tools.

Graves depicts these Belgic invaders as technologically superior and, supposedly, one of the new tools they brought was the ox drawn plow. This, and their superior iron tools, supposedly allowed them to farm in places where the defending tribes could not. Perhaps this gift helped ease their acceptance in Britain. Amathon, the god of the plow, would have smiled favorably on this new and superior tool. Likewise, his people would have been happy to see that invading forces were content with inferior lands, which the natives considered uninhabitable. Other historians argue that the earlier British Celts were no less advanced than the invaders but Graves clings to his theory because it upholds his own belief that technological advancements inevitably encroach upon older paganism.

In retrospect, Graves is creating a theory of trans-European invasion. This invasion supposedly began near the Black Sea and resulted in the capture of Io and the destruction of Knossos. It then swept into Europe, eventually reaching Gaul. By then the invaders had lost much of their identity and merged with the Celts. They occupied Gaul for years before unifying again as the Belgae and passing into Britain. In Britain, they teamed with earlier invaders already established there and overthrew the older cult of Bran worshipers From Britain they proceeded to Ireland where they were labeled the Tuatha Dé Danaan. This theory is unlikely and Graves draws from conflicting historians to support it, but it does lend support to the legends found in the *Book of Invasions*. Graves has bent ancient history to validate Irish mythology. He's also set the stage for his own theories on a universal goddess culture and laid down the required invasion and trade routes to convey his ogham system from the Black Sea to Ireland.

CHAPTER X

WELSH TRIADS AND IRISH KENNINGS

While examining *The White Goddess* we should examine another aspect of early Welsh literature, which may illuminate Graves's claims. The collection of saying and stories known as *Trioedd Ynys Prydein*, or the *Triads of Britain*, are central to understanding Welsh bardic poetry. Concealed within their cryptic references are early records of Welsh tales, which later bards drew from. Within the triads, we find early mentions of Arthur, Taliesin, Maelgwn, and the various disasters, which left Britain defenseless against later invading Saxons. These tales and their characters are grouped in triplets under a single theme or subject matter. Examples include the "three golden shoe makers" and the "three heroic sovereigns of the Island of Britain". Such triadic groupings of popular tales served as mnemonic aids to reciting bards and were easily framed into a question and answer format for bardic students. However, the triads were more than simple mental lists.

Many triads have accompanying commentary, which elevates them above mere question and answer format. In a way, each triad becomes a miniature tale and the collective whole embodies the bulk of Welsh traditions. The triads preserve many details unknown outside of their triadic form, and hints of lost tales permeate the surviving triads. It's long been suspected that the triads were memorized by bards and formed the core of their education; although exactly when this process originated is unknown. In short, the Welsh bardic canon was entirely oral, existing only in the minds and mouths of the bards, and the triads served as an index.

Because the triads were developed over several generations dating them as a whole is impossible. Many experts agree that the majority are earlier than the mid-eleventh century and predate the earliest written copies of the *Mabinogion*. Early bards were obsessed with the contents of the triads and several manuscript copies survive to attest their popularity throughout the medieval period. Later bards continued to hand copy the triads even after the invention of the printing press although these same bards had often forgotten the tales, which the triads indexed. This problem was compounded by the fact that many of the triads were vague to begin with. By their very nature, the triads were meant only as a memory aid and not as a complete collection of Welsh lore. Possibly, the surviving hand written manuscripts were memory exercises.

From the thirteenth century onward, Welsh bards began to lose touch with older traditions despite their devotion to the triads. Welsh poetry from the thirteenth to the sixteenth century reveals this. Twelfth-century oral tradition still retained a firm bardic foundation but by the fifteenth century this foundation had crumbled under political pressure and a desire for more worldly learning. With most of the supporting tales lost, the triads became merely an empty index of names, locations, and forgotten battles. Later bards often plundered the triads for old names, which they could sprinkle into their poems to create an air of past Celtic glory. Bards who didn't know the true stories of these characters created new legends in which they attempted to explain their mention. This resulted in many late corruptions to authentic Welsh mythology. The *Mabinogion* abounds in such errors and the corruption of Caridwen's image has already been noted.

Graves cites the triads ten times within his work but never reveals which translation he uses. His reference to triads by their number implies a translation with numbered entries. Yet, before 1948, there was no complete translation of the triads and those partial translations which existed, varied in their numbering. However, when Graves's numbering is placed against his sources an interesting pattern is revealed.

Eight of the ten triads used by Graves appear in the footnotes to Guest's *Mabinogion*; each listed by the correctly corresponding number. Apparently, Graves simply gleaned his references from Guest and Davies. The matching numbering system used by Graves and Guest is substantial evidence for this assertion. A quick comparison between Guest's use of the triads in question and Graves's nearly identical use confirms our suspicion. In most cases, Guest fails to reproduce the entire triad but merely offers those lines relevant to her argument. In each of these cases, we find that Graves also fails to reproduce the entire triad and depends entirely upon the portions, which Guest quotes.

Twice within *White Goddess* Graves mentions that the battle of *Cad Goddeu* was among the "three frivolous battles of Britain". Guest mentions the same fact within her footnotes (Guest 324). Graves's second reference to the three frivolous battles relates the tale of Morvan, Caridwen's ugly son and one of the few survivors of the battle of Camlan. Guest relates the same tale within her footnotes on page 429 and refers the reader to her own earlier reference to the same legend on page 318. Graves, following this cross reference, found both mentions of the frivolous battles and Morvan's survival at Camlan. He needed no further sources to support his brief mention of the legend.

Likewise, Graves mentions that Kai was one of the "three diademed chiefs of battle". Guest mentions this triad three times within her notes (Guest 351, 360, 417). Additionally, Davies mentions this triad in his *Mythology and Rites of the British Druids* and may be a possible alternate source for Graves's statement. Aranrhod appears twice in Graves's triad references; once as the mother of the twins Gwengwyngwyn and Gwanat, and again as the "silver circled daughter of Don". Both references derive from a single paragraph of Guest's notes (Guest 301). Graves may also have gleaned the same idea from Davies (Davies 1809, 205, 268). Chapter eighteen also mentions triad 24 and the "three crimson stained ones of Britain". Graves cites the triad as listing Llew Llaw and Arthur as two of the three "stained ones" and fails to mention the third member of the triad. Once again, Guest cites the same triad on page 301 and mentions Llew and Arthur in the same order as Graves; likewise failing to mention the third member of the triad.

The "three tribal herdsmen of Britain" also appear in both books. In chapter nine of *White Goddess*, Graves reveals the names of all three of these herdsmen. All three are also given by Guest (Guest 318). Additionally, the most famous of the three (Gwydion) is mentioned again in relationship to this triad earlier in Guest's book (Guest 300). Lastly, chapter six of *White Goddess* compares references within triads 61 and 50 to a legendary prison known as Oeth or Anoeth from which Arthur was rescued by Goreu. Guest refers to this prison twice and cross-references her citations (Guest 332, 406). Davies, in his *Mythology and Rites*, also references this triad and equates Oeth and Anoeth with Caer Sidi (Davies 1809, 404, 407).

These references explain all but two of Graves's triad citations. The two triads, which Graves doesn't extract from Guest's footnotes, include his reference to triad 54 and an unnamed triad which mentions Britain as the "honey island" (Graves 1993, 60, 86). Graves uses triad 54 to support the legend that the Welsh descended from Gomer, son of Japhet. This legend is then connected to Geoffrey's claim that the British descended from Trojans. Graves's mixing of Celtic, Biblical, and Greek genealogies suggests that he may have found references to triad 54 within the works of Davies. Guest fails to produce the relevant triad but, interestingly enough, her footnotes refer the reader to Davies's works regarding the legendary Welsh ancestor Hu Gadarn and his role in the Deluge (Guest 327). References to the honey island also occur within Guest's notes and Davies's *Mythology and Rites* but both fail to mention the relationship to the triads. Guest instead cites this phrase from one of Taliesin's poems (Guest 293).

From this, we learn that Graves could have discovered nearly all of his triadic material from the footnotes of Guest's *Mabinogion* and three of Graves's citations are found within a single page (Guest 301). The two triads, which she fails to quote directly, are indicated by cross references to both Edward Davies and the works of Taliesin;

two sources, which Graves already knew. We now understand why Graves hesitates to depend too heavily upon the triads. He almost certainly lacked a full translation.

In addition to the triads, we should also consider *Cad Goddeu* in light of poetic kennings. Kennings were a variation of simile in which the phrase became consistently linked to the noun in question. Examples include calling a slot machine a "one armed bandit" or one's spouse as "my better half" or "the ball and chain". Such kennings were popular in Irish and German poetry until the end of the Renaissance. Welsh poets also indulged in this technique but, unlike the Irish, no formalized system survives.

Interestingly enough, the Irish fili created kennings for the letters of the ogham alphabet. These could serve poets as either a memory system for the ogham, or vice versa, the ogham could serve as a memory aid to the poetic phrases during impromptu poetry recitals. Like the triads, and the ogham listings discussed earlier, the kennings could be put into question and answer form and serve as a test for bardic students. Each letter was given an accompanying poetic phrase, which was supposedly connected to the letter by some sort of symbolism. This symbolism was so obscure and varied that modern experts fail to see the connections between the majority of them and the letters they represent. Some kennings were connected to the tree associated to the given letter. Thus, one of the kennings for *duir*, the oak, was "most exalted tree" because the oak was held in highest regard within Celtic lore. Other kennings were based not on the tree itself but on things made from that particular type of wood. One of the kennings for *fearn*, the alder, was "milk container" because milk buckets were often made of alder wood. "Shelter of a lunatic" is given for *quert*, the apple, because both Merlin and Suibne concealed themselves in apple trees after going mad. Other kennings are more obscure and their meanings are hopelessly lost. We may never know why *onn* was called "wounder of horses" or why *huathe* is "most difficult at night".

Three systems of ogham kennings exist, each named after a

character of Irish myth. They are *Briatharogam Morainn mic Moin*, *Briatharogam Maic in Oc*, and *Briatharogam Con Culainn*: ogham of Morann, ogham of Mac Ind Oic, and ogham of Cuchulainn respectively. These mysterious kennings could serve poets as a way of secretly expressing the letters of the ogham in their speech or could be used as stock phrases for their poetry when writer's block struck them. If ogham kennings could be put into poetry, could they be found within *Cad Goddeu*? If so, this would give tremendous evidence to Graves's theory that *Cad Goddeu* concealed the ogham alphabet.

Unfortunately, we find no known ogham kennings in either *Cad Goddeu* or *Hanes Taliesin*. We shouldn't be surprised. Ogham kennings, like the ogham itself, are an Irish invention and it's unlikely that we would find either concealed in medieval Welsh poetry. Of course, it can be argued that a large amount of Irish mythology and culture did infiltrate Wales but ogham didn't seem to make this transition. Undeniably, *Cad Goddeu* contains a handful of cliché themes and many cryptic phrases similar to the Irish kennings, yet we find no evidence of any concealed meanings to the poem beyond the obvious riddles. Riddles exist within *Cad Goddeu* but ogham isn't one of them.

Although Welsh poetry contained no formalized system of kennings or riddles whose answers were ogham letters Graves continues to press his argument. Where he couldn't find kennings and riddles he creates them by rearranging the lines of both *Cad Goddeu* and *Hanes Taliesin*. Chapter five of *White Goddess* displays this method as Graves rewrites Guest's translation of *Hanes Taliesin* to create riddles, which he then answers. The logic behind Graves's answers is debatable. For the curious, the answers to the riddles Graves "found" in *Hanes Taliesin* are given at the opening of his sixth chapter. To arrive at the answers Graves needed he was required to delve into a larger pool of literature than any medieval bard could realistically be credited with. Graves clearly overestimates the ability of the bards in their construction of the poetic riddles and in doing so raises an interesting question.

Exactly how well read were these Renaissance bards and how did the integration of non-Celtic literature impact bardic poetry? In short, bards from the fourteenth century onward were surprisingly well read in classical Greek and Latin texts, yet it was exactly this education, which caused them to neglect their native Welsh traditions. The invention of the printing press, the increasing accessibility of texts, and the resulting increase in worldly education contributed enormously to the death of bardism. Before the fourteenth century, bardic education in Greek and Latin were sporadic and this lack of education limited bards to mastering their own language and legends. These poets had access to a wide range of Celtic sources, including Nennius, Geoffrey, the *Gododdin*, the triads, the *Mabinogion*, and the texts carried out of Ireland after it had "saved civilization". Bards of the late fourteenth century onward were confronted with a wider range of literature, including classical mythology and history, the Bible, and an influx of Arabic learning. Foreign characters such as Hercules, Alexander, and Solomon quickly infiltrated bardic poetry and imply that bards wished to tie Welsh traditions into a larger literature. Yet even these bards could not have possibly drawn from all of the sources Graves claims were available to them while creating their riddles.

The entire situation was a contradiction. Early bards couldn't have possibly had the required education needed to hide ogham in a series of non-Celtic riddles. Renaissance bards may have possessed a better education but they had no motive to create riddles concealing an obscure Irish alphabet, which they never used. Their increased education was forcing them away from Celtic traditions. Their riddles didn't convey their knowledge of Welsh mythology but rather revealed their ignorance.

In reality these riddles were little more than idle guessing games and even the most uneducated listener would find no challenge in guessing the correct answers. Many such riddles may have evolved from earlier Welsh kennings although such kennings were never formalized into a concrete system; nor did they conceal ogham. The riddles usually implied particular characters of Welsh legends without actually naming them and the listener was expected to recognize the character intended. Yet, the hints were never difficult. A riddle whose answer was Jesus might consist of three lines stating:

I was born in a stable
I wore a crown of thorns
I was crucified

Few of the riddles found in Renaissance Welsh poetry are more difficult than this. If these riddles were truly used as methods of teaching Welsh mythology then they serve as sad evidence of the unfortunate state of education at the time. Most likely, the use of these riddles traced back to truly pagan times when more difficult riddles were used in earnest to teach a complete Celtic mythos. Such question and answer dialogs have long been popular within Celtic tradition and may trace back to questions framed around the triads.

However, riddles referring to characters of Welsh mythology were scant before the fourteenth century. After that date, we find greater commonalties between the Welsh romances and bardic court poetry. The implication is that there was little communication between the two schools until late, just as Graves argues. This suggests that the riddles within *Cad Goddeu* are a late addition. They cannot be part of an original sixth century poem because most of the actions attributed to these characters are themselves late corruptions drawn from the *Mabinogion*. A real sixth century Taliesin couldn't have riddled upon Blodeuwedd's creation from flowers because, in the sixth century, that tale hadn't yet been invented. At this point, most critics abandon the hope of finding an original sixth century *Cad Goddeu* behind these corruptions, but Graves chooses another path. He suggests the theory of two Taliesins, a real sixth century bard and a later Gwion who modified the poem to conceal the ogham.

The riddles within *Cad Goddeu* reveal no secrets of Celtic mythology but instead derive from the *Mabinogion*; particular interest was paid to the second and fourth branches of the collection, *Branwen Daughter of Llyr* and *Math Son of Mathonwy*. It seems that the author was familiar with the *Mabinogion*, and perhaps knew no other Welsh mythology. This indicates the late state of the poem. Either these lines are late corruptions of an earlier poem, or the entire poem dates to a later time when only the *Mabinogion* and its related tales survived in popular story telling. Either way, the poem as it stands is of the late Middle Ages. Any earlier versions of a pre-Christian poem within *Cad Goddeu* were lost long ago; if they ever existed. *Cad Goddeu* does contain elements of paganism but only those elements which could have been drawn from the *Mabinogion*, itself a late corruption of earlier tales. In short, everything in *Cad Goddeu* could be found in the *Mabinogion* expect for those line dealing with the magic battle of trees.

Yet, it's exactly this magic battle of trees that comprises the core of the poem. *Cad Goddeu*, after all, is supposedly a poem of the battle of the trees. Those lines, which were inspired by the *Mabinogion* may be easy to identify as corruptions, but they are not the point of the story. Behind these lines is a collection of other lines telling of a battle in which trees fought as soldiers. Exactly why they fought or who led them is debatable but the popular tradition given in *Myvyrian Archaiology* should not be lightly discarded. In all probability, there was an earlier draft of *Cad Goddeu*, credited to Taliesin, which dealt mainly with Gwydion's animation of trees to fight against otherworldly forces. This poem was written as a tribute to Gwydion's battle and was popularly credited to Taliesin, but later bards confused the matter, and claimed that Taliesin himself was also present at the battle.

An alternate theory regarding the origin of *Cad Goddeu* suggests that it was based on an earlier Irish poem attributed to the visionary poet Suibhne. Suibhne's poem contains kennings upon various trees, including oak, alder, blackthorn, and yew. These kennings depict the oak as "high above trees" and yew as "conspicuous in graveyards"; a fact Joyce also noted (Joyce 1:359). The ash tree is portrayed as useful for weapons, the bramble is covered in blood, and the birch tree is entangled near its top. Each of these images is reminiscent of the later *Cad Goddeu*. The mention of the entangled birch is striking and forces the reader to reconsider Graves's assertion that the similar image in *Cad Goddeu* is a metaphor for literary struggles.

Suibhne's poem also bears significant similarities to the Welsh poem *Apple Trees*, popularly credited to Merlin. The mythic accounts of Merlin and Suibhne depict both poets as madmen living in woods and clinging to a form of natural mysticism. Merlin supposedly lived before Suibhne but the existent copies of his poems are later than the Suibhne poem. Therefore, transmission from Ireland to Wales seems likely and we must wonder if both *Apple Trees* and *Cad Goddeu* were influenced by the earlier Suibhne material. The commonalties between the works of Suibhne, Merlin, and Taliesin contributed to confusion between them and the possibility that all three derived from a common legend cannot be overlooked. It has even been suggested that Merlin was the original protagonist of *Cad Goddeu* (Tolstoy 136).

In light of all this we must ask: what is Edward Davies's stance on the poem? After all, it was Davies who suggested to Graves that *Cad Goddeu* implied a druidic alphabetical secret and we expect to see more of Davies behind Graves's reading of the poem. However, readers searching for an inspirational translation of *Cad Goddeu* from the pen of Edward Davies will be disappointed.

Like his treatment of the Taliesin legend, already mentioned, Davies fails to address the complete *Cad Goddeu*. Once again, Davies has begged off any attempt to interpret the meaning of such a mystical poem. Instead, *Mythology and Rites* offers his usual fragments and Davies admits that he has little clue regarding *Cad Goddeu*'s meaning (Davies 1809, 538). His only conclusion is that the poem is full of Arkite lore and he sides with earlier critics who labeled the poem "eminently incomprehensible".

Davies claims that he is only offering the "conclusion of Taliesin's *Cad Goddeu*" and cites only 108 lines of the original Welsh text. This partial listing is broken into seven sections and within each section, Davies provides prose translations, which even an amateur would dismiss when placed against Nash, Skene, and Ford. The only interesting items within the Davies translation is his suggestion that the nine types of flowers were used during a ritual purification of the bard in the Arkite religion and his mention of a gem encrusted shield reminiscent of the biblical breastplate of *Exodus* (Davies 1809, 540, 544). Davies concludes with the claim that Jesus was included in the poem merely to give it an air of Christianity and conceal its druidic flavor. Graves later claimed that many druidic poems used the same trick.

Celtic Researches offers even less analysis of *Cad Goddeu*. Here, finally, we find Davies's suggestion that *Cad Goddeu* was a battle of ideas. Furthermore, Davies interprets the hundred-headed toad as a symbol of the human race in general. It's an odd interpretation but not without some ingenuity; one hundred heads or one hundred families was the definition of a *cantrev*, the ancient land divisions of Wales. Davies argues that the battle "in the recesses of his head" imply a mental struggle in the minds of the Celts. Graves borrows this idea but avoids Davies's translation.

Davies concludes his notes to *Cad Goddeu* by stating that his partial translation is offered "in order to exercise the ingenuity of better mythologists" (Davies 1809, 538). Davies knew that *Cad Goddeu* was beyond his understanding and he hoped that future mythologists would sort it out. Davies has dropped the gauntlet at the feet of his fellow researchers and, nearly 140 years later, Graves accepted the challenge. As we've already noted, Graves felt that poets such as himself were exclusively qualified to interpret poetical and mythological symbolism and resolve issues of iconotropy. In light of this attitude, how could he allow *Cad Goddeu* to go unresolved? Graves considered it not only an interesting puzzle but also his duty as a poet to salvage the poem's meaning from Davies.

Davies was, after all, not a poet but a nineteenth century Christian historian.

As we know, Graves believes *Cad Goddeu* contains concealed references to the ogham and he reorders the lines to support this view. The equally obscure *Hanes Taliesin* undergoes a similar transformation in Graves's hands. These two poems are the core of *The White Goddess* but they are hardly the only poems Graves rewrites during his research. In chapter twelve of *White Goddess,* the Irish *Song Of Amergin* receives a similar revision as Graves searches for concealed references to ogham. Like *Cad Goddeu* and *Hanes Taliesin,* the *Song Of Amergin* is a collection of independent "I have been" statements and therefore lends itself well to Graves's divide and conquer method of interpretation. Amergin himself has several parallels to the Welsh Taliesin and Graves draws on Macalister's views in his discussion of the poem.

CHAPTER XI

RENEWAL OF CONFLICTS

Most of the fourth branch of the *Mabinogion* deals with Gwydion's training of Llew in magic and combat. It's Gwydion's magic that makes Llew a man by the threat of a phantom army and creation of a magical woman as Llew's wife. Thus, Gwydion trains Llew in love and war, the two primary interests of young men in primitive societies. The enduring popularity of the *Mabinogion* undoubtedly hinged on its use of these two timeless themes.

Gwydion guessed Bran's name because Bran carried an alder branch into battle and the words *Bran* and *alder* are linguistically connected in the original Welsh. Apparently, Bran wasn't too intelligent for carrying his namesake into battle. Gwydion and Amathon prevailed and the secret name of their female commander was not guessed. However, from the Nash quote Graves provides we know that the unguessed name is *Achren*, meaning "trees".

Bran also means *crow* or *raven* as Graves argues. He suggests that the Bran cult came from the Aegean long before Gwydion's people made the same journey. He then draws resemblances between Bran and Aesculapius, a Pelasgian hero also symbolized by the crow. Aesculapius is portrayed in the *Iliad* as a mortal who had learned the art of medicine from the Centaurs. He was eventually killed by Zeus in punishment for raising the dead and thereby contesting Zeus's powers. Although Homer depicts Aesculapius as mortal, he was worshiped as a god of healing by later Greeks. He was often depicted as a bearded old man with a snake wrapped around his walking staff. This staff was the caduceus, still used as the symbol of the medical profession today. Graves believes Aesculapius was the "king of the Thessalian crow-totem tribe of Lapiths" (Graves 1993, 52).

This same crow tribe had an earlier king named Coronus, or Cronos, also meaning crow. Coronus was killed by Hercules and it's no accident that Graves believes Hercules was the sacred hero of the tribe of Amathaounta, the very tribe, which he claims the Tuatha De Danaans descended from. Now we begin to understand the hostilities between the armies of Achren and Bran. The battle of *Cad Goddeu,* where Achren defeated the crow god Bran, is a continuation of an earlier conflict between the Lapith crow tribe of Coronus and the Amathaounta tribe near the Aegean. A battle starting near the Aegean at the outset of the proposed invasion spills into Europe where the same religious conflict inspired the Belgae to overthrow earlier Celts in Britain. In both instances the crow tribe was defeated by the son of the goddess; first Hercules, then Gwydion. A dark omen was slowly spreading over pagan Europe. For the first time, the Son was eclipsing the Moon. This intrusion of patriarchal solar worship into druidism is exactly the same conflict Davies complains of in his *Mythology and Rites* and Graves's theory is an elaborate substantiating of Davies's conjecture.

Yet, this shift was slow and subtle. The battles between these pagan religions were fought over several generations and a wide geographic area. Perhaps nobody at the time could have linked the capture of the goddess' temple in Argos with the fall of Bran's worship in Britain. Indeed, there may not have been a direct connection. We are only reconstructing those parts of history, which uphold Graves's theory. The objections to this theory are many.

However radical Graves's theory sounds, we must remember that it doesn't entail the total destruction of goddess cultures at this point. The sweeping invasion out of Greece and into Ireland was not an extermination of paganism, the druids, or goddess worship. Both sides of the battle were goddess-worshiping pagans who honored the moon and sacred trees. Both also worshiped the divine son of the goddess and sacrificed their kings as his earthly counterparts. The difference between the two sides rested in the degree of homage they paid to the goddess in comparison to her son, and how frequently they sacrificed their kings because of this. The invaders, represented by the Amathaounta tribe and the Tuatha De Danaans, called for less frequent human sacrifices. This extension of the king's life also extended his power and he used his influence to further downplay the need for his own sacrifice.

Much of this theory depends on the connection between those Celtic tribes who worshiped Bran in Britain and the Lapith tribes who worshiped Aesculapius. The unifying factor is the crow, which was supposedly the totem of both tribes. The names Bran, Aesculapius, Coronus, and its variant Cronos all have connections to the word crow. However, Bran's connection to the crow appears forced and Graves gives little supporting evidence for it. Later he mentions that Cronos derived from the root word *cron* or *corn*, meaning crow and this equated Cronos with Bran, the Celtic crow god.

This is merely circular logic. Graves has stated that Bran equates to Cronos and therefore means crow. Then, as evidence for this, he mentions that Cronos equates to crow and must therefore connect to Bran. The entire argument is a closed loop in which A equals B because B equals A. No outside evidence is ever considered and from reading *The White Goddess* alone we assume none existed.

Luckily for Graves, there is evidence that Bran equates to the crow and raven in Celtic myth, despite his failure to it. Examining the parallel translations in Nash's *Taliesin* confirms the fact. Where *raven* appears in the English translations we find that Nash was translating from the Welsh *bran,* or one of its variants (Nash 93, 100, 156, 203). Davies had also compared Bran with the raven long before Nash (Davies 1809, 401, 505). In 1908, Edward Anwyl had suggested that *Bran* equated to *raven* in the Welsh language, and the confusion between crows and ravens in Celtic myth is well documented. By 1911, J. A. MacCulloch used Frazerian methods to claim that Bran may have been one of several Celtic "bird-gods" and suggests that such a bird-god cult is hinted at in the magic birds of Rhiannon found in the *Mabinogion* and the *Triads* (MacCulloch 215).

Additionally, both ravens and crows symbolize death in Celtic mythology, as the *Gododdin* illustrates.

Yet, it's not surprising that Graves's Bran theories appear confused. Eventually, Bran become symbolic of nearly all pagan gods whom represent the divine son in Graves's hypothetical pagan world. As such, Bran represents the traditional god of those pagan societies before the rise of patriarchy. He is son, lover, and victim of the goddess before the newer pagans began emphasizing the importance of the divine son and modify this cycle.

Graves needed to mold Bran into this role if he was to support his interpretation of the battle of *Cad Goddeu*. Unfortunately, this also meant equating Bran to so many mythic figures that he risks losing his identity. Throughout *The White Goddess* Graves equates Bran to Cronos, Saturn, Jehovah, Apollo, Phoroneus, Orpheus, Q're, and Iahu. Nor is the crow his only bird. Graves also connects Bran to the barnacle goose, raven, and wren. Lastly, as his name implies, Bran is a god of grain. Based on these alleged crow connections, Graves draws further links between Bran and Aesculapius.

Because Aesculapius often appears with a dog, and *Cad Goddeu* was fought over a stolen dog, Graves believes the tribe of Bran descends from the tribe of Aesculapius. As further evidence, Graves relates Hercules's task of stealing the dog Cerberus from the Greek underworld, a task similar to Amathon's theft of a dog from Annwn. In each story, the dog served as a watchdog and his theft implied the loss of protection. The dog's protective role derives not only from these myths but also from Davies's *Myth and Rites*. Davies dedicates two pages to dog symbolism within Arkite religion, credits the dog with "fidelity, vigilance, and sagacity", and claims that anything protecting pagan temples may be symbolized by dogs (Davies 1809, 232-234). Lastly, Davies notes that dog symbolism appears in the Eleusinian mysteries, Isis was assisted by dogs when searching for Anubis, and Ceres was accompanied by dogs.

Hercules used a drugged cake to overpower Cerberus. This trick was familiar to Graves. He had used it as early as 1916, in his poem

Escape, to describe his own near death experience during World War I. From this poem, we learn that Graves considered his "death" an initiation or a mythic rebirth. Graves was reborn by the grace of the goddess, "Dear Lady Proserpine", who allowed him to skirt Cerberus and return to life. Once again, Graves was breathing his own life experiences into *The White Goddess* as a way of validating his argument and then validating his own experiences through the argument he created.

Hercules had also once stolen a roebuck from the grove of Artemis and Graves links this to the theft of the roebuck of *Cad Goddeu*. He claims that in both instances the roebuck symbolized concealment of religious secrets. The roebuck's ability to elude hunters, or lure them deeper into the woods was not lost on Graves. Examples of such futile hunts are found in the *Mabinogion*, Arthurian legends, and Grimm.

So far, Graves has included the symbolism of the dog and roebuck because he considers them major elements in the battle, which *Cad Goddeu* commemorates, and of the earlier Greek battles, which began the invasion. By linking Gwydion's tribe to Hercules Graves is able to make the dog and roebuck symbolic of his pagan religion. However, the dog and roebuck were not the only animals stolen from Annwn. The triads indicate that a third animal was stolen as well and Graves has a harder time accounting for the third member of his trinity.

The triad in question declares:

> The three frivolous causes of battle on the Isle of Prydein: The first was the battle of Goddeu, which was caused about a bitch, a roe-buck and a lapwing; and in that battle 71,000 men were slain.

The mention of the lapwing proves that variant versions of the legend of *Cad Goddeu* were known in medieval times. The result was that some bards knew of the lapwing and some didn't. Idealistically, all bards were trained to meet the high standards set by the triads but in reality, many bards fell short. The author who recorded the story of *Cad Goddeu* in the *Myvyrian* collection omits the lapwing. Conversely, Nash cites the lapwing from the triadic version. Obviously, Graves was familiar with both versions.

Graves places particular emphasis on the triad mentioning the lapwing. However, it's unnecessary for him to consult this triad and there is no reason to draw the lapwing into the argument. Graves could have simplified his argument by ignoring the triad in question and eliminating both the lapwing and the numerous explanations used to justify its inclusion. Few readers would have been aware of the triadic description of *Cad Goddeu* and his failure to mention it would raise no eyebrows. In light of this, we must ask why he places such importance on the triadic version of *Cad Goddeu*.

The answer lies in Graves's mythic hero, Hercules. Besides stealing the dog from Hades and the roebuck from Artemis, Hercules once stole the tripod from Herophile, a priest of Delphi. Coincidentally, Herophile's father was Zeus in the form of a lapwing. So, while Hercules hadn't actually stolen a lapwing, he had stolen from the temple of Delphi, which was guarded by a descendant of a sacred lapwing. Graves argues that the lapwing symbolizes disguise and the intentional confusion of pagan secrets in attempts to conceal them. In making the lapwing sacred, Graves claims the Celts are following an age-old pagan tradition, which can be found in various religious texts, including the Bible and Koran.

He believes Leviticus's claim that the Lapwing is unclean is a taboo of a non-Semitic origin, proving that the lapwing was sacred before its introduction into the Bible. His evidence for this is that many of the unclean birds on the list are alien to the Semitic lands and most were sacred in Greece or Italy. The implication is that the lapwing was a sacred bird to the matriarchal pagans of Greece, but Graves has little supporting evidence. Granted, many of the unclean foods on the Leviticus list are there because they are pagan symbols. However, this may not be true of the lapwing. Graves claims all birds on the list were sacred in Greece or Italy, but if he knew of any specific examples of the lapwing being sacred, he fails to cite them.

Graves speculates that since many of the animals on the list are foreign to Semitic lands the list must be of non-Semitic origin. He overlooks the consideration that by outlawing such animals the Jews were prohibiting contact or trade with non-Semitic people and prohibiting themselves from eating food outside of their own homeland. These laws were made to keep Jews out of touch with non-Semitic pagans in an attempt to limit pagan corruption to Jewish religion. Graves should have realized this motive behind these prohibitions; the opening chapter of *King Jesus* uses a similar argument to explain the Jewish ban on priestesses.

As further evidence that the lapwing is sacred Graves cites the Koran's claim that the lapwing was one of King Solomon's prophetic birds. Unfortunately, the identity of the lapwing in both the Bible and the Koran are disputed. The King James calls this bird the lapwing, but the New Revised Standard Version prefers hoopoe. Other sources agree and claim that the hoopoe was considered unclean because it eats bugs from cow manure. The lapwing in the Koran is also occasionally translated as hoopoe.

Confusion between the lapwing and hoopoe is common in mythology and early historic accounts. The occult significance of both birds is documented well into the Renaissance and their organs are frequently mentioned ingredients in occult manuscripts. Graves knew of this confusion but insists on the questionable King James translation and thereby gives his lapwing ideas validity. It's odd that Graves prefers lapwing to hoopoe in such ambiguous cases; the hoopoe's occult lore is greater and more fitting to Graves's views.

With the above connections established, Graves places one more piece into his puzzle. He cleverly links the battle of *Cad Goddeu* to earlier religious battles in Greece. He establishes that the defeated Bran is the British equivalent to Aesculapius and the defeated Cronos. Hercules becomes the victorious hero who stole the dog, roebuck, and (symbolically) the lapwing during these earlier battles. Amathon, his British counterpart, accomplished the same thing when he stole dog, roebuck, and lapwing in a single raid into Annwn. His brother, Gwydion, was victorious in the ensuing battle against other worldly forces when he guessed Bran's religious associations to the alder tree. In Britain, the cult of the male hero had stolen glory from their more matriarchal cousins, as they had done in countless battles before. The sacred dog, roebuck, and lapwing became the symbols of the new cult.

Thus, Graves writes that *Cad Goddeu* uses "elements of a Hercules myth" to tell how the Tuatha De Danaans captured important shrines from the Bran cult. He dates the actual battle to c.400 BC and claims that this is about the time of the Celtic La Tene phase and the first Belgic invasion of Britain. As evidence, he cites Geoffrey of Monmouth's war between Belinus and Brennius, which he believes to be confused account of the battle. Graves equates Belinus and Brennius to Bran and Beli. Beli is father to Arianrhod, Gwydion, and Amathon in the Welsh triads. Thus, Graves says Amathon entered the battle of *Cad Goddeu* as a representative of his father Beli.

There are several things wrong with this argument. First, Geoffrey's pre-Roman history is suspicious. Graves dates the war of Belinus and Brennius (and thus the battle of *Cad Goddeu*) by the fact that Rome was sacked by Gauls in 390 BC under a leader named Brennus. Graves identifies this man with the Brennius of Geoffrey. While the sacking of Rome by Brennus is a fact, that doesn't prove the entire story. This Brennus may not be the same man as Brennius and even if he is, this doesn't prove Geoffrey's story. Lastly, even if Geoffrey's story is true, there's no proof that this war between Belinus and Brennius is a confused account of the battle of *Cad Goddeu*. Graves has already stated that *Cad Goddeu* was not a literal battle, yet Geoffrey is clear that Belinus and Brennius fought literal battles in their war.

Graves implies that *Cad Goddeu* tells how an invading Brythonic tribe helped a British alliance of agricultural tribes capture the most important temple from the Bronze Age priesthood of Bran. The temple was Avebury and was the center of the Bran cult. Graves even suggests that Avebury was their national necropolis. He may not be far off in calling it such. Avebury is a mere seventeen miles north of Stonehenge and the entire area around both monuments has a high concentration of burials.

Although there are no ancient burials located within the sarsen circle of Stonehenge there are burials within the perimeter of the outer ditch. Additionally, many of the Aubrey holes of Stonehenge contain cremations, although this may not have been their original purpose. Some of these burials are newer than Stonehenge and contain pieces of the Stonehenge stones. Overall, there are almost 350 burials in a radius of a few miles around Stonehenge; more burials than any other area of equal size in Britain. Some of these burials date to between 3000-2000 BC, predating Stonehenge, and we must wonder if Stonehenge or Avebury were intentionally placed near the burials or if later burials were intentionally placed near the monuments.

The other British tribes, who united with the new invaders, worshiped Beli rather than Bran. These people were farmers and Graves believes their demigod was Amathon, the god of plowmen. He bases this on Rhys's assertion that the Celtic root word *ar* implies "plowed land" and Guest's rendering of *Amathon* as "husbandman" (Guest 323). With the help of the invading Brythonic tribe (who worshiped Gwydion) they displaced Bran and Arawn as demigods under the supreme deity. Amathon and Gwydion then became the new demigods under this supreme deity and the supreme deity itself became Beli. In plain English, the Tuatha De Danaans kicked out the Bran cult, installed new demigods and redefined the ultimate god as Beli, their own supreme being. This theory making Beli a violent intruder into older Celtic paganism derived from Algernon Herbert's 1838 *Essay on the Neo-Druidic Heresy*, extensively cited by Nash (Nash 240-41). This victory was reached because the British Amathaonians gave the Brythonic tribe some sort of secret knowledge about the Bran cult.

Just what was the secret that the Amathaonians gave the new

invaders?

Graves implies that this secret was the name of the supreme deity of the Bran cult and that Bran and Arawn were lesser deities serving under this unnamed deity. Who was this deity? Graves won't reveal this name until chapter sixteen, but instead quotes Caesar's comment that the druids believed they descended from the god *Dis*, sometimes given as *Dis Pater*.

Dis is the Latin god of the underworld so we can assume that Caesar didn't actually mean the druids descended from Dis, but that they believed they came from a Celtic god who was equated to Dis in the Latin pantheon. The true name of this "Celtic Dis" isn't recorded by Caesar. Caesar also claimed that Gallic druids came to Britain to study. Based on this Graves concludes that the seat of the "Celtic Dis" cult was in Britain. The implication is that the "Celtic Dis" cult was centered at Avebury and was controlled by a druidic priesthood who saw Bran and Arawn as demigods under this mysterious "Celtic Dis". This is the cult Amathon and Gwydion's people defeated when Gwydion revealed the true name of the "Celtic Dis".

Later in *White Goddess* Graves suggests that this Celtic Dis was a god named *Jievoao*. The method Graves uses to arrive at this conclusion is complex and questionable. Indeed, it's the prime secret of the battle of *Cad Goddeu* and one of the largest points Graves attempts to prove in *The White Goddess*.

Yet, even if we disregard Graves's conclusion we are not left completely in the dark regarding the identity of this mysterious Celtic Dis. We may not be able to place a name to this deity but perhaps we can give him a face. Salomon Reinach has identified several figures of what he believes to be the Gallo-Roman Dis Pater and reproduces several in his *Bronze Figures*. Cook also reproduces two such statuettes (Cook 1: 97). This deity is commonly shown wearing a wolf skin and holding a deep pot or cauldron while leaning on a staff with his other hand. MacCulloch inclines towards a similar assessment and mentions that the staff of Dis Pater is sometimes replaced by a hammer and that this deity can tentatively be linked to Cernunnos (MacCulloch 31).

Returning to Gwydion, Graves equates him to the Norse god Odin or Woden, whose symbol was the ash tree *ygdrasill*. By doing, so Graves supports the theory that the invading Belgic tribes had a Germanic origin. Rhys made similar suggestions in his *Hibbert Lectures* and *The Welsh People* and Charles Squire followed suit in 1905. Graves cites all three sources within *White Goddess* and may have taken the theory from any. By linking Gwydion to Odin Graves establishes the ash tree as Gwydion's symbol. The Belgae themselves had always claimed a Germanic origin and *Germani* had been the name of an early Celtic tribe. Caesar himself had confused Germans with Celts during his invasion of Gaul.

Graves next claims that there were at least two places known as Annwn, or the Celtic other world. One was in the Prescelly Mountains of Pembrokeshire, where the bluestones of Stonehenge originated. The other was in Wiltshire, the county where Avebury is located. Graves may be partly correct here but not exactly on target. Annwn is the Celtic other world and as such it is never clearly defined. It may have never meant to be understood as a literal place on the face of the earth but may have been seen more as another dimension, a metaphysical world or parallel universe, which overlapped into our world. It was generally believed to be in the north, although the west is a close runner-up and was the choice supported by Davies. Exactly where in the north was never clear and was relative to the location of the speaker at the time. No matter where you were, Annwn was always considered North of you and similar ideas surface in the earliest Wiccan books (Gardner 1991, 24). The souls of the dead were believed to go to Annwn, but dying wasn't the only way to get there. Like most pagans, the Celts believed the living could enter the other world via magic rituals or a sacred location that served as a magic gateway. Just as Greeks believed that deep caves could lead to Hades, the Celts believed that caves, wells, or springs could lead to Annwn. Thus, each Celtic community could have its own local entrance to Annwn.

When Graves says there was an Annwn at Wiltshite and at Prescelly Mountains he implies that there were local entrances to Annwn at these places. These local entrances could have been any impressive natural feature that had a mystic air about it. Caves and springs are typical examples. Mountains would also be suitable although the Celts seemed to prefer the idea that Annwn was underground like Hades and not on a mountaintop like Olympus. The entrance in the Prescelly Mountains may have been an exception. A mountain with a cave may offer the best of both worlds, placing Annwn on a mountaintop and underground simultaneously; certain Celtic poems do suggest that Annwn is both below and above the world of the living. The megalithic structures and stone circles of Britain may also have been considered entrances to Annwn at one time and there are Bronze Age megalithic burials in the Prescelly Mountains. Several authors are convinced that such megalithic structures were regarded as entrances to the other world by the Celts.

We can be sure that the Celts didn't build these megalithic sites. These structures were already in ruins when the Celts discovered them, but they did use them continuously until the Roman conquest. The Celts didn't know what they were but they must have realized they were religious in purpose and were built by a vanished people whose identity they could only guess at. To the Celts, megalithic structures took on an air of magic and became symbols of the dead. Even if the Celts failed to understand the uses of megalithic structures it would only be natural for them to attribute magic powers to the sites and perhaps convert them to their own religious uses. Therefore, druids didn't build Stonehenge, but the discovery of Celtic burials in the area implies that they used it in some way.

Graves places the battle of *Cad Goddeu* at the Annwn in Wiltshire, before Gwydion's people invaded South Wales. He declares Stonehenge is unsuitable for Bran's temple because it's "unsuitable for the worship of an alder god" (Graves 1993, 58). Instead, he suggests Avebury for the center of the Bran cult. His conclusion is that Stonehenge is Beli's prime temple, and is constructed in an

"Apollonian style" as opposed to the crude appearance of Avebury. Davies had made a similar suggestion in his *Mythology and Rites* when he commented that Stonehenge was a temple to the Celtic Apollo (Davies 1809, 502).

Graves raises some good points here but as usual he has missed some facts, or has chosen to misread evidence. It's true that Avebury's stones aren't tooled like those of Stonehenge and this gives Avebury a crude appearance. This may be because Avebury was earlier and represents a more primitive skill level, or it may be because Avebury served a different purpose than Stonehenge and the stones didn't need to be as precise. The result is that Avebury appears primitive compared to Stonehenge. More evidence in favor of Graves's temple theory is that Avebury is older than Stonehenge, just as it would be if Bran's cult was centered there. Some historians suggest the possibility that stones from Avebury were moved to Stonehenge, implying a shift of importance from one site to the other. While it can't be proven that stones were moved this way, stones are missing from Avebury and some of the stones at Stonehenge appear to be taken from another structure. Conversely, all these things can also be explained by the theory that the same people built both circles and that Stonehenge is an upgrade in skill, knowledge, and technology. If this were true, it would only be natural to salvage stones from the older, obsolete Avebury and shift importance to Stonehenge once it was completed.

Graves next probes the origin of the Celtic god Beli. By linking Beli with Belus (Father of Danaus) and through Belus to Bel the Babylonian fertility and agriculture god (counterpart to the Cananite Baal) he finally claims that the original was Belili, a Sumerian equivalent of the White Goddess. This linking of Beli to Baal and Bel derives from Joyce's *Social History* and is also suggested in *The Greek Myths*, where Belili appears as a Palestinian and Mesopotamian goddess. Belili was a goddess of trees, love, the moon, and the other world. She was sister and lover of Tammuz, the corn and pomegranate god mentioned in Dan.11:37 and Ezek 8:14

and the willow was sacred to her.

Graves uses popular etymology to link the Babylonian Bel with the Celtic god Beli from whom Gwydion and Amathon descended. What he doesn't tell us is that the Babylonian Bel was primarily a rain and thunder god and that the Celtic Bel is usually linked with fire or light and can hardly be considered a god of dark, stormy skies. Graves claims Beli is a pan-Celtic solar god and compares him to Apollo much as MacCulloch did earlier (MacCulloch 26). Indeed, Beli may be the god Caesar equated to Apollo and Rhys suggested his pan-Celtic status by equating the British Beli to the Irish Bile (Rhys, Brynmore-Jones 43).

Graves should have known Bel was associated with solar fire in Celtic mythology. Many of his sources mention Bel's connection to fire, the sun, and heat. MacCulloch suggests that Bel was a solar deity and Frazer speaks frequently of May 1st being the pagan holiday of Beltane and the tradition of lighting Beltane fires; sometimes containing animal sacrifices. This tradition is a continuation of an ancient Celtic practice in honor of Beli, who is often portrayed as a solar deity. The Beltane fires themselves may have been used as sympathetic magic to fuel the sun's return in spring and sacrificial victims were likely burnt from time to time, if not on a regular basis. If so, then these may have been the same sacrificial fires Caesar mentions.

Nor were these the only sources that claimed Bel's solar attributes. Rhys suggested as early as 1888 that the Celtic root word *bel* implied typical solar imagery such as heat, fire, the sun, and burning. Interestingly enough, Rhys also suggests that *bel* implied murder, war, and death (Rhys 1888, 38). From these associations it's likely that *bel* implied destruction by fire, which in turn may imply sacrifice in the form of the Beltane fires. Finally, Davies connects Belus to the sun in *Celtic Researches*.

An image of Belenus found at Trunholm depicts him carrying a solar disc in his chariot, thus linking Bel with fire and the sun yet again. Lastly, the ancient Celtic writer Publius Terentius Varro mentions a druidic fire walking ritual, which Lewis Spence later identified as the *Gabha-Bheil*, the "trial by Bel". Thus, Graves had all the evidence needed to show Beli was a solar fire deity, yet refused to do so. It seems Graves is selective about the facts he acknowledges in order to uphold his views. This isn't the only time that Graves ignores Frazer's evidence despite his overwhelming admiration for Frazer's theories.

Nor does Graves mention that *Bel* in Babylonian wasn't the name of an actual deity but a general title that could be applied to any god. Bel simply meant "lord". This explains the many versions of Bel and Baal (its Hebrew spelling), such as Baal-Hazor, Baal-Hermom, Baal-Berith and Baal-Zebub. It's easy to see how Marduk took the name Bel once he became all powerful. It would only be normal for *Bel*, lord, to refer to the most powerful god at the time. Marduk was originally a god of storms, thus they could easily become confused with each other or be identical. However, this Babylonian Bel doesn't fit well with the solar Beli of Celtic myth. There's probably no link between the two. This is not only a blow to Graves's theory but also to fundamentalist Christians who ignorantly accuse the druids of Baal worship. This misunderstanding, or their intentional misreading of mythology, has led many Christians to equate druidism to Satanism and claim that Halloween (Samhain) is a satanic holiday. Iconotropy is still alive and well in the modern world.

Once Graves links Beli with Belili he suggests the Sumerian Belili was a goddess of the willow. Thus, Beli was son of Belili and god of the willow who became a god of light and divination. Amathon was Beli's son and he invoked Beli's power to help him overcome Bran's alder cult in fourth century BC Britain. Graves says this battle between willow cult and alder cult in Britain may be a later reflection of a similar battle in Palestine. His evidence for this is that the feast of the tabernacles was also called the day of the willows and that willow branches were carried during the feast while alder branches were forbidden; possibly, because it was a symbol of the opposing alder cult of Astarte and her son.

Thus, Amathon (symbolized by the alder) replaced Bran (willow) and Gwydion (ash) replaced Arawn (whose tree is unknown). Notice that Graves has changed his tree association with the gods. In chapter three, he linked alder with Bran but now has linked it with Amathon instead and has assigned Bran the willow. Furthermore, Graves believes that the writer of the *Romance Of Taliesin* must have known Amathon as Llew Llaw. This seems unlikely. Gwydion and Amathon are brothers and Llew is their nephew. Llew and Amathon couldn't be one and the same.

In chapter four Graves explains the history of the Danaans. The word *Danaan*, like Achaians, is used by Homer to describe the Greeks who besieged Troy. It's also used in the phrase *Tuatha De Danaan*, "the children of the goddess Danu", already mentioned. Because Danaan is used both ways, Graves believed the Celtic Danaans were descendants of the Greek Danaans. To support this he cites the *Book of Invasions*, which says the Tuatha De Danaan originally came from Greece.

Incidentally, Geoffrey of Monmouth claims the first British inhabitants were Trojan refugees. If so then the Tuatha De Danaan wouldn't be Greeks, but their enemies, the Trojans, making Graves's theory wrong. Yet, while Graves accepts Geoffrey's ideas on Belinus and Brennius he ignores Geoffrey's theory of Trojans founding Britain because it undercuts his own theory. Of course, the claim that Trojans founded Britain is ridiculous and deserves to be rejected. Yet, Graves chose to cite Geoffrey's equally inaccurate story of Belinus and Brennius. Again, Graves is stacking the sources in his own favor.

To understand who Graves believes the Danaans were, we must first understand his view of ancient Greece. This is best accomplished by placing *The White Goddess* beside *Hercules*, his 1945 novel, which reconstructs Thessaly's history. Graves claims that the original natives of Thessaly were Satyrs, Lapiths, Aethics, Phlegyans, and Centaurs. (Graves follows Harrison and depicts Satyrs and Centaurs as human tribes rather than the mythical creatures envisioned today.) These tribes worshiped the triple goddess under various names and suffered multiple invasions of increasing violence. First, came the Greek Ionians from the area of the Danube. The Ionian invasion was rather peaceful and more of a migration than a bloody conquest. The later Aeolians and Dorians were increasingly violent and posed the first serious threat to Greek goddess worship.

These later invasions seriously injured Thessaly's Bronze Age goddess culture as the invaders repressed the religion of the indigenous people. A huge wave of refugees flooded out from Thessaly in all directions. These are the people Graves calls a tribal confederacy of the second millennium BC; Egyptian documents labeled them "people of the sea". They were the Dorians and the flood of refugees they inspired: a combination of Bronze Age goddess tribes, Ionians, and Aeolians who had invaded earlier. Over time, some of these Sea People developed into the Danaans who sacked Troy while others invaded Syria and also defeated the Hittite empire and Palestine. Others went on to Britain and Ireland via trade routes. This, Graves explains, is the connecting link between the Greek Danaans and the Irish Danaans. In short, Graves believes that the myths of the Celts, the ancient Greeks, and ancient Palestine were all influenced by the myths and culture of the Sea People or Danaans.

Next Graves uses questionable etymology to explain the root of the word *Danaan*. He says Danu, Danae, and Don are all the same deity who also "appears in Roman records as Donnus" (Graves 1993, 61). Note that Graves is gender bending his names again and freely switching between the female Danu and Danae and the male Donnus. Also, notice that he mentions Roman "records" but is actually citing Roman mythology. This implies that Graves was already accepting Roman myth as a sort of poetic history.

The Roman Donnus was the father of Cottius, the sacred king of the Cottians, a confederacy of Ligurians. They occupied Liguria, a region of Southeast France and Northwest Italy. The Cottians gave their name to the Cottian Alps and settled in Liguria about the sixth century BC. Graves mentions that "cotys appears as a dynastic title in Thrace" from the fourth century BC to the first century AD and also several variations of the word *cott* or *catt* are used in British tribe names (Graves 1993, 61). In summary, Graves is trying to show a link between the Danaans and the British tribes whose names contain the *cott* or *catt* root. He believes that the Ligurian Cottians are related to these British tribes because both of them descend from a deity whose name is based on Don, which is itself the root of Danaan. Put simply, they are both descendants of the Sea People who were pushed out of Greece earlier.

Just how the Ligurian Cottians influenced the Celts is unclear and Graves fails to explain it. However, the Ligurian language did influence the development of the Celtic languages so it's possible that the variations of *cott* entered the Celtic languages in this way. Ammianus Marcellinus stated that the druids of Gaul taught that the Celts were the result of the mixing of an aboriginal people of Gaul and a people from beyond the Rhine, near the North Sea. According to this tradition, these people supposedly drove the Ligurians out of the majority of Gaul and back to the foothills of the Alps. Ammianus claims the reason for this invasion was that the North Sea had flooded the surrounding low lands, driving these people inland. Strabo tells the same story and quotes Ephoros who also agrees. The identity of the people from beyond the Rhine is unclear but it's likely that they were the Celts themselves.

While the druids may have claimed that the Celts were the result of a mixing of Ligurians and an unknown northern people, in reality the Celts were that northern people from the North Sea and the mixing they did with the Ligurians was more like a slaughter. Possibly, the Ligurians were the pre-Celtic or proto-Celtic people who later became the Celts and this may explain how Ligurian language influenced Celtic languages, but this theory doesn't explain why ancient writers always differentiated between the Celts and the Ligurians.

Graves says these various *cott* tribes took their names from the goddess Cotytto or Cotys found in Thrace, Corinth, and Sicily. He mentions Strabo's comparison between her frenzied ritual, the Cotyttia, and the cults of Demeter and Cybele. His *Greek Myths* designates Cotytto a lunar goddess and equates her with Semele and Thyone. By linking Cotytto with Demeter, Cybele, Semele, and Thyone, Graves takes a considerable step towards unifying all Mediterranean goddess into the single goddess needed to uphold his universal ancient matriarchy. Davies set the example decades earlier when he equated Venus, Derceto, Isis, Ceres, Proserpine, and Latona on a single page and later lumped together Selene, Isis, Cerse, Rhea, Vesta, Cybele, Archia, and Niobe into a single concept (Davies 1809, 178, 184).

Thus, Graves establishes a link between the Celtic Danaans and the Greek Danaans via their common worship of a goddess named Don, Danu, or Danae. Never mind that his theory has flaws which he has ignored or that he has stacked the cards in his favor by being selective in his sources and ignoring conflicting evidence. For the sake of argument, we will accept this theory that the Celtic Danaans and the Greek Danaans are indeed the same people, or at least related.

Once Graves connects the Irish and Greek Danaans he begins expanding the formula by claiming that Greek mythology depicts Cottys as the brother of Briareus and Gyes, the monsters who assisted in Zeus's battle against the Titans. These two monsters were called the *hecatontocheiroi*, the hundred handed ones. These hecaton-tocheiroi, which assisted the upstart Zeus in his war against the older order of the Titans are identical to the Danaan tribes who swept across Europe establishing their more patriarchal brand of paganism over the earlier forms of matriarchy. In short, the myth of Zeus and the hecatontocheiroi overpowering the Titans is a mythical account of how the new pagans overpowered the old. Based on the works of Tatian and Thallus, Graves dates the victory of Zeus and the Hecatontocheiroi to c. 1505 BC. The Cottians and Hecatontocheiroi are the same people who would later be called the

Danaans. Thus, according to Graves:

Tuatha De Danaan=Danaans=Cottians=Hecatontocheiroi

Graves's use of the Cottians and Hecatontocheiroi derives directly from a nearly identical theory within *Celtic Researches*. Davies had used the root word *cott* to connect a number of Asian, Mediterranean, and European people to establish a migration route from Asia to Celtic Britain (Davies 1804, 201-210). He contends that this vast migration is nothing less than the dispersal of tribes after the confusion at the tower of Babel. These tribes migrated west and eventually became the Belgae. Their defeat and relocation is recorded in Greek myth as the tale of Cottys, Briareus, and Gyes; the monsters that rose up against the rightful gods and were punished accordingly. Davies's theory is laughable and Graves modifies it to make it fit his own model. However, both authors share the key elements, which depict the Cottians and Hecatontocheiroi as a wave of rebellious pagan migrations moving from East to West and eventually entering Belgic territory.

Graves argues that the Achaeans entered Thessaly roughly1900 BC and became the earliest Greeks to enter Greece. This is basically correct in the fact that the Greek Mycenaen culture was founded when a race of Indo-Europeans entered Greece from the North around 2000 BC. These Indo-Europeans were forerunners of the Greeks whom we think of as classical Greeks today. They likely entered Greece from the North and eventually reached Thessaly before going further south to establish Mycenae and becoming the Achaeans. Graves claims these people were patriarchal herdsmen who worshiped a trinity of male gods.

He suggests this trinity may originally have been the Indian gods Mitra, Varuna, and Indra found in the *Rig-Veda*. These three gods and their legions of lesser deities were known as the *Adityas*, children of the goddess *Aditi*. They warred with the *Danavas*, their supernatural enemies. Significantly, Danavas means "children of Danu". Thus, we either have a link between the Indian Danavas, the Greek Danaans, and the Irish Tuatha De Danaan, or an incredible coincidence.

Now Graves's equation can be further elongated:

Tuatha De Danaan=Danaans=Achaians=Cottians=Hecatontocheiroi

Graves's theory is that an Indo-European tribe who worshiped the Adityas entered into Thrace around 2000 BC and became the Achaians. They invaded Thessaly and mixed with the indigenous people already there, the Pelasgians. There was friction between the Achaians and the Pelasgians, resulting in some of the Pelasgians fleeing to various locations. Their destinations included Lesbos, Chios, Cnidos, Thrace, and the Troad. Among those Pelasgian tribes who remained behind were the warlike Centaurs, who welcomed the Achaians as allies in their raids against the Lapiths. Thus, Graves explains the myth of the Hecatontocheiroi helping the gods defeat the Titans as an allegory of the Centauars helping the Achaians defeat the Lapiths.

Perhaps now is a good time to pause and ask exactly what has Graves accomplished in connecting so many tribes and mythical characters by such a slender thread. If we examine his formula, we notice that he is slowly uniting various pagan cultures and drawing an invasion route for the new school of patriarchal pagans. In doing so he follows the model of Davies who believed "the mythology and the rites of the Druids were the same, in substance, with those of the Greek and Romans" and assumes "these superstitions are reducible to the same principles, and that they proceeded from the same source" (Davies 1809, 89). Graves, like Davies, upholds a model of worldwide paganism. Yet, where Davies argues that this paganism was a corrupt version of Old Testament religion, Graves instead claims that this universal paganism was divided by two equally pagan warring factions.

In Graves's model, a nomadic tribe from the Eastern fringe of the Indo-European expansion has abandoned the goddess to worship a male trinity. Spreading west they bring warfare to Greece. Certain Greek tribes flee further west, while others unite with the invaders. Eventually, a snowball effect is achieved as the invaders continue westward uniting various tribes under their new system of male power and male godhead. In myth, they are the Hecatontocheiroi who support Zeus's rebellion against the old gods. At the siege of Troy, they are the Achaians or Danaans. When they reach Ireland, they are the Tuatha De Danaan, the superhuman race of warrior-magicians who claimed to have fallen to earth in a flash of lightning. Centuries later, this same legend of an undefeated master race inspired Hitler's blitzkrieg to sweep across Europe. *Blitzkrieg* itself means "lightening warfare" and Hitler's "master race" was based on the Aryan idea of blonde haired, blue eyed warriors such as the Tuatha De Danaans.

Meticulously, Graves has depicted the new school of patriarchal paganism as an oppressive regime sweeping from the East, into the Mediterranean, and across Europe in a wave of slaughter equal to that of World War II. Incidentally, Christianity followed the same route and the parallel between the Danaan invasion, Christianity, and the Nazi blitzkrieg are strongly implied. To Graves, each of these invasions were made possible by mistakenly elevating the importance of a male savior. Step by step Graves has led readers to reach the same inference.

CHAPTER XII

THE LESSER POEMS

We've already seen Graves reinterpret Celtic mythology and Greek history to create his patriarchal invasion. Keystones to this model are *Cad Goddeu* and *Hanes Taliesin*. However, these aren't the only poems Graves reinterprets. He also cites lesser-known poems to suggest that druidism secretly survived into the Middle Ages. Those poems include many obscure titles and often their occurrences in *White Goddess* are the reader's first encounter with them. Most of these poems play a minor role and few are quoted in their entirety.

The most interesting of these minor poems is *Preiddeu Annwn* ("*The Spoils of Annwn*"). Like *Cad Goddeu* and *Hanes Taliesin*, *The Spoils* is traditionally credited to Taliesin but has been dated to the thirteenth century by Stephens. Nearly all translators of *The Spoils* have commented upon both its difficulty and obscurity; most have chosen to depict it as either worthless gibberish or Taliesin's most mystical and druidic work. Stephens called the poem "one of the least intelligible of the mythological poems" (Nash 211). Sharon Turner declared the poem unintelligible and concludes that "all connexion of thought seems to have been studiously avoided" within it. Davies (predictably) believes the subject of *The Spoils* is "the mythology of the deluge, and the mysteries that were celebrated in commemoration of it" (Davies 1809, 516). Guest avoids the entire poem in her *Mabinogion* and cites only the first stanza of an original translation from "a distinguished Welsh scholar". Her opinion is that an "exact interpretation is by no means easy to discover" and concludes that the poem is "a mystical poem which appears to be full of allusions to traditions now no longer intelligible" (Guest 287; Nash 211). Ironically, Nash believes *The Spoils* to be "one of the most interesting and instructive pieces" credited to

Taliesin and claims that it's a key to understanding most of Taliesin's others works (Nash 210). Nash's favoring of the poem seems contradictory to his anti-mystic stance but, as we will soon see, Nash's explanation is the least mystical of all.

The plot of *The Spoils* is confused but a few points are certain. The author, supposedly Taliesin, laments that he is the sole possessor of certain Celtic tales and ridicules the ignorance of his fellow bards who are unfamiliar with his stories. He appeals to the reader by stressing his own importance and belittling his bardic competitors. He repeatedly asserts that he is "a candidate for fame" who "will not allow praise" for lesser bards. This attitude is in perfect keeping with the bardic bragging of *Cad Goddeu* and typifies the conflict between the high and low schools of medieval Welsh poetry. However, *The Spoils* is bardic bragging *writ large*. In it, Taliesin brags of knowing certain tales, which, besides being lost today, were apparently obscure even when the poem was written.

The Spoils cites several lost tales. References to "the first word from the cauldron", "the brindled ox, with his thick head band", and the vague silver headed animal are all lost upon modern readers. Like those bards whom Taliesin criticizes, we fail to understand the importance of the nine maidens who warmed the cauldron or the six thousand men who stood upon the wall. We don't know what kept Cwy from traveling to Devwy. We don't even know who Cwy is.

Despite these obscurities, there are certain inferences, which can be extracted from *The Spoils*. The title alone implies a raid into Annwn to capture either people or goods. The poem seems to recount a military raid led by Arthur. The objective of this raid is unclear but apparently Arthur took three shiploads of troops with him and only seven men returned alive. It has been frequently stated that Arthur attempted to steal the magic cauldron mentioned early in the poem. Alternately, he may be attempting to free an imprisoned character named Gwair who is also mentioned. Possibly, Gwair equates to Mabon, the imprisoned hero, which Arthur frees in *Kilhwch and Olwen*. Gwair may also equate to Pryderi who was magically imprisoned in a fortress when he touched a cauldron suspended from chains; a cauldron, a fortress, and a prisoner in chains are all elements of *The Spoils*. Ultimately, Gwair, Mabon, and Pryderi may all derive from an earlier tale of a hero who was imprisoned while attempting to steal a magic cauldron and was later freed by Arthur during his own successful theft of the same cauldron.

Graves, like most readers of *The Spoils*, is intrigued by the mention of several *Caers*, or fortresses, within the poem. Each stanza of *The Spoils* introduces a new fortress name. The version, which Graves uses, gives a total of eight such fortresses. It has long been suspected that the key to understanding the poem lies in the correct translation and identification of these fortresses. Unfortunately, their identification is the most problematic aspect of *The Spoils* and it's not even certain how many fortresses are mentioned. Some critics have suggested that the eight fortresses are all different locations. The majority of researchers, including Graves, believe that most of these names are alternate titles for a single fort. These differing approaches influence the translations. Authors wishing to depict the fortresses as identical often struggle to translate the names into synonymous images. Translators who see them as different locations feel no need to draw parallels between them.

Graves never reveals which translation of *The Spoils* he used. He knew of the Davies translation but (wisely) avoided it. Nash fails to translate the poem himself but instead offers the Stephens translation; minus the final stanza, which Nash and Davies both claimed to be spurious. Surprisingly, Graves's version doesn't match the Stephens-Nash version either. Nor does Graves's version match that offered by Skene. In fact, Graves's translation conflicts with all known sources. It seems that Graves is either depending upon an undocumented translation or has complied his own translation from those sources already mentioned. A careful examination of Graves's version supports the latter theory.

The versions offered by both Stephens-Nash and Graves contains

48 lines. Skene's total is also 48 once the spurious final stanza has been removed. Davies renders his translation in prose rather than poetry, making his line count irrelevant. The Nash, Skene, and Graves translations are so similar that comparison is difficult but it seems that Graves created his version primarily from Nash and with occasional reference to Skene. Graves closely follows Nash though out the poem but the first hint of Skene's translation appears by the fourth line. Graves's version reads "Through the *spite* of Pwyll" while Nash gives "Through the *permission* of Pwyll" (Graves 1993, 107; Nash 212). Davies offers "Through the *mission* of Pwyll" (Davies 1809, 515). Thus, *permission* and *mission* are preferred by Graves's two primary sources but Graves favors *spite*; the same word chosen by Skene (Skene 264). It may be premature to conclude that Graves compiled his own version from Nash and Skene based on this single example but evidence favors this conclusion. Graves couldn't read Welsh and his two known sources gave similar terms which Graves shunned in favor of another word which, coincidentally, matched Skene.

This leads us to wonder if Graves consulted Skene for *The Spoils*, why did he ignore the eight lines of *Cad Goddeu*, which Skene translated and Nash did not? Why did Graves rely once on Skene but not again? Possibly Graves's version of *The Spoils* "restored the missing lines in the spirit of the original" just as he did in *English and Scottish Ballads* (Graves 1969, xxiv). If Graves did compile his version of *The Spoils* from multiple earlier translations he may have felt justified. Nash confessed that he had also doctored the Stephens translation (Nash 211). If Nash could alter his translations to avoid mysticism, Graves likely felt justified in mixing translations to insert mysticism back into the poem.

However, all of this is mere hair splitting. The true test of Graves's translation, and his motives, is his depiction of the various fortresses already mentioned. The mysticism of *The Spoils* revolves around these fortress names and if Graves intends to argue a mystic interpretation of the poem it will depend on these fortresses. Graves does not disappoint us. Once again, he combines all his known sources to arrive at an original solution.

Graves lists the fortress names as: Caer Sidi, Caer Rigor ("the royal castle"), Caer Colur ("the gloomy castle"), Caer Pedryvan ("four-cornered castle"), Caer Vediwid ("the castle of the perfect ones"), Caer Ochren ("the castle of the shelving side"), and Caer Vandwy ("the castle on high") (Graves 1993, 106). Davies gives: Caer Bediwyd ("the enclosure of the inhabitants of the world"), Caer Mediwyd ("enclosure of the perfect ones"), Caer Rigor ("enclosure of the royal assembly"), Caer Golur ("gloomy enclosure"), Caer Vandwy ("the enclosure resting on the height"), and Caer Ochren ("the enclosure whose side produced life") (Davies 1809, 516). Notice that Davies intentionally translates the names in imagery consistent with his belief that these terms all signify Noah's ark. Graves rejects Davies's interpretation and instead favors the belief that the fortress is symbolic of the Celtic other world.

Comparing Graves's listing to Davies, we see that the best matching translation is Caer Rigor; Graves translates this as "the royal castle" and Davies gives "enclosure of the royal assembly". Next is Graves's Caer Colur and Davies's Caer Golur; both translated to mean "gloomy". Graves's Caer Vediwid becomes Davies's Caer Mediwyd but both authors suggest that it contains "the perfect ones". Both men offer "on high" as translations for Vandwy. A significant disagreement occurs with Caer Ochren; Graves gives "castle of the shelving side" while Davies provides "enclosure whose side produced life". Lastly, we have Graves's Caer Pedyvan and Davies's Caer Bediwyd, which are so different that we might conclude they aren't equivalent at all. Graves depicts it as a "four-cornered castle" while Davies insists upon "the enclosure of the inhabitants of the world".

From this overview, we see that Graves didn't draw exclusively from Davies's translation. Furthermore, Graves didn't use the Stephens translation favored by Nash. (Stephens appears to have drawn on Davies himself and most of their interpretations agree.)

Skene's fortresses also fail to match Graves's version. Skene depicts Caer Sidi as an island, Caer Pedryvan as a quadrangular fort or Roman camp, Caer Wydyr as a fortress of glass, and Caer Vandwy as a corrupt form of Caeramond or Cramond (Skene 410-411). Graves has again departed from Davies, Nash, and Skene to arrive at a solution, which is independent yet similar to his forerunners.

By combining the images of the various fortresses Graves creates a convincing argument that a tomb or round barrow is implied. In short, he interprets *The Spoils* as a myth of the death and rebirth of the male hero. This is the same life, death, and life cycle which Graves mentions in chapter one as the antique story in thirteen parts. He argues that this myth was central to many pagan cultures who took the story literally. However, allegorical aspects within the poem are strongly implied.

This descent into Annwn symbolizes the trance state of inspired poets. In both cases, the main character descends to an underworld to drink from a source of primal knowledge. Only the best poets and heroes return unharmed. Countless others become lost in the other world and fail to return with their needed knowledge; others return but bear lasting damage from their encounters below. Graves's interpretation suggests that the seven heroes who returned alive are the seven heroes of other allegorical descent myths, which teach the same lesson. Thus, Arthur is equated to Jesus and several other legendary heroes who have braved the other world to capture knowledge or insight.

Fifty years ago, this interpretation of *The Spoils* was considered unique. Today, in the wake of *The White Goddess*, it's considered cliché. The merger between Graves's personal poetic style and Celtic paganism has become so strong that nearly every pagan author since Graves has chosen to imitate his interpretation of *The Spoils*. However, turning back to the earlier research of Nash and Skene reveals two highly divergent approaches to this poem and reveal that Graves's path is not the only option.

Nash denies all mysticism within *The Spoils* and claims that its difficulty lies in the fact that it doesn't deal with traditional poetry, or even Celtic mythology, but instead deals with contemporary romantic tales which have since vanished. Basically, *The Spoils* refers to events in unknown and relatively unimportant stories. We don't understand the poem because we don't have the stories in question. These lost stories have become lost specifically because they were not central to Celtic belief. In Nash's mind "the first word from the cauldron", "the brindled ox, with his thick head band", and the cauldron warmed by nine maidens are unimportant minor tales with no impact on Celtic mythology or even later bardic poetry. The fact that the author of *The Spoils* complains that his tales are unknown is evidence that these tales weren't as popular as the mainstream tales.

Skene also denies the mystic interpretation of *The Spoils* and favors a strictly historical perspective. He depicts Caer Pedryvan as a Roman camp. The six thousand men who stood upon the wall equate to a Roman legion; the wall referred to is obviously Hadrian's wall. The three boat loads of soldiers who followed Arthur may have been the very army used to defeat Mordred. Skene attempts to identify Mordred with Medraut, a British prince who supposedly led the Scots and Picts in rebellion against Arthur (Skene 59). The decisive battle between Arthur and Medraut supposedly occurred at Camelon, which Skene equates to Camlan, Arthur's traditional final battle. In all, Skene concludes that *The Spoils* tells of Arthur's men crushing a combined army of Picts, Scots, and Saxons beyond Hadrian's wall. Arthur circumnavigated the wall and won the battle but suffered heavy losses. Skene also reveals that Arthur captured several fortresses in earlier stages of this campaign; probably the very fortresses mentioned in *The Spoils*.

Readers wishing to cite this interpretation as evidence of Arthur's existence should be warned. Nowhere in his work does Skene state that *The Spoils* is based on historical fact. He merely contends that someone once *believed* this story was true and wrote a poem about it. Hardrian's wall is real and six thousand men do equate to a Roman legion. Camelon is an authentic site and is believed to be a Roman camp. Yet none of this proves that a man named Arthur defeated a man named Medraut during a Scottish-Pictish rebellion. Skene merely observes that at some point before the thirteenth century, this story was placed upon these places and events and *The Spoils* draws from this legend.

The problems with *The Spoils* are identical with those of *Cad Goddeu*: we have no truly ancient manuscript from which to work. Possibly, *The Spoils* is no older than the single surviving copy. If so, then Taliesin isn't the author. Conversely, if Taliesin is the author then the surviving copy is not from his hand and could contain multiple corruptions. Considering the number of known corruptions in other Celtic poetry this possibility is almost certain. Either way, we know that *The Spoils* isn't a Taliesin poem directly from the hand of Taliesin and the disjointed style of the poem make it difficult to measure any corruption.

Next, we will examine *Anrhyfeddonay Alexander*, which Graves found mentioned in both Nash's *Taliesin* and Davies's *Celtic Researches*. This poem originally appears in the *Red Book of Hergest* and Graves claims it is a parody of a thirteenth-century Spanish romance in which Alexander is confused with Merlin. Nash holds a similar view but considers the substitution of Alexander for Merlin to be accidental rather than parody. Graves briefly mentions this poem, quickly dismisses it, and moves on. We are left wondering why he mentioned it at all. At this point Graves has already pursued a complex debate concerning the secret meaning behind an obscure medieval poem. Now he pauses just long enough to introduce an even more obscure poem and associate it to a virtually unknown Spanish romance. Then, without breaking pace, he resumes the original argument. We are again reminded of Mehoke's comment: "Graves does not feel the casual reader is worth stopping for and can be purposely difficult when he chooses to be so".

Celtic Researches suggests that *Anrhyfeddonay Alexander* may have confused Alexander with Hercules as well as Merlin, a view, which likely interested Graves. Davies tries to rationalize the myth of Hercules in much the same way that Graves attempts to rationalize several other myths, including Hercules. Not only does Davies attempt to understand the Hercules myth using the same method as Graves but he also studies of one of Graves's favorite mythical characters, Hercules himself. Graves's fascination with Hercules predates *The White Goddess* and extends, logically enough, into his *Greek Myths*. Perhaps his most interesting use of Hercules appears in his poem *Hercules at Nemea*.

Concealed within this ten-line poem are almost too many implications to list. The poem supports Graves's claim that what is expressed in poetry can't be rendered directly into prose. Included among the poem's many ideas are several which are central to *The White Goddess*. The idea that Hercules serves the goddess, the symbolic importance of the fool's finger, the White Goddess subtlety implied by her white teeth, and the witch's mark are all seamlessly integrated in two short stanzas. This poem stands as a prime example of how Graves incorporates ideas from *The White Goddess* into his poetry.

Graves mentions that Cicero listed six different characters named Hercules. Varro suggested there were no less than forty-four heroes of that name. The mention of Cicero and Varro again reveal the depth of Graves's research. Yet, it wasn't research for *The White Goddess*, which brought these authors to his attention but *Hercules, My Shipmate* which led Graves to their accounts. Graves mentions both historians within the appendix to *Hercules*. Furthermore, this gives credibility to Graves's account of the writing of *The White Goddess*.

Nor is this the extent of that research. His *White Goddess* concepts were fairly solidified before the publication of *Hercules*, as the appendix reveals. There, on multiple occasions, Graves refers to the White Goddess and on one page makes mention of her no less than three times (Graves 1945, 461). Even at this stage, Graves was already linking various goddesses of Greek religion to a single deity.

He refers to the White Goddess as Isis, Samothea, Rhea, Artemis, and Marianae (Graves 1945, 461-462, 464).

What is more interesting is that Graves foreshadows his ogham theories in *Hercules* when he claims that the Greek mysteries supplemented standard Greek religion by teaching secrets to those members who could be trusted. These secrets, like druidic teachings, were seldom written down, and when they were, they were written in cypher (Graves 1945, 462). This sounds suspiciously like the ogham theories within *The White Goddess* and we wonder exactly how much ogham research Graves had done by the time he had written *Hercules*. Did Graves read Davies's account of Hercules and Orpheus while researching for *Hercules*? It seems odd that Graves consults a Celtic researcher to find an account of the Greek poet Orpheus. Yet, Davies believed that the dance of trees caused by Orpheus was an allusion to a cryptographic secret and Graves later accepted this idea himself. Furthermore, Davies places an Orphic slant on the Argo myth and mentions a version of the story, which depicts it as a Orphic allegory. Graves later accepted these ideas as well and it appears within the appendix of *Hercules*. If Graves was researching for both *Hercules* and *The White Goddess* simultaneously, he may have easily found Davies's views on Orpheus and incorporated them into both books. This implies that *The White Goddess* wasn't written in the white hot trance Graves claims; nor was it written directly after *Hercules*. It was actually being developed in the back of Graves's mind as he finished *Hercules* and at least some of his research for one book was equally applicable to the other.

In conclusion, we see Graves simultaneously researching Greek and Celtic materials as he wrote *Hercules*. We know Graves did a large amount of research for *Hercules*, and we know his claim that this influenced his *White Goddess* ideas. Yet, the reference to the cryptographic secret in Orpheus's dance of trees reveals something new. Graves consulted Davies *before* the publication of *Hercules* and did so not as part of his *Hercules* research, but as research for *The White Goddess*. Davies is not the only source Graves used for both

books. Both books also mention Malinowski's *Sexual Life of Savages*.
Yet, what the Davies research implies is that Graves was going out
of his way in his research of *Hercules*. This out of the way path was
a diversion into the creation of *The White Goddess*.

Near the end of chapter eight Graves prepares the reader to
accept his reconstruction of *Hanes Taliesin*. This reconstruction
reveals the ogham alphabet, which he claims spells out the life
events of Hercules. Just before summing up his evidence Graves
pauses to give the following lines from the poem *Angar Cyvyndawd*
("The Hostile Confederacy"):

> I have been a roebuck on the mountain,
> I have been a tree stump in a shovel,
> I have been an ax in the hand.

The source is Nash's *Taliesin*, although Graves also encountered a
muddled version from Davies. Graves claims the lines are confused
and gives the correct order by reversing the final two lines. He
explains that the tree must be cut down and the stump burned to
ashes before it fits into the shovel to be used as fertilizer on the
fields. This is another example of Graves's iconotropy, but to what
purpose? Graves draws on this poem again in chapter twenty-one,
but not these particular lines or any of their aspects. He has drawn
on a few lines of a completely unrelated poem simply for the sake of
solving its iconotropic problem. Yet, the mystery doesn't stop with
Graves citing this unrelated poem.

We must wonder not only why Graves introduces the poem at
this point, but also why he solves it in this manner. Granted, the
lines make little sense in their original form and Graves's idea does
create some sort of logic. Yet, what indication do we have that
Graves's logic corresponds to the original meaning of the poem?
Graves works under the assumption that the lines are somehow
related, despite the fact that there may be no connection. Celtic literature is full of similar poems containing lines beginning "I have

been" and there is no reason to believe that such a line in any given poem is related to the following line. Rather, it seems from the examples given, that each statement of "I have been" is unrelated to earlier lines or those that follow. Each such line is a complete statement and the collective intent of several such lines is not to produce a logical order but to recite a chain of unrelated incarnations depicting the various experiences the poet has obtained.

Graves disagrees and reorders the lines to produce a more unified meaning. To him, most of these poems are differing accounts of a calendar theme. His renderings of *The Song of Amergin*, *Cad Goddeu*, and *Hanes Taliesin* make this clear. Yet, in this particular case, what has convinced Graves that the end result of the poem is a shovel full of ashes to fertilize a field? Neither a field or fertilizer are mentioned and although a tree stump, shovel, and ax are mentioned, there is no assurance that the last two lines of the poem are linked in any way.

Graves returns to the poem *Angar Cyvyndawd* in chapter twenty-one while discussing the alphabet supposedly created by Nennius. This is a fairly obscure legend and Nash makes only a brief mention of it, claiming that it is no older than the ninth century. Nash fails to reproduce the alphabet itself and merely dismisses it with a short commentary. Graves instead must draw on the works of James Ussher to reproduce the alphabet. Graves claims that the British bards had used an alphabet for centuries before the arrival of the Saxons and that Nennius's alphabet must have been intended as a joke against the Saxons.

As expected, Graves searches for hidden meanings in the letter order of the Nennius alphabet, this leads him to reorder the letter names to resemble the order of the ogham and then to translate the letter names into Greek. Once Nennius's alphabet has been mutilated, Graves claims to have uncovered a secret "Egyptian Christian" formula. According to Graves, this formula is expressed in a Greek pentameter, which resembles Luke 2:35. In reality, there is little resemblance.

In explaining this concealed formula, Graves again cites the poem *Angar Cyvyndawd*. We expect that his second mention of the poem would in some way build on what he has already established, yet it does not. Instead, Graves only makes a brief mention of the poem as supporting evidence for the larger argument regarding his Egyptian Christian formula. More astonishing, Graves cites a totally different line of the poem. There is absolutely no relevance between the two excerpts and the reader is expected to grasp the relationship between two quotes from the poem, which have both been taken out of context.

Edward Davies, Graves's source for *Anrhyfeddonay Alexander* and the resulting Hercules theories, is also the source of his argument regarding the "uneasy chair above Caer Sidin" found in *Hanes Taliesin*. Following Davies, Graves suggests that Caer Sidin is actually Cader Idris, one of the highest mountains in North Wales. Both authors freely exchange Cader Idris for Caer Sidin based on the fact that Caer Sidin cannot be positively identified and because other Celtic poems habitually interchanging the names of mythic places, (as seen in *The Spoils*.)

Local legend tells that anyone spending the night on Cader Idris will be found in the morning, either dead, mad, or a poet. Incidentally, the line between poet and madman is a thin one, as Merlin's legend illustrates. Rhys had even gone so far as to say, "The association of poetry, prophecy and idiocy is so thoroughly Celtic as to need no remark" (Rhys 1888, 99).

Davies suggests that there was a primitive observatory upon the peak of the mountain from which the Celts observed the motion of the stars. For once, Davies has made a plausible suggestion. As Graves proves, there are many astrological hints in Celtic poetry, which express an interest in the movement of the heavens. Within *Hanes Taliesin* Taliesin claims, "I know the names of the stars from the North to the South" and mentions a "whirling round without motion" which may imply the movement of the heavens around the pole star. Lady Guest's translation of the same poem includes the lines "my original country is the region of the summer stars" and "I have been on the galaxy". Furthermore, Graves cites John Macneill to argue that the "cattle of Tethra" in the *Song of Amergin* is also a veiled reference to the stars.

With all of this implied astrological meaning, and Davies's suggestion that Cader Idris housed an observatory, it's interesting that Graves didn't make a similar claim. Perhaps this idea conflicted with his preexisting ideas on the hidden meaning of *Hanes Taliesin*. Considering the amount of time Graves dedicates to astrological and astronomical features of Celtic paganism we might assume that he would have liked to have argued that there was an observatory on Cader Idris. However, in order to arrive at the ogham letters, he was required to attribute this line to Rhea and not Idris.

The next poem examined, *Marwnad y Milveib* or *The Elegy on the Thousand Children*, appears in Nash's *Taliesin* under an alternate title. Graves quotes this poem regarding Celtic reincarnation beliefs and mentions that pre-Christian Europeans believed that only kings, chieftains, poets, and magicians were reincarnated. The idea that only privileged people reincarnated may seem odd by today's standard. Those who believe in reincarnation tend to believe that all souls have equal opportunity for the afterlife, yet this mindset wasn't necessarily widespread in pre-Christian times. It would be easy for the socially elite to cultivate a belief in selective reincarnation and this would help maintain their elite status. Graves claims that the Celts supported this idea, despite offering little solid evidence of it. Gerald Gardner later drew on this idea of selective reincarnation in *Witchcraft Today*. There Gardner states that only Wiccans were reincarnated among their former tribe or family (Gardner 1954, 68).

The discussion of ancient reincarnation beliefs leads Graves to comment on Pythagoras, that favorite philosopher of armchair theorists. Supposedly, Pythagoras and his followers had a strong taboo about eating beans, partly because they were believed to contain human souls. These souls were seen as breath or wind and this in turn, explained why beans cause flatulence. Internal gas was evidence that you had swallowed the breath or soul of another living thing. Exactly how Graves arrived at this conclusion is unclear but the concept of breath or wind being equivalent to the soul is common to pagan cultures. The basic concept appears in *Prolegomena* and later in *The Greek Myths*. He also mentions the unusual belief that to eat beans was to eat your parents head, another idea taken from Harrison (Harrison 627).

The White Goddess also mentions that Pythagoreans had a taboo on eating fish. This, and the bean taboo, are Graves's first mentions of Pythagoras or his followers. While Graves bases his comments on accepted ancient writings, we should remember that Pythagoras left behind no surviving material. Some historians suggest that refusal to commit anything to paper was in itself part of Pythagoras's beliefs. Such refusal to record religious beliefs is common among early pagan cultures; Caesar said the same of the druids.

By far the most interesting of the lesser poems quoted in *The White Goddess* is the transformational formula given by Isobel Gowdie in her 1662 witchcraft trial:

I shall go into a hare
With sorrow and sighing and mickle care,
And I shall go in the Devil's name
Aye, till I come home again.

Graves claims that this transformation was merely symbolic. Then he proceeds to reconstruct the rest of Gowdie's formula with a series of changes related to his own seasonal calendar. This reconstructed poem appears in chapter twenty-two of *The White Goddess* and also appears in Graves's 1955 *Collected Poems* under the title of *The Allansford Pursuit*. The same poem is also addressed in his *English and Scottish Ballads*. Graves latter omitted *The Allansford Pursuit* from his official canon. It's a clever work of speculation, and an interesting exercise in his analeptic methods, but fails to meet Graves's usual high standard.

Graves may have first encountered Gowdie's trial in Murray's works and his treatment of Gowdie's testimony shows heavy influence from *Witch-Cult*. We find such Murrayite traits as the fact that male members of the cult were dominant, mention of a horned goat-god, sexual union with the devil via an artificial member, and circle dances. These are primary traits of Murray's witch-cult and Murray also claimed that Gowdie's shape changes were considered symbolic rather than literal and that Gowdie simply mimicked each animal named within her dance. These factors also contributed to Graves's recreation of Greek paganism in *Hercules*.

The suggestion that Gowdie merely mimicked the animals of her dance enables Graves to utilize the religious function of the dance while also rejecting those supernatural elements, which he found distasteful. Like many pagans, Graves favors a mystical worldview but questions individual manifestations of the supernatural, leading him to reject historical accounts of earlier manifestations. His assertion that Gowdie's dance is merely symbolic derives from the interpretive method he applies to mythology; supernatural manifestations in either myth or historical accounts are usually depicted as allegories by Graves. This approach was anticipated as early as the sixteenth century by Dr. John Weyer who said much the same thing years before Gowdie's trial.

However, it's unlikely that the formula represented such symbolic transformations. It's more likely that Gowdie believed that she had literally shape shifted via magical powers. While this may be impossible, it was still considered possible within seventeenth century Scotland. Shape changing was one of the main charges against Scottish witches of the time and John Weyer's argument against this was slow to penetrate the remote regions of Scotland. Alexander Carmichael's *Carmina Gadelica* devotes considerable space to so called *fith-fath* poems that supposedly transformed humans into animals. Men were believed to become horses and bulls while women became cats, hares, or hinds (Carmichael 1: 22). Ireland had a similar spell, the *feth-fiada*, which caused either shape changing or invisibility (Joyce 1:246). St. Patrick supposedly used this spell, proving its continued existence between the fifth and seventeenth centuries. Gowdie had likely recited a version of the fith-fath and believed in its powers to transform her into a hare. The strange part of Gowdie's confession is that her recited fith-fath rhymes in English. This implies that it was written in English rather than in her native Scottish Gaelic. Apparently, the belief in the fith-fath was strong enough to provoke seventeenth century poets to construct English versions.

From their reading of witch trials Graves and Murray should have known that most transformation cases were taken literally in the Middle Ages; Graves had even read *Carmina Gadelica* (Graves 1993, 412). Many witch trial accounts contain similar impossible testimony, which suspects claims to have witnessed. Whether these suspects honestly believed they witnessed or partook in shape changes, or whether they simply claimed to have done so to satisfy their torturers is irrelevant. Either way, they wanted the courts to take their stories literally and this implies literal belief in shape shifting.

Despite the diversity of the above poems, they all share a single trait, quotation within the text of *White Goddess* itself. However, one of the most influential poems to influence Graves's argument receives no direct quotation in the text and is mentioned only in passing. Near the end of the book Graves reveals this poem as one of only three titles he openly cites as part of his own suggested canon. The poem in question is *Piers Ploughman* the fourteenth century alliterative allegory told in the form of a dream and commonly attributed to William Langland. *Piers* paints a vicious satire upon the church, its clergy, and nearly all of England's elite. Like *White Goddess* and the *Book of Lambspring, Piers Ploughman* is a call for personal and societal unity. Graves was intrigued not only by this call but by the dream device used to present it. Although there are no direct quotes of *Piers* within *White Goddess*, its themes run like an invisible undercurrent throughout the text and Graves's criticism of modern society often echoes the complaints of Langland roughly five centuries earlier.

Translator J. F. Goodridge summarizes *Piers* in phrases, which could equally apply to *The White Goddess*. Goodridge reveals that Langland satirized the mindless and soulless desire for wealth, the arbitrary powers and lack of love or mercy within the church and state, and the "scramble of self-interest" within the political scene (Goodridge 262). In short, Langland attacks everything, which Graves considers symbolic of the "nowdays" mentioned in the forward of *White Goddess*: "a civilization in which the prime emblems of poetry are dishonoured" (Graves 1993, 14). Drawing from Langland (and hints of *Don Quixote*) Graves pictures himself as one of the last hard working and honest men in a world of corruption. This attitude recurs throughout *White Goddess*; but Langland's impact takes other forms as well.

Graves's claim that Judas hung himself from an elder tree derives from *Piers* and is the only direct citation of Langland's work Graves provides (Graves 1993, 185). Other items Graves utilized include Langland's use of the Latin word *cardo*, a hinge. Graves could have discovered this from his own reading of *Piers*, but it's revealing that the most authoritative study of *Piers*, that made by W. W. Skeat in 1886, provides a footnote in which *cardo* is cited as the source of Langland's imagery. Skeat mentions that Langland's image of closing gates ultimately derived from the Latin *cardo* and that the power of the hinges is central to the passage in question (Skeat 2:14). Skeat's footnote undergoes a strange metamorphosis during Graves's creative process and becomes central to his explanation of the goddess Cardea, who presided over door hinges and thereby became connected to Janus, Roman protector of doors and gates.

Roman poet Ovid credits Cardea's powers as "to open what is shut; to shut what is open". Graves believes Ovid's statement may be a fragment of a pagan religious formula. What he fails to acknowledge is the overt sexual symbolism of Ovid's words. Possibly, Cardea's worship contained fertility aspects or addressed the powers of virginity or childbirth. If so, this explains another image within *Piers*; the representation of Eve and the Virgin Mary as closed and open gateways to salvation. Langland depicts Eve as the sinful woman whose actions barred mankind from heaven while Mary's role in the nativity is depicted as reopening the gates of salvation. Langland's subtle imagery implies sexual abstinence is central to salvation. Mary's "gateway" had only opened once and by doing so offered salvation to the world. This interpretation perhaps derived from a reinterpretation of Ovid's depiction of Cardea. Ovid was highly read during Langland's time; Chaucer, Spenser, and Shakespeare were all familiar with his works.

Piers may also have influenced Graves's depiction of the partridge as a sexually lascivious bird. Graves mentions the super-stition that female partridges can become impregnated by the mere breath of the male and cites Aristotle and Pliny as sources for this belief. Significantly, Langland cites the same belief and Skeat's footnotes refer the reader to the same Aristotle quotation (Skeat 2:177). Possibly, Graves even confuses Langland's references to the partridge with his similar references to the peacock. *Piers* depicts both birds as lecherous, Skeat's footnotes equate the two, and Aristotle commented upon both birds as well (Skeat 2:230). It's doubtful that Graves consulted Skeat's footnotes while writing *White Goddess* but he was possibly thinking of them, as well as Aristotle, *Sirach*, and the Bible, as he wrote his partridge passage.

What most Graves scholars recognize, and most pagans do not, is the subtle undercurrent of another poem flowing through *The White Goddess*. The poem is Skelton's *Garland of Laurel*, already mentioned for its tree listing. Like *Piers*, this poem is never directly quoted and is mentioned only once. Yet, its themes drive much of Graves's argument both within *White Goddess* and in much of his other works. Skelton had been a long time favorite of Graves and *Laurel* provided him with more than merely its tree listings. Many of Graves's points were anticipated by Skelton's works five centuries earlier.

Laurel tells the story of Skelton's achievement of poetic recognition. It begins as Skelton, in his early 30's, wanders through the woods and comes to rest against a blasted oak. As he ponders the meaning of life, he falls into a dream or trance, that favorite poetic device of the Alliterative Revival. In his dream, he meets the Queen of Fame (fame personified) and Dame Pallas (wisdom personified). Fame reveals that Pallas has commanded her to record Skelton in her book of fame despite the fact that Skelton has written nothing memorable. Fame admits that Skelton is gifted with poetic ability but complains that he's wasting time instead of writing. She insists that if Skelton doesn't write a good poem soon she will erase his name and condemn him to obscurity.

Pallas defends Skelton by arguing that fame and poetic ability don't always coincide; many hack poems have become famous while many good ones go unrecognized. She argues that the masses are uneducated and it's not Skelton's fault if his intelligent works aren't appreciated. Given the choice between fame and intelligence, Pallas argues that Skelton should choose the last.

Queen Fame and Pallas demand that Skelton write a poem and both shall judge whether he is worthy of the laurel. The result is an adventure spanning over 1600 lines, most of them irrelevant to our study. Skelton meets the ghosts of former poets and has visions of his female friends weaving his garland of laurel. The poet dedicates several stanzas to these women; most of whom have been identified by historians. They represent an assortment of ages and Skelton addresses them with various forms of admiration. Next follows some typical references to Greek and Roman mythology, astrology, and Skelton's semiserious bragging. Near the end occurs the imitation of Ovid, already mentioned. Eventually, Skelton returns to Queen Fame and Pallas and is rewarded with his garland of laurel. Skelton is elated with his prize but we suspect he's humoring us a bit. There was never really any contest; Skelton's name was already in Fame's book and the women were weaving his laurel before he finished the poem.

The commonalties between *Garland of Laurel*, *The White Goddess*, and many of Graves's other sources are many; as are the commonalties between Skelton and Graves. The greatest common factor is perhaps the hardest to define and lies in the general tone of Skelton's poem. As one critic states, *Garland of Laurel* is about "the survival of poetry in an antipoetic world" and Skelton repeatedly depicts poetry as a difficult and challenging rite of renewal rather than the pastime of a few effete literary posers (Brownlow 11-12). Skelton sees poetry as an "occult art" capable of defeating time and mingles his poetry with classical paganism and astrology. This attitude is common to much of *White Goddess* as well. Throughout *Laurel*, Skelton adopts an attitude, which both ridicules the ignorant masses and exalts his own intelligence. Skelton's taunts and confidence reminds us of Taliesin's monologues. The taunting of the masses by both poets has a slight resemblance to Graves's own taunt in the forward of *White Goddess*, where he questions the loyalty of other poets. Lastly, Graves may have favored Skelton because he had attended Oxford after a brief stint at Cambridge; Graves always favored his *alma mater* over its archrival.

A more concrete contribution derives from stanza 146 of *Laurel*. In modernized English it runs:

How Dame Minerva first found the olive tree, *she red*
And planted it there where never before was none: *unshred*
A hind unhurt, hit by casualty, *not bled*
Recovered when the forester was gone: *and sped*
The harts of the herd began for to groan, *and fled*
The hounds began to yearn and to quest: *and dread*
With little business stands much rest. *In bed*

We find a hind sheltering itself from dogs by hiding beneath an olive tree. This is the origin of Graves's allegory of the hind, roebuck, or unicorn of poetic inspiration, which occurs in *White Goddess* and *Unicorn and the White Doe*. Skelton's image, possibly combined with an early reading of the *Book of Lambspring*, resulted in Graves's allegorical roebuck. An image representing the allegory appeared on the first edition dust jacket of *The White Goddess*; a reminder that the book had originally been titled *The Roebuck in the Thicket*.

Lastly, the mythic, astrological, and alchemical references within *Laurel* caught Graves's eye. In three short stanzas, Skelton mentions seven of Hercules' labors. Other stanzas mention Ixion, the goddess Fortune, and the phoenix; all minor players in *The White Goddess*. When Skelton awakes from his dream, he discovers that it's new year's eve and has a vision of the double faced Janus amid the stars. The 105th stanza provides an alchemical list of seven metals and the planets that rule them. Additionally, Skelton fills his poem with astrological symbolism and it's even been suggested that the exact time of the poem's creation is cleverly expressed in astrological terminology within the text (Brownlow 52-53). The existence of an acrostic within *Laurel* suggests that Skelton occasionally enjoyed being cryptic; possibly *Laurel* does contain specific astrological dates or other acrostics waiting to be found. Graves knew of the first acrostic and may have searched for others. Whether or not he found other hidden messages is unknown but Graves's approach to *Garland of Laurel* would later influence his treatment of *Cad Goddeu*.

CHAPTER XIII

THE WHEEL

A central theme of *White Goddess* is the recurring pattern of life, death, and rebirth. This cycle was sacred to the pagans of Europe and the Mediterranean, and its symbols permeate Graves's book. The lunar cycle, the progression of Earth's seasons, and the turning of the night sky around the pole star all symbolize death and rebirth to pagans much as Jesus' birth, death, and resurrection symbolize the same concept for Christians. To many pagans, nature's patterns suggest a constant attempt to return to the point of origin after a lifelong quest for knowledge and experience. It's a basic tenet of most paganism that life runs in such cycles but never returns to exactly the same starting point. Upon starting over we find that we face similar problems but past experiences have enhanced our perspective and given us fresh understanding.

Graves argues that pre-Christian pagans viewed their lives in much the same way. This cycle found particularly strong parallels in the life of the king, the poet, or anyone dedicated to the welfare of the people, or the creation of Muse inspired art. Eventually these kings and poets became substitutes for the common man who was eager to relegate the more macabre rituals of this religion to community leaders. The king and poet then became living symbols of this recurring cycle. From that point forward, their lives are dominated by taboos and obligations removing them from the human world and making them archetypes for their followers.

This rise and fall of the divine king is exactly the theory advanced in *The Golden Bough*. Yet, Frazer's theory couldn't be lifted and placed *in toto* into *White Goddess*. Graves modified it by choice and necessity. The most significant change Graves instituted was the connection between divine king and poet. Frazer was primarily interested in the divine king from an anthropological standpoint and neglected the connection between king and poet. Graves, on the other hand, used Frazer's works to found his personal religious beliefs by applying the model of divine kingship to his poetic life. The result is that the poet takes precedence in *White Goddess* and moves though the same stages as Frazer's divine king. To Graves, the poet and king both live their lives as divine models dedicated to the goddess and are eventually sacrificed in order to return with greater knowledge. Furthermore, if Graves's hypothetical goddess religion was a reality, then it's safe to say that king and poet symbolize a process of life, death, and rebirth, which all members of society had once undergone as part of their religious training.

Day by day, season by season, and year by year the king and poet slowly tread out their lives on a sacred path, spiraling inward and upward towards a summit. From there they are cast down again, like Sisyphus, to resume their climb from the bottom. Along their sacred route, they often stop for ritual observances and rites of passage, which clarify their sacred mission to themselves and their observers. These rituals mark the stages of their journey. Graves labels these stages as "stations of the year" and claims that each of them have their own privileges and responsibilities. Knowing what phase or station the poet is at allows him to write better poetry. More importantly to pagans, recognizing these stages enable the pagan to better relate to the world around him and, on a mystical level, allow increased control of the supernatural elements which pagans often call magic.

Graves lists the five stations of the year as "Birth, Initiation, Marriage, Rest from Labor, and Death" (Graves 1993, 138). Everyone must experience these stages, in this order, to live a complete life in Graves's poetic paganism. Neglecting any of the stations resulted in an imbalanced life and therefore an imbalanced mind and, worse yet to Graves, an imbalanced soul. Denial or refusal of any of the five stations was dangerous to the average man but outright heresy to the poet who is sworn to honor and celebrate life in all its stages. Anyone declining any of the five stations could never become a true poet and couldn't hope to become a fully developed adult. Poetry and paganism, to Graves, are keys to human development.

This acceptance of life's stages appears again in chapter twenty-three as Graves states that poets aren't required to free themselves from physical desires as required of Indian mystics. Instead, poets embrace the concept of love in all of its aspects. This leads to physical desire and the desire for continued existence. In short, poets must love the idea of love itself and be willing to live their lives in order to feel that love. This concept contradicts most Eastern philosophy and contributed to Graves's dislike of Eastern mysticism. Graves may have occasionally fancied an escape from poetic duty but shirking any of the five stages was considered unmanly.

Obviously, at least two of Graves's five stages are inevitable. Birth and death are normally beyond the realm of human control. Through medicine and birth control, we can postpone or hasten the birth of others, but we can hardly tamper with our own births. By the same token, we can postpone or hasten the deaths of others, or even our own deaths. However, medical advancements can only delay the inevitable.

On the other hand, initiation, marriage, and rest are choices we consciously encounter. Of these three, initiation is the most difficult to define and consciously peruse. From Graves's work, we gather that initiation means initiation into adulthood, but even this can be a vague definition. Because of the nebulous aspects of initiation, it becomes the one station where most people stumble, or manage to avoid completely. On a strictly biological level, this initiation occurs at puberty but the onset of puberty seldom signifies the arrival of adulthood in Western society. Indeed, in many people puberty precedes their most immature phase.

In various Christian denominations, the ritual of confirmation symbolizes initiation into adulthood. Many denominations have shifted this ritual from immediately after birth to a time closer to puberty to acknowledge that the soul develops concurrently with the body. Pagan cultures have recognized initiation into adulthood in other ways. Their methods are too numerous to list, yet, sexual education, spiritual guidance, and (for men) martial training are typical traits. Pagan women may lose their virginity in a ritual of sexual instruction. Tribal elders may instruct males and females in the symbolism of their religion. Lastly, young men may learn to defend the tribe in either mock combat or authentic battles. Both Frazer's *Golden Bough* and Malinowski's *Sexual Life of Savages* offer examples.

Graves understood the purpose of this initiation and our society's failure to embrace it. As a teenager, his own confirmation had been a dismal anticlimax. The lack of inspiration he felt eventually convinced him that Christianity had lost its spiritual impact and degraded into mere ritual and rhetoric. As his poem *Escape* reveals, Graves wouldn't feel fully initiated into adulthood until his near death experience on the battlefield. Afterwards, he searched for other methods to achieve this sensation and, for a short time, advocated ritual drug use to replace listless Christian confirmations. During his own drug use, he attempted to create the needed atmosphere by listening to recorded pagan invocations and examining photographs of pagan artwork.

Details of experimental drug use don't appear in the first edition of *The White Goddess*. Gordon and Valentina Wasson, the couple who convinced Graves of the importance of psychedelic drugs, first wrote Graves in January of 1949 when they requested information concerning the poisoning of Claudius. Graves had suggested that he had been poisoned with toxic mushrooms and the Wassons had independently developed a similar theory. Their correspondence quickly increased and Wasson eventually visited Graves at Majorca in 1953. Together they experimented with psychedelic mushrooms for the first time on January 31st, 1960. This experience left a lasting impression on Graves and later editions of *White Goddess* were duly supplemented with Graves's mushroom theories.

The appeal of hallucinogenic drugs was short and by 1962, Graves claimed he no longer enjoyed them. Initially, Graves called some of his trips illuminating and spoke of them in positive tones. He advocated drug use within his *Poet's Paradise* lectures, included mushroom theories in *The Greek Myths*, and rewrote much of *White Goddess*, substituting fly agaric for aconite in his reconstructed pagan rituals. Other sources claim Graves's experiences weren't always pleasant. A particular bad trip, led Graves to swear off the transcendent value of drugs and the entire psychedelic movement.

Before his experiments, drugs held a mysterious appeal for Graves. He saw them as possible shortcuts to inspiration and an easy path for those who weren't poetically inclined. However, bad personal experiences changed his view. Fly agaric was no longer the layman's route to mystical experiences but a risky gamble that could injure the irresponsible. Drugs had certain advantages under the right circumstances, but most people were better off without them. Eventually his view on all drugs narrowed until he finally dismissed them as useless and their users as shallows thrill seekers looking to escape life's stages rather than embrace them.

Graves's short-lived drug use was the culmination of several factors beyond the Wassons. Besides Graves's suggestion that Claudius was poisoned by mushrooms, he also mentions hunting mushrooms as a child at his Grandfather's manor (Graves 1957, 22). Graves had once licked a hallucinogenic mushroom as a child and been frightened by the strange reaction it induced in him. Possibly, this experience was the origin of his later interest in hallucinogens. Graves may have considered the experience akin to some form of revelation similar to his battlefield initiation and poetic trance.

Graves underwent another hallucinogenic initiation in 1947 when he was bitten by a poisonous snake and began to hallucinate the revolving island of Celtic mythology. His life was saved by a treatment of wild olive leaves. To hear Graves tell the story we would believe that anyone receiving a similar poisonous bite would also hallucinate the legendary island. Yet we can't rule out the suggestive power of Graves's mind. He had already encountered legends of the revolving island and the glass or crystal palace in his Celtic sources. Additionally, he had read *The Crystal City Under the Sea* at an early age and the book's description of an underwater glass palace remained with him for decades (Graves 1969, 68). Furthermore, Cook's *Zeus* suggests that the ancient Celts saw the other world as a revolving tower or castle. These literary sources contributed to Graves's vision. His knowledge of Celtic paganism had conditioned him to see a revolving silver island upon his death, and faced with death his mind reacted accordingly. Similarly, countless non-pagans have envisioned a long tunnel of light upon near death and we suspect this is the result of similar cultural conditioning and wonder if these same people would have hallucinated a revolving silver island if they had been raised as pagan Celts.

This snakebite may have contributed to Graves's interest in hallucinogenic drugs, the visions they cause, and their effect on mythic and religious ideas. But the story of the snake bite is more interesting than it first appears. Because we know when Graves was bitten, we can date his statement within *White Goddess* to sometime after 1947. This can be confirmed by setting the enlarged edition against the first edition. Doing so reveals that the story of the snakebite is missing from the first edition.

Of further interest is the fact that Graves had read White's *Selborne* early enough to cite it in the first edition. Thus, when he received the snakebite, Graves was already familiar with the passage in *Selborne*, which advocates "common salad oil" as a cure for snake venom (White 51). Graves claims that a local doctor prescribed wild olive leaves for his bite. Did the doctor prescribe this cure independently or did Graves request this specific cure because he was already familiar with the olive oil treatment? Possibly, Graves saw his bite as a mythic accident that required the corresponding mythic cure or a symbolic initiation, which required the correct symbolic reply.

The next station of life, marriage, is often confused or merged with initiation. Unmarried individuals often claim allegiance to nobody and are free agents in society. This attitude is particularly pressed upon unmarried men and the bachelor lifestyle is typified as one of independence and promiscuity. By characterizing marriage as a loss of freedom many people are inclined to believe that marriage, instead of initiation, marks entry into adulthood and the obligations that come with it. People today envision marriage as "growing up" and "settling down" to become mature adults. In Graves's pagan model, nobody would hope to marry until they had reached adulthood independently.

This explains the pagan's disdainful attitude towards virginity. In an idealistic Christian society, both partners would remain virgins until their wedding night. Indeed, many Christian men wouldn't marry a woman who had lost her virginity beforehand, and retention of virginity has often been the very definition of a "good girl". To the pagan, this attitude is nonsensical. In most pagan cultures, loss of virginity is equated with initiation rather than marriage. A man marrying a virgin would immediately question his partner's maturity and may hesitate to even consider her as an adult. This reveals one reason why Canaanite women prostituted themselves at the temple of Astarte. It was their religious duty to lose their virginity before marriage. Most Canaanite women had no trouble finding pious pagan men (or faltering Christians) to accommodate them.

To many of us, "Rest from Labor" hardly seems a station of life and its exact definition eludes us. We may look forward to retirement from a job, or other obligations, but we may see this as our journey's end rather than another station in itself. Yet, retirement doesn't mean complete withdraw from the world but rather a time in which we can offer our experiences to others. This resting phase is when we adopt the image of the wise man or crone aspect of the goddess.

Initiation, marriage, and rest are the three stages we must consciously embrace. When coupled with birth and death we arrive at a pentad serving as a guide for those wishing to live by Graves's system. Graves transposes the life of the poet into this pentad cycle in order to liken the life of man to the progression of the seasons. Wiccans use a similar technique to show mankind's place in the wheel and have developed the myth of the dying and returning god whose life is bound up with earth's fertility. In creating this myth, Wiccans draw heavily on Graves's system. Although the myth of the goddess's dying consort has existed long before Graves it was Graves who revived it long after Western religions had abandoned it. Many pagans are fully aware of the antiquity of this myth and enjoy researching its earlier incarnations. However, most of those who do so view this pagan past through the lens of Graves's work and unconsciously project his model backwards onto past cultures.

Most Wiccans perform rituals on the sabbats to honor and celebrate the progression of the god though the wheel of the year. These rituals have forced the Wiccan wheel into a degree of uniformity and the symbolism of Wiccan ritual has solidified into something more concrete than the symbols of Graves's pagan lifestyle. The Wiccan myth of the god's seasonal life has lead several Wiccan denominations to connect stages of the god's life to the various sabbats. Exactly which life stage is connected to which sabbat depends upon the denomination.

Collectively, these sabbats comprise a Wiccan liturgical calendar similar to those used by Judaism and Christianity. Most Wiccan sabbats have their equivalents in these other religions. For example, winter solstice is observed as Yule, Hanukkah, and Christmas respectively. The overlapping symbolism between paganism and other religions and the question of continuity often leads to controversy regarding which celebrations are older. Although critics can rightfully claim that most pagan rituals were created in the latter half of the twentieth century, they also acknowledge that these rites are often reconstructions or revisions of authentic pagan rites predating most monotheist religions.

These holidays are the high points of the Wiccan year. The

repetition of this cycle is an integral part of paganism and pagans search for meanings in the passing of the year, the raising of crops, the turning of the stars, the generations of man, and in the symbolism of the tarot card called the Wheel of Fortune. Belief in reincarnation or transmigration of the soul is the logical result. Although pagan denominations differ in their interpretations of this cycle, reincarnation is often a fundamental tenet. As with paganism, so is with Graves's poetic system. Both are based on the belief that repetitive seasonal changes imply a universal cycle of death and rebirth.

It's no accident that Graves's pentad cycle resembles the pagan wheel of the year. Not only did later pagans draw from Graves; Graves drew from earlier conceptions of the wheel motif. In *King Jesus*, Graves places seasonal and cabalistic interpretations on *Ezekiel*'s cryptic vision of wheels within wheels (Ezek 10:10). He reveals that each cherub represents a wheel of four spokes; each spoke representing a solstice or equinox. These astronomical events divide the year into four seasons and each season is represented by an animal. These symbolic animals are akin to Ezekiel's vision but not identical. Ezekiel first mentions man, lion, ox, and eagle then lists cherub, man, lion, and eagle (Ezek 1:10, 10:14). Graves combines both statements and offers ox, lion, eagle, and man. Following several earlier authors, he then associates Ezekiel's vision with the similar list within Daniel. Daniel's vision included a winged lion (or griffin), bear, winged leopard, and an unidentified monster comprised of elements from each of the others (Dan 7:12). In *King Jesus* we find Jesus meditating within a magic circle divided into four quarters; each quarter contains one of these beasts, symbolizing temptations to be overcome (Graves 1984, 232-233).

Graves's adoption of this idea places him firmly in an occult tradition extending well beyond pagan practice. Attempts to correlate man's life to seasonal cycles derive from the larger desire to equate man to the universe. This relationship between man (the microcosm) and the universe (or macrocosm) is a key element to paganism and derives primarily from medieval and Renaissance Neoplatonism. During this era, many prominent philosophers combined elements of Neoplatonism, the cabala, and Hermetic texts to produce a mystical interpretation of Christianity, which depended on pagan and occult inspirations. Their works laid much of the foundation for the later pagan movement.

One of the Hermetic laws has resulted in the often quoted pagan adage "as above, so below". The smallest part must reflect the whole and, therefore, man's well being depends on his ability to identify with the universe as a whole. Most Hermetic philosophers promoted this concept; Pico Della Mirandola, Marsilio Ficino, Henry Agrippa, and Giordano Bruno, among others. Later scientific advancements refuted the Hermetic approach but latecomer Robert Fludd carried the mystical Hermetic worldview well into the seventeenth century.

Each of these authors attempted to equate humans to the cosmos and often expressed this concept via emblematic illustrations, which united man and creation. Agrippa offers several circular emblems of supposed magical or spiritual significance, including one, which places man over a pentagram (Tyson 347). Comparisons to Graves's five stations, pagan wheel of the year concepts, and the tarot are revealing. If Agrippa's circle represents the wheel of the year then the figure within is expressing the same idea found within Graves's five stations.

Fludd's illustrations elaborated upon this theme. Taking a cue from Agrippa, earlier philosophers, and possibly Leonardo Da Vinci, he imposes man over the universal emblem in an attempt to reveal their corresponding proportions. In other works Fludd depicts man's internal world, his mind and soul divided and organized into (comparatively) easy to understand compartments.

The logical deduction from these wheel symbols is the belief in reincarnation and an examination of Graves's works reveal that reincarnation is a recurring theme. Although he never claims to have been reincarnated, he does imply that he has lived before, and the majority of his references to reincarnation favor the idea. Graves had even written an article entitled *Reincarnation* in which he boasts that Londoners preferred belief in reincarnation over typical Christian conceptions of heaven and hell. Additionally, he observes that early Christians themselves had embraced reincarnation until the church condemned the belief as heretical (Graves 1969, 76).

In another of his stories, Graves's main character is trapped in a collapsing building. He finishes the tale by claiming that he must have been killed because his next memory was that of a small child being lifted to a window to watch Queen Victoria pass by (Graves 1964, 153). It's no coincidence that Graves's own first memory was that of being held to a window to watch Queen Victoria pass by. This memory impressed him enough to record it within the first paragraph of his autobiography. The implication is obvious but Graves never makes a direct statement regarding his own past lives. He was aware that past life memories were not to be trusted. However, Graves may have privately believed he possessed past life memories and such beliefs may have played a role in his ability to write fiction or project his mind backwards via analeptic memory. Such possibilities lead to several historical and theological questions.

Graves addresses one of these questions in the opening of chapter nine, when he asks if there is any escape from the wheel of reincarnation. The question is central to Graves's beliefs and he claims it's the core of both druidic and Orphic religions. Graves had already dealt with this question in chapter thirteen of *Hercules*. There, Orpheus, the eponymous leader of the Orphic religion, explains: "We are all caught on a wheel, from which there is no release but by the grace of the Mother. We are whirled up into life, the light of day, and carried down again into death, the darkness of night; but then another day dawns red and we reappear, we are reborn" (Graves 1945, 125). Orpheus further claims that a man may even be reborn in the form of an animal. We are left wondering how much Graves is speaking from his personal belief and how much is only reconstruction of ancient Orphic thought.

While belief in reincarnation has suffered periods of unpopularity, it's never truly died out since pre-Christian times. Many influential pagan cultures have embraced reincarnation, including the ancient Egyptians, Greek Orphics, Buddhism, and Hinduism. Theories of reincarnation also became credited to some early philosophers including Plato and Pythagoras. Graves was hardly the first author to suggest a connection between Pythagorean and Celtic reincarnation beliefs. Similar comparisons had been made as early as the third century by Ammianus Marcellinus and as recently as 1903 by D'Arbois de Joubainville. The possible connection between Pythagoras and the Celts has been fertile breeding ground for many crank theories. The fact that none of Pythagoras' works have survived, only fuels such theories.

There are two basic approaches to reincarnation, which may be termed *Eternalists* and *Escapists*. Neither can truly be said to be superior to the other but the wheel can take on different meanings depending on which approach you choose. Both schools are found within paganism and traits of both can often be found within the same individual. Graves displays this ambiguity in much of his work.

The Escapists are easily the larger group. They believe the world is caught in a cycle of life and death, which prohibits the development of the soul. To them reincarnation is only for those who need to re-experience the world in order to learn a lesson. The true goal isn't to be reborn but to develop spiritually so that there is no longer a need to be reborn. Escapists view the world as a place of suffering, either in the poor conditions of human existence, or in the simple fact that life in this world is somehow separate from the divine. They believe union with the divine takes place on a nonphysical level, thus each reincarnation is a further delay in this union. They seek to escape The Wheel through spiritual development. Living a good, pure life and spending much time in self-improvement and self-reflection are the keys to escaping further incarnations. Many believe that criminals and sinners can be purified by certain rituals and that those who refuse purification are punished by being reincarnated in lower life forms such as animals. Buddhism is the best-known example of Escapist beliefs and the first Buddhist principle is that all life is suffering. The Orphics are another such group and many Greek philosophers developed their ideas from Orphic religion. Purification through reincarnation also influenced many of the occult lodges and groups, which appeared during the occult revival in the late 1800's and early 1900's. Similar beliefs influenced Iolo Morganwg as he forged out what he believed to have been druidic beliefs in *Barddas*.

On the other hand, the Eternalists believe that The Wheel turns forever and they happily accept this. They see the world as everlasting and themselves being reborn repeatedly through reincarnation. Time is eternally repeating its cycles and there is no escape. There is no need to escape or any desire to break the cycle. It is not a punishment to be here but a privilege that should be indulged in. The world is good and we should enjoy it. Eternalists are the smaller group probably because most of us prefer to believe that there is a better place we can eventually reach. It takes greater effort to face this world and believe it's worth revisiting an infinite number of lifetimes. Eternalists are obligated to continually look at the bright side rather than simply throw their hands up in anguish and claim "I must be working off bad karma" or neglect this world in favor of rewards in the next world.

Both of these schools of thought exist within the pagan community today. Eternalist pagans argue that paganism is a nature religion and thus it must take pleasure in the physical world of nature. They may believe in a sort of "heaven on Earth" idea. They often argue that this world may be the only world and we should enjoy it, do everything we can to protect it, and enjoy that we are reincarnated into it again. Escapists pagans are also protective of nature and the world but see them as a testing ground. Those who pass the test through proper living are excused from future incarnations and pass on to some more spiritual existence in another world.

Both schools advocate reincarnation despite their different opinions of its purpose. However, these two schools of thought do not represent the entire pagan community. Some pagans do not accept any reincarnation theory but instead opt for something akin to "genetic memory" to explain memories of past lives. Graves hints at this possibility during a 1970 interview and refers to the experimental research of James McConnell as evidence (Norris 2).

Graves was apparently an Escapist, or at least wrote as one when he asked if there was any escape from The Wheel. Just where he encountered the Escapist philosophy is unknown but he was well read in history, myth, and religion and had been aware of it for years. Laura Riding, a devout Escapist herself, likely instilled some Escapist beliefs into Graves as well. The desire to escape mundane reality through human development occurs repeatedly in her works and may derive from cabalistic thought. It also appears in Graves's works after 1926, when Riding came to England.

On the other hand, Gerald Gardner seemed to be a sort of Eternalist, but a rather selective one who never takes a clear stance on the subject. It was a tenet of early Gardnerian Wicca that only Wiccans were reincarnated with their friends and families (Gardner 1954, 32, 42, 68). Gardner claimed that non-Wiccans were not reincarnated at all, or if they were, they were reincarnated with strangers. Early Wiccans seemed to take pleasure in reincarnation and believed the other world was full of people waiting to return to the world of the living, where they could enjoy themselves again. Eventually they would be reborn, but with no memory of their past lives. These memories could be reclaimed through Wiccan ritual and Gardner offers the poem *The Witch Remembers Her Last Incarnation* as evidence of this. While it could be said that Wiccans are Eternalists, Gardner also makes statements that sound like typical Escapist theories as well. After having said that Wiccans use ritual to ensure rebirth, Gardner then claims that the goal of the Wiccan is to escape the wheel of rebirth and become one of the "Mighty Ones" or "Mighty Dead", the guiding spirits of Wiccans who have died and not reincarnated (Gardner 1954, 140). In this respect, Wicca reflects earlier pagan ancestor worship akin to Celtic, Greek, and Native American beliefs.

Early Gardnerian Wiccans resembled the Orphics who believed that the dead went to Hades unless they had performed the proper rites. While we may link Hades to the Christian Hell, the two were far from identical. To the Greeks Hades wasn't a place of eternal punishment but a place of temporary gloom and depression. You could be punished forever in Hades, but only if you were exceptionally evil. Even then, your punishment wasn't so much painful suffering but was more akin to the pointless labors of Tantalus or Sisyphus. The common man's soul went to Hades and faded into obscurity until it was reincarnated. In Hades past life memories were lost by crossing the river Styx or by drinking from certain wells. Various Greek pagan cults offered ways to reclaim your past life memories or retain them while in Hades.

Orphic initiates were buried with golden plates containing ritualistic instructions on how to behave in Hades so that they could be reborn with their memories intact. A few such plates have been recovered and Graves used their material to write the song, which he places in Orpheus's mouth in *Hercules*. He also admits, in the appendix of that book, to drawing on druidic mythology and Frazer's *Totemism and Exogamy* to flesh out his religious depiction. Obviously, Graves sees a close connection between druidism and the Orphics, as have many other writers both before and after him. Davies also found similarities and believed that Celtic terms appear in the Orphic hymns and that "All the accounts of Orpheus agree with Druidism" (Davies 1804, 131, 144). Following Davies, *Hercules* suggests that Orpheus brought his mysteries from the druids.

Was Graves right in depicting the pagan Celts as Escapist? A look at Celtic literature suggests otherwise. Caesar reported that Celtic warriors had no fear of death because the druids taught reincarnation. These warriors fearlessly rushed into battle because they knew they would reincarnate. Had they been Escapists they would have shirked death as one more needless birth. Yet, the valor of Celtic soldiers was well known in the ancient world and stories of them charging against the ocean or fighting to the death over the "hero's portion" are common. Caesar also mentions that Celts loaned money with the idea that it could be repaid in the next life. Their own literature also suggests the Celts looked forward to being reincarnated. Multiple examples exist of Celtic heroes who are encouraged to bear children to ensure their own rebirth. Pwyll and Cuchulainn are prime examples.

In the end, it may be more important to know Graves's own stance than the stance of the ancient Celts. Was Graves an Escapist or an Eternalist? Was he even decided in the matter? As already stated, it seems that Graves was writing as an Escapist when he asks if all things must continue forever. However, in chapter twenty-three Graves supports some Eternalist thought and tries to link it to Western poetic traditions. In the end, we might conclude that Graves is an Eternalist, but perhaps a rather unhappy one who is not entirely comfortable with the possibility of eternal incarnations.

CHAPTER XIV

THE WORD AND THE SIGN

Graves's impact on paganism includes more than theories of reincarnation. *The White Goddess* also helped define much Wiccan terminology, ritual, and symbolism. The word *witch* itself was given a new popular etymology, which varied from commonly accepted scholarship. The pentagram, which Graves alludes to several times, became the most widely accepted symbol of pagans. Even minor references to foreign ceremonies became incorporated into pagan traditions. From *The White Goddess* these things entered into the growing pagan community, often via Gerald Gardner, and merged into typical Wiccan practice.

Foremost among these changes was Graves's derivation of *witch*, *wicker*, and *wicked* from the word *willow*. While this etymology is questionable, it exerted profound influence on Wiccan literature and reinforced various associations among pagans. Foremost among these is that *witch* is wrongly linked to *wicked* as the result of Christian propaganda during the medieval witch trials. This may contain a grain of truth and the term *wicked witch* can be dated to at least 1475 (Kieckhefer 84). Both *witch* and *wicker* are believed to derive from the old English root *wic*, meaning "to bend". Isaac Bonewits was the first pagan to claim this etymology and he extended it to the older Indo-European root *weik* (Bonewits, 104). Thus, *wicca* has been tied to *wic* and *weik*, two different European roots meaning to bend. The leap from this to *wicker* is a good example of popular etymology. In popular logic *wicker*, like *witch*, derived from *wic* because wickerwork is created from flexible wooden strips.

Bonewits argues that *wicca* also derives from *wic* because Wiccans bend reality through magic ritual. Yet, it's unlikely that

Gardner knew this etymology when he used *wicca* to describe his witch-cult. Gardner probably knew that the old English *wicca* or *wicce* was associated to *witch* but he may not have known of the earlier *wic* or *weik* roots. Not that it mattered. Gardner knew enough to establish the needed link. Gardner was only interested in linking his coven to earlier ideas of witches, not to vague Indo-European root words. Graves later adopted Gardner's etymological claim, giving it further strength (Graves 1964, 551).

In reality, the word as Gardner gives it is *wica*. How the word went from *wica* to *Wicca* is unclear but it's been suggested that Gardner was dyslexic; or at very least a horrible typist (Kelly xv; Frew). Either way, we can assume Gardner borrowed the term based on its association to *witch* and also to the old English *witan*, itself a term of uncertain origin. As early as 1016, Wulfstan II preached against the *wiccan* and while he never clearly defined the term, he linked it with pagan worship, witchcraft, and sorcery. In the fourteenth century, *Piers Ploughman* uses the word *wicchecrafte* and provides the connecting link between the older *wiccan* and the modern witchcraft (Skeat 2:251). Less than a century later the term "wicked witch" appeared and the transition was complete. Regardless of what Wulfstan intended, *wicca* now meant witchcraft and *wiccans* were witches of either sex.

Besides redefining the word *witch*, Graves also redefines the names of the fingers in his discussion of his ogham key-board and assigns each finger a planetary attribute. Graves's planetary attributes are:

Index or fore-finger, Jupiter
Middle finger, Saturn
Ring-finger, the Sun
Little finger, Mercury

He then links popular cheiromancy to the ogham. Thus, the index finger becomes the oak finger because Jupiter was often depicted as an oak tree or carved oak pillar. For reasons never explained Graves connects the Saturn finger to the Christmas Fool. Because of connections between Apollo and the Sun, the ring-finger becomes the Apollo finger in Graves's system. Finally, the little finger symbolizes death because Mercury leads the dead to the underworld. These attributes are questionable but the overlap between mythological characters is so wide that nearly any attributes could be given to any deity and it's best to avoid splitting hairs at this point.

Graves's finger system draws almost exclusively from Roman mythology with the single exception of the Greek Apollo. This is because Graves draws from cheiromancy sources, which are themselves connected to astrology, and the planets are named after Roman deities. Graves includes Apollo because it's vital that he connects his mythical ogham system to his earlier theories regarding the rise of Apollonian logic and poetry.

In his discussion, Graves mentions the Latin Blessing, a gesture commonly seen in Roman art and medieval paintings. This gesture involves raising the thumb, index finger, and middle finger of the right hand and was often displayed by ancient Romans before giving a public lecture. This tradition is continued today by the Pope, who uses the same gesture for benediction. Graves mentions a Phrygian bronze votive hand dedicated to Zeus depicting this gesture. A reproduction of this artifact can be found in Cook's *Zeus* and this is almost assuredly the source of Graves's data (Cook 1: 391). Furthermore, Cook describes one of the earliest known depiction of the Christian god with arm raised and fingers extended in this gesture of benediction. This carving dates to c. 300 AD and provides evidence of the gesture's transition from pagan to Christian blessing (Cook 2: 289).

In the same paragraph Graves mentions the so called "devil's blessing", the gesture of two fingers up and three fingers down, which is today popularly associated with rock concerts. According to Graves, it was originally an invocation to the horned god, one horn being lucky and the other being unlucky. It reminded pagans that the horned god ruled over both good and evil. This gesture is one of many currently used in Italy to repel the evil eye and is likely to be of ancient origin. Religious writers had connected this gesture to Satan as early as the first half of the thirteenth century (Russell 118).

Displaying the gesture itself or, more commonly today, wearing a pendant in the shape of a hand displaying the gesture, is common practice for protection from evil. Such pendants were originally made of coral but have been replaced by cheaper metal trinkets. Besides an invocation to the horned god, the devil's blessing has also been interpreted as an invocation to the moon or a moon deity. The "horns" of the gesture become symbolic of the crescent moon and the hand is often kissed before raising it skyward. Honoring the moon by kissing and raising the hand is documented by *Job 31:26-28*, where exactly this sort of behavior is forbidden to Jews. This may have suggested a practice found in Leland's *Aradia* (Leland 49). Similar rituals of greeting the moon were practiced as far apart as Scotland and Arabia as late as the mid nineteenth century (Carmichael 1:122; Doughty 1:412). Pagans occasionally do this but it is assuredly a case of pedantry and not an unbroken tradition dating back to either Scotland or biblical times. Graves himself often bowed to the new moon (Graves 1958, 61). During an especially stressful night in New York, Graves nervously paced Manhattan's streets until he found the moon over the skyline. Fellow poet Alastair Reid accompanied him on this walk and noted that the sight of the moon seemed to calm Graves (Graves 1995, 270).

The devil's blessing appears only in later editions of *The White Goddess* and leads to questions of where and when Graves found it. This could have been one of the subjects discussed between Graves and Gardner when they met in 1961. It's already known that Gardner drew from Graves to develop his Wiccan beliefs. It would be ironic if Graves then drew this item from Gardner and used it as further evidence of an existing witch-cult. Any Wiccan group using this gesture would have avoided the term "devil's blessing" in an attempt to distinguish between Wicca and Satanism. Yet, if Graves received the information from Gardner, Gardner may have made no such distinction. Although Gardner was at pains to separate Wicca from Satanism, he was also an expert on much more than typical Wiccan symbolism. Gardner had already read *The White Goddess* before his visit to Majorca and may have been eager to contribute this bit of knowledge to Graves's collection of lore.

Graves also attempts to explain the gesture of the *digitus impudicus,* or middle finger. To Graves the middle finger is linked to the goddess Venus, ruler of erotic love and sexuality. Yet this is an unlikely origin for what has become the most common obscene gesture in the world. It has long been suspected that "the finger" has its origin in the various gestures displayed while casting or repelling the Italian "evil eye". The evil eye itself dates to classical times and a wide variety of hand gestures have become associated with its casting and repelling. The upraised fist or any number of fingers pointed at the victim are other variants of the insulting evil eye and may be the ultimate origin of the belief that it's not polite to point.

Graves neglects to mention another obscene evil eye gesture commonly known to the ancients as "the fig". This insult was performed by placing the thumb between the first and middle finger of a closed fist. This gesture has almost completely vanished as an insult and is sometimes seen in combination with the upraised fist or the crossed arm gesture. The fig is irrelevant to Graves's work but his failure to mention it may reveal something. This gesture appears in two early studies of phallic worship: *A Discourse on the Worship of Priapus* by Richard Knight (1786) and *The Worship of the Generative Powers* by Thomas Wright (1866). Graves's failure to mention the fig may imply his failure to read either book. This is significant because Harding drew from Knight, while Murray drew from Knight *and* Wright. In addition, both Knight and Wright address various other topics, which Graves would have found interesting.

Wright's book discusses, among other things, ritual acts of various medieval cults and stereotypical images of witch sabbats. In particular, Wright discusses medieval allegations of nude circle dances and charges of gathering herbs by night while nude. Today many pagans recognize such traits as possible origins of Gerald Gardner's insistence on the use of ritual nudity, or worshiping "skyclad". Wright also mentions that many early pagans made obviously false conversions to Christianity only from social pressure and continued to practice paganism under their thin veneer of Christianity. Additionally, he mentions *Robin Goodfellow, his mad pranks and merry gests*, a booklet that Graves cites in *White Goddess*. Wright links Robin Goodfellow with phallic deities much as Graves does, and claims that witchcraft was the last form of phallic worship in Europe. Yet, there is no hard evidence that Graves drew directly from Wright. Instead, it appears that Graves arrived at the same idea via Murray, who reproduces the same argument and even the same woodcut.

Other interesting items from Wright include the belief that the witch mark was often found on female sexual organs. This agrees with common ideas of the witch mark but clashes with Graves's own theory. Wright also mentions that it was commonly known that the Christian calendar adopted many earlier pagan holidays and cites Easter as an example. The Christian usurpation of pagan holidays has become a standard element in pagan texts; *Golden Bough, Carmina Gadelica,* and *White Goddess* all cite examples.

Knight, who wrote eighty years before Wright, is even more interesting in light of Graves's ideas. Knight wrote of silver amulets in the shape of the fig, linked the moon to fertility and menstruation, discussed the horns of Alexander and Moses, and bull worship in Egypt. He repeatedly argues that even the most ludicrous ritual or symbol contains true religious meaning to the believer. These believers protect the true significance of their icons from outsiders resulting in a secret doctrine intelligible only to the elect. However, as with Wright, Graves could have found all of these ideas in Murray's works instead, leaving us no proof that he had read Knight.

Nor are the works of Knight and Wright the only sources where

Graves may have encountered the fig. Cook mentions this gesture in the second volume of *Zeus* and lists several other sources in his discussion. Cook suggests that the gesture was used by pagans initiated into the cult of Demeter. Additionally, he claims that a fig may have been revealed to the initiate during the initiation ritual much as an ear of corn was revealed during the initiations at Eleusis. These ideas would have appealed to Graves and his failure to mention the fig or the initiation ritual in which it was used suggests that Graves did not completely read Cook's *Zeus*.

Graves next claims that the medieval witch-cults in Britain also used the "finger alphabet". As evidence he offers the so called "witch mark", often mentioned in witch trials after the fourteen century. He cites Joseph Glanvill's *Saducismus Triumphatus* regarding the location of the witch mark in the case of the Somerset witches of 1664. This same case appears in Murray's *Witch-Cult* (Murray 1996, 89). Both books mention that the witch mark was placed on "the fourth finger of the right hand between the middle and upper joint". Assuming they included the thumb the mark would have been placed on the ring finger.

Notice Murray's influence on Graves as he completely accepts her theory that the witch mark was a tattoo. He can't be wholly blamed. Murray's tattoo theory sounds credible, however, in order to accept the tattoo theory you must accept her larger theory, as Graves had obviously done.

In reality, the witch mark was a late element of witch persecutions and consisted of part fact, part fantasy. Far from being any secret insignia it was more a vague concept that included nearly any physical irregularity suiting the witch finder's needs. While it's true that in Britain and New England the witch mark was most often found on the hand it could easily be on any part of the body and the shoulder or sexual organs are close runner ups. Murray herself gives contradictory statements regarding the mark's location. *Witch-Cult* cites instances of its occurrence on the hand, shoulder, thigh, and wrist (Murray 1996, 75, 83-89). *God of the Witches* further claims that the mark had "no special place on the body" but the left shoulder was commonly cited (Murray 1970, 100).

Murray's tattoo theory prompts Graves to mention that British sailors once tattooed a star between their thumb and first finger as a good luck charm. This is the first of several occasions where Graves alludes to the pentagram without actually naming it. Other examples include his reference to the pentagon shaped slabs lining the Pharos seaport. Graves never uses the term pentagram but he mentions pentagrams in relation to the witch mark and thereby links the star to witchcraft. Graves clearly links the pentagram to the goddess and thus sets the grounds for modern Wiccan symbolism. However, is he the first to do so? Where did Graves learn to link the pentagram to the goddess?

While it's commonly linked to everything from Wicca to Satanism and cabalistic ritual, the pentagram is merely a star devoid of any single meaning. The names and meanings placed on the pentagram are of importance and not the star itself. Most pagans call it a pentagram but other names are "the witch's foot" and more interestingly, "the druid's foot". This implies a connection between witchcraft and druidism, as Graves postulates, but the exact relationship remains unclear. The pentagram has also been called the "seal of Solomon" by some cabalistic students, but most agree that because cabalism is an offshoot of Judaism the seal of Solomon was logically the six pointed Star of David. Both Aleister Crowley and S.L. Mathers utilized the pentagram and although it's unlikely that Graves read either of their works his familiarity with other occult material has been noted.

Followers of the Greek philosopher and mathematician Pythagoras supposedly called the pentagram the *pentalapha* and used it as a symbol of recognition within their cult. Pythagoras believed in the mystic power of the triangle and the letter A, both of which occur in the pentagram five times. Pythagoras lived c.500 BC and Greek vase paintings attest to the existence of pentagrams in Greek art at the time.

Many Wiccans claim it's the symbol of pagan Europe and it has become especially connected to modern Wiccan practice. It represents the power of the spirit over the lesser elements: fire, air, earth, and water. The origin of this idea is unknown but Eliphas Levi mentions these elemental attributes and may have derived them from Danish astronomer Tycho Brahe's 1582 *Calendarium Naturale Magicum Perpetuum*. While Brahe doesn't display the pentagram with the elemental attributes he does put all the same symbols in one column showing a pentagram with human body imposed and the elements listed nearby. Obviously, he was implying an association between the elements and the points of the pentagram.

Some pagans claim that the pentagram's origin lies in the design of an apple when cut in half, as Graves himself mentions. A horizontal cut through an apple reveals a pentagram shape and apples were the sacred fruit of the Celts. Yet to suggest that the druids used the pentagram in any way is almost laughable. While magic apples are common in Celtic myth, their internal pentagram is never mentioned. If the Celts truly venerated the apple because of the pentagram, we would have examples in Celtic art. No such examples are known.

This is the first mention in *The White Goddess* of either a star or pentagon and Graves avoids the word pentagram entirely. However, he was obviously thinking of the pentagram when he wrote about pentads, stars, and pentagons. Many Wiccan readers of *The White Goddess* believe that Graves was hinting at the pentagram as a Wiccan symbol with its standard symbolism of the four elements and the spirit. However, it would be impossible for Graves to associate the pentagram with Wicca because at the time of Graves's writing Gardner hadn't yet published any of his Wiccan writings. Gardner's first book to deal specifically with Wicca was *High Magic's Aid* in 1949, yet even it never mentions the words Wicca or pentagram.

In chapter twenty-three, Graves touches on the significance of the pentad in various pagan religions and again avoids the term pentagram. His views on the pentagram and the role it plays in ceremonial magic probably helped Gardner choose the pentagram as a Wiccan symbol. While the pentagram has traditionally been linked to witchcraft, we have few (if any) references to it during the witch trials of the Middle Ages and Murray fails to incorporate it into her witch-cult theory.

Exactly where did Graves find the pentagram and why did he link it to goddess worship? Did he read some religious, magical, or occult work that linked the pentagram to paganism or did he simply find mention of a pentagram by some historian in a pagan culture and draw his own conclusions about its meaning? We know that he had read some occult works and had encountered the cabala before. Lastly, we know that Graves detested Yeats for his occult involvement, so we can assume that Graves knew something of the nature of this involvement or of the nature of the Golden Dawn. He could have encountered the pentagram in any of these sources.

The pentad underlies much of *The White Goddess* and pagan theology. The fivefold stations of life are Graves's own creation, although Frazer addresses four of the five stages. Although Graves defines the goddess as fivefold, he primarily focuses on her triple aspects of temptress, mistress, and destroyer. Because the fivefold goddess is Graves's modification of the triple goddess, he finds it easier to address the three better-known aspects. The two remaining aspects are not nearly as well documented in his sources and Graves neglects them because even he considers them less important than the usual three. Graves attempts to define all five aspects within *King Jesus*; labeling them "The Spinner, Fame, the Queen of Heaven, Repose, Wailing" (Graves 1984, 215) The tasks assigned to each lesser goddess include spinning the thread of life, flattery of the hero, sexual reward (or sexual corruption), rest (or death), and honoring the dead hero. This description is the nearest Graves approaches to fully explaining all five aspects of the goddess. Significantly, *White Goddess* itself fails to expound on all five aspects and even within *King Jesus*, we find Jesus continually shuffled between three Maries, not five.

CHAPTER XV

JUDEO-CHRISTIAN IMPACT

Graves lost his devotion to Christianity long before 1948. Yet, it wasn't a loss that he took lightly and his abandonment wasn't the typical hostile rejection common with some pagans. Instead, he underwent a slow change as his early faith was eroded by historical research and personal experience, to be replaced with a type of paganism. Repeatedly we see his refusal to completely abandon biblical authority and ultimately Graves opts to rewrite many biblical accounts rather than reject them entirely. His reasons for this include his refusal to deny those early emotional experiences which mainstream religion had provided and his belief that Christianity had once been a better religion.

His claim that the early books of the Bible are based on sacred images captured by Israelites at Hebron allows Graves to introduce iconotropy into the argument. By suggesting that Israelites captured sacred images of earlier paganism, Graves implies that Judaism and Christianity contain a strong infusion of the matriarchal paganism, which he supports. Additionally, he provides a convenient excuse for the absence of any evidence regarding this pagan religion by suggesting that later Jews and Christians absorbed it into their own faith and destroyed those aspects they disliked. These Israelite misinterpretations liberate Graves to rewrite biblical stories without facing accusations of iconotropy. In his own mind, Graves is only correcting the already corrupt versions of biblical tales rather than twisting them to suit his needs.

We've already seen Graves's iconotropy theory develop from a simple idea of misunderstanding existing images to a creation of images which he assumes to have existed. Now this method is applied to the Bible. We shouldn't be surprised. The direct attack on the Bible was inevitable considering Graves's religious standpoint. Graves, like Frazer, seeks to undermine biblical authority. Unlike Frazer, however, Graves makes both the covert implications and the brazen frontal assault.

A minor example of this method is his treatment of the twelve tribes of Israel and their connection to the jeweled breastplate, which formed the central piece of the priest's ephod, mentioned in *Exodus*. Graves postulates a connection between the ephod's jewels and ogham's letters. This allows the ephod to become an oracular device. Priests manipulating phosphorus strips behind the jewels spelled out appropriate messages and duped their followers into obedience; an idea Graves uses in *King Jesus*. How Graves reached this unorthodox conclusion is unknown but he may have drawn inspiration from Milton's *Paradise Lost*.

Near the end of *Paradise Lost*'s third book Milton merges his interpretation of the breastplate with solar imagery and mentions the twelve stones "and a stone besides" (Milton 109). This extra stone brings the total to thirteen, just as Graves suggests. His use of solar imagery seems to imply that the breastplate lit up and later, in the sixth book, Milton mentions "radiant Urim"; again suggesting that the stones were illuminated.

Exodus provides explicit instructions for the creation and use of the ephod, including a listing of the jewels to be used for the central breastplate. However, biblical references do not indicate that all twelve stones were used during divination. Common belief states that only two stones were used, Urim and Thummim. These two stones attached to the ephod above and beyond the original twelve and their usage is repeatedly mentioned within the Bible without reference to the other twelve stones (Num 27:21; 1 Sam 28:6). Urim and Thummim may be identical to those inscribed stones mentioned in Exodus 28:9-10; each of which bore the names of six of Israel's tribes. Assuming that the six names were each inscribed upon a different facet, it seems that Urim and Thummin were merely two standard six sided dice inscribed with the names of the twelve tribes and used for divination. Similar dice methods were also used by pagans of the same era (Lane-Fox 208-13).

Whether these stones were dice or not is irrelevant to Graves's argument and the dice theory is a far cry from Graves's contention that all twelve of the gems were used during divination. Rather, it seems that Graves's vision of the ephod was impacted not only by its mention in *Exodus* and *Paradise Lost* but also by the mention of two other similar devices within *Judges*. These references reveal that the ephod of the Tabernacle wasn't the only ephod in existence. Two others were created by the idolaters Gideon and Micah when they abandoned the biblical god. Gideon had made his from gold, as *Exodus* instructs, while Micah forged his from silver (Judg. 8:26-27; 17:4-5). The exact appearance of these ephods isn't recorded and no mention of gemstones is made but Gideon and Micah clearly used their ephods for pagan rituals. The biblical claim that "all Israel went thither a whoring after it" implies that Gideon's ephod was consulted as an oracle. Danite spies also asked Micah's priest to consult with god, again implying that his ephod was consulted as an oracle (Judg. 18:5). The Danites later stole Micah's breastplate. Possibly, they regarded it as a magical device and believed they had gained supernatural abilities by possession of it much as possession of the ark of the covenant was regarded as auspicious.

Graves's religious upbringing alerted him to the relevant biblical passages regarding his ephod theory. However, other sources exist. Charles Doughty's *Travels In Arabia Deserta*, another of Graves's sources, mentions the "ancient divining stones, which were set one for a tribe, in the vesture of the chief priest of Israel", suggesting that all twelve stones were used for divination (Doughty 360). Murray also mentions Urim and Thummim and their relationship to casting lots (Murray 1970, 156). *Piers Ploughman* may also have provided inspiration. The opening passage of its second book depicts *Mede*, the personification of bribery and corruption, adorned with rubies, diamonds, sapphires, amethyst, and beryls. Finally, Davies mentions a similar jeweled shield within his *Mythology and Rites* and equates the shield's gemstones to the zodiac signs (Davies 1809, 544). This Arkite shield is highly reminiscent of the biblical breastplate and the similarities are probably intentional on the part of Davies, whose Arkite theory depended upon biblical symbolism.

A significant amount of twisting is required to make ogham correspond to the biblical twelve jewels. Graves assumes such a connection is possible and then declares that the jewels listed in the Authorized Version are completely erroneous. Next, he rebuilds the jewel sequence with the help of J. I. Myers, a source he fails to fully cite. Finally, he reorders the jewels in a seasonal order because he believes the biblical sequence was intentionally confused. Supposedly, Solomon was also familiar with ogham tree symbolism. Graves believes the verse in *1 Kings* 4:33: "He would speak of trees, from the cedar that is in the Lebanon to the hyssop that grows in the wall; he would speak of animals and birds, and reptiles and fish" implies Solomon's familiarity with ogham.

In both the mention of the jeweled breastplate and Solomon's knowledge Graves assumes that the true religious beliefs were hidden and there was a puzzle to solve. He then rearranges obscure sources to suit his assumption. Basically, he has created his own problem and then solved it to his own satisfaction much as he assumed there was a hidden meaning to *Cad Goddeu* and *Hanes Taliesin*.

His desire to reinterpret Christain texts also explains his use of the *Book of Enoch*. Graves sides with biblical experts who claim that *Enoch* is the key to understanding the words of Jesus. The similarities between the Gospels and *Enoch* are too many to be coincidence and are not easily explained. If Jesus was an authentic person, he may have been familiar with the contents of *Enoch*. Alternately, if Jesus was an invention of the Gospel writers, the words of *Enoch* may have been attributed to him at a later date.

Graves's sources for his *Enoch* data reveal four biblical experts by name: Charles, Burkitt, Oesterley, and Box (Graves 1993, 83). Here, in an unexpected windfall, Graves has given us four of his sources in a single line. Who are these authors?

Charles is assuredly R. H. Charles, author of multiple biblical studies, including *A Critical and Exegetical Commentary on the Revelation of St. John* (1920). Charles also edited an edition of *The Apocrypha and Pseudepigrapha* (1913). These titles imply that Charles was familiar with both Revelations and *Enoch*, perhaps the most influential Jewish and Christian texts to impact the writing of *White Goddess*. Significantly, William Oesterley wrote the introduction for Charles's translation of *Enoch* and contributed material in conjunction with George Herbert Box. Box had also independently authored *Judaism in the Greek Period from the Rise of Alexander the Great to the Intervention of Rome* (1932). F. C. Burkitt was author of titles such as *The Gospel History and it's Transmission* and *Jewish and Christian Apocalypses*; both published before 1915.

All four authors wrote early enough to be included not only in *White Goddess* but also to serve as sources for *King Jesus*. Secondly, each author explored Christian and Jewish apocalyptic writings and favored the New Testament time frame, which Graves utilized for *King Jesus*. Because they favor apocalyptic texts these authors were familiar with the similarities between Revelations and the mystical visions of Enoch and Ezekiel, which Graves believes to have influenced Essene mysticism. After all, all four men insisted that *Enoch* was central to understanding Jesus.

Graves likely discovered these authors while researching for *King Jesus* but it's unknown whether or not he found them independently. Charles, Oesterley, and Box collaborated within *The Apocrypha and Pseudepigrapha*, a book frequently cited within the *Jerome Biblical Commentary*, another of Graves's sources. Alternately, they may have been suggested to him by someone such as Joshua Podro. Podro, an expert on rabbinical literature, first met Graves in the early 1940's. Together they spent many hours discussing early Jewish and Christian texts and Podro advised Graves during his writing of *King Jesus* (Seymour 289-290; R.P. Graves 1995, 78).

Two of Graves's *Enoch* citations deal with the divisions of time into years, days, and hours. Considering *Enoch*'s astronomical and astrological bias this is hardly surprising. *Enoch*'s detailed divisions of time and categorical listing of angels make it one of the most mystical of Judeo-Christian texts. It's often been compared to the mystical visions of Ezekiel and cited as an early influence on those later cabalistic and Hermetic authors who rank legions of angels into a strict hierarchy. This astronomical-astrological bias and angel listings are Judeo-Christian variations upon the older pagan system of astral magic, which involved meditation upon various planets, stars, and their divinities as a form of spiritual development. Each planet and zodiac constellation possessed its own protecting spirit, which could be consulted during the planetary hours mentioned by Guest and Davies. Thus, proper time keeping and astronomical observation were central to this regime of meditation.

Paul alludes to this practice when he complains that the Galatians worship the elements and "observe days, and months, and times, and years" (*Gal. 4:9-10*). Graves notes that Cyprian's *Confessions* reveal a similar pagan practice. Cyprian's initiation involved musical instruction, herbal lore, and lessons regarding the birth and death of physical bodies. Spirits were equated to the seasons and Cyprian watched dramatic performances in which their lessons were enacted. Finally, the new initiate had visions of trees. In short, he was instructed in the vast correspondences of astral magic. If Cyprian's initiation sounds suspiciously like modern Wiccan initiation, we shouldn't be surprised; his experiences are the classic model of the pagan mystery cults which Wicca emulates.

This pagan system of astral magic centered upon the twelve zodiac signs but quickly expanded as various interpretations were placed upon the signs. The original twelve were divided into both positive and negative aspects for a total of twenty-four. Then, each of these twenty-four were again divided into a period of rising power, a period of peak power, and a final phase of declining power. This produced six different interpretations for each zodiac sign, three good and three evil and brought the system to a total of seventy-two influences (*decans*), which affected the worshiper for good or evil. Prayer, meditation, and ritual helped the pagan align the decans to his advantage and much pagan and early Jewish and Christian occultism revolved around describing and appeasing the seventy-two spirits of the decans. *Enoch* attempts to Christianize this system and equates the ruling spirits to legions of angels serving Jehovah.

By the third century, this system inspired the hermetic texts already mentioned. Corruptions of this system appeared in Europe after the twelfth century, with the influx of Arabic education, and by the sixteenth century, this system was hopelessly corrupted in various English and Latin texts. The *Steganographia*, written by the Spanish monk Trithemius is a typical example; Graves cites this work in the last half of *White Goddess* (Graves 1993, 426). Other examples include Dr. John Weyer's examination of the seventy-two demon princes and Agrippa's corrupt and incomplete listing of the decans in his *Three Books of Occult Philosophy*. The most amazing preservation of astral magic in Celtic literature is perhaps the prayer recorded in the 1800's and presented within *Carmina Gadelica*:

Uiriel shall be at my feet
Ariel shall be at my back
Gabriel shall be at my head
Raphael shall be at my side (Carmichael 1:95)

This Scottish prayer reflects the Enochian ordering of angels and suggests hints of a lost accompanying ritual. Pagans will recognize this prayer as a likely source for the *Lesser Banishing Ritual of the Pentagram* used by the Golden Dawn. Similar imagery appears in the cabalistic *Sepher Yetzirah*.

Several other astrological manuals survive from sixteenth-century Wales, proving the popularity of astrology during this era (Levack 168). The reference to planetary hours within the *Mabinogion* and the *Auraicept*'s mention of the seventy-two scholars suggest that astral magic was corrupting Celtic traditions by at least the time of our surviving copies of these texts. The seventy-two scholars of the *Auraicept* are derived from the seventy-two Jewish scholars of cabalistic tradition. Therefore, it seems astral magic didn't reach Ireland until after the confusion of the seventy-two decans resulted in the creation of the seventy-two Jewish cabalists, probably sometime after the Spanish cabalistic boom of the tenth century.

Graves was marginally familiar with the cabala and his use of *Lambspring* reveals a limited familiarity with Hermetics, but he was apparently ignorant of the astral magic system from which both evolved. He knew the zodiac and had discovered the importance of timekeeping in paganism and early Jewish and Christian texts. However, much astral magic eluded him. Twice he erroneously refers to the "Great Year" as equivalent of eight standard years when in reality the Great Year is a Hermetic term for a single revolution of the zodiac; a 26,000 year process. He refers to the number seventy-two repeatedly but is unfamilar with the decans. Instead, he believes the importance of the number derives from the total number of strokes in the ogham alphabet. We can't blame Graves for his ignorance. A full listing of the seventy-two decans, their descriptions, and planetary hours only exist in rare magical manuscripts, which he was unlikely to consult.

His ignorance of the system forces him to work the problem backwards. With only the zodiac and a few references to ancient timekeeping, Graves has correctly assumed that such an astral system once existed and attempts to reconstruct it himself. However, the details of his final result differ considerably from the authentic system. Graves's introduction of European sources into this basically Mediterranean and Arabic system, diverts him towards a creation which he can then equate to the ogham. Basically, Graves concludes that this system was universal and spanned Europe, the Mediterranean, and the Middle East. This allows him to incorporate late corruptions without checking their accuracy and enables him to project his universal magic system backwards into remote history.

How familiar were medieval or Renaissance Welsh bard with either the character of Enoch or the *Books of Enoch*? Had they known of him they would have found him appealing. His claim to divine knowledge is comparable to Taliesin's hubris and certain lines of *Enoch* are highly reminiscent of Taliesin's poems and the long history of manuscripts, which preserved them. The fortieth chapter of *Enoch* tells how Enoch has learned all things directly from the mouth of God and wrote them into books. Enoch had claimed, "I know all things, and have written all things into books" (*2 En.40:2*). Among Enoch's knowledge was astrology and he bragged that "I have measured and described the stars" and asks, "What man has seen their revolutions, and their entrances?" (*2 En.40:3-4*). Surely, Welsh bards saw parallels between the divinely inspired Enoch and Taliesin. It's even possible that some of the late Taliesin material was intentionally written in imitation of Enoch's boasting and that this material may have impacted the later versions of *Cad Goddeu* or *Hanes Taliesin*.

As shown, later Welsh bards had access to an impressive amount of literature and *Enoch* may have been included. *Enoch* has the advantages of being both a pious text, which illuminates the Bible and also a somewhat cabalistic text with occult undertones. *Enoch* describes how God ordered the ten levels of heaven and organized armies of angels, archangels, cherubim, and seraphim by rank and file. Several of the most powerful angels, including Uriel, Michael, and Gabriel are explicitly named and divisions of heaven are enumerated. Medieval readers found this data easy to correlate to cabalistic and Hermetic occultism. The Renaissance period saw not only the death of bardism but also the rise of occultism in the forms of grimoires such as Agrippa's *Three Books Of Occult Philosophy*, Hermetic texts such as *Lambspring*, and cabalistic authors such as Robert Fludd. Indeed, the bardic riddle asking, "how many angels can stand on the point of a knife" may have derived from the imagery of legions of armed angels in the *Enoch*.

The probability that Welsh bards were familiar with *Enoch*,

Hermetic texts, and other non-Celtic mysticism leads us to wonder how such sources influenced late bardic poetry. Possibly, the philosophy credited to Taliesin wasn't ancient druidism but rather Neoplatonic mysticism drawn from contemporary Hermetic and cabalistic texts. If so, then Graves and many other Celtic mystics have reversed the flow of ideas. Rather than claiming that druidism survived into the Renaissance to affect later mysticism, we should investigate the possibility that Christian mysticism was projected backward and paganized to fit Renaissance misconceptions of earlier druidism. The similarities between Renaissance mysticism and the supposed beliefs of the druids may be a product of the Renaissance itself and confirmation or denial of this theory becomes difficult due to the absence of earlier manuscripts to compare against.

The astral magic of *Enoch* is also hinted at in another of Graves's Christian sources, the *Book of Tobit*. *Tobit* is divided into fourteen short chapters, which tell the story of Tobit, a blind Israelite of the Naphtali tribe, and his family. Sarah, a distant relative of Tobit, has married seven times and upon each of the seven wedding nights, her husbands have been killed by the demon Asmodeus. In answer to her prayers, the angel Raphael is sent to intervene. Raphael convinces Tobit's son, Tobias, to marry Sarah. Upon their wedding night Tobias repells Asmodeus with the smell of a magic burning fish, much as the smell of burning sheep flesh was believed to repel evil and burning leather repelled fairies in Scotland (Carmichael 2:243, 355). After the demon is defeated, Tobias uses the same magic fish to restore his Father's sight.

Graves cites *Tobit* twice within *The White Goddess* but the reference in chapter eight is the most significant. There, Graves links the seven murdered husbands to Frazer's sacred king theories. The similarity of Frazer's seven-year reign to the seven yearly husbands of Sarah is not lost on Graves. He declares that Tobit is the "lucky eighth" while the demon Asmodeus is an incarnation of Set, who is responsible for the murder of the sacred king. This tallies well with Frazer's claim that the king may offer a substitute sacrifice for seven years but upon the eighth year must offer himself. In reality, the seven-year cycle is a creation of Frazer and not an anthropological fact. However, it's an idea which fits well with *Tobit*. Graves claims that the dog, which accompanies Tobias, is a hint that Tobias is playing the role of the sacred hero. However, a close reading of *Tobit* reveals that this dog is only mentioned twice in fourteen chapters.

Tobit ends with a summary of the visions of Jonas (Jonah) and the tale of Jonas and the whale may somehow relate to the magical fish used by Tobias. Likewise, this magic fish may also relate to the fish symbol used by early Christians. Similarities between the biblical prophet Jonas, the Celtic prophets Merlin and Taliesin, and a real poet named Jonas Athraw (who lived sometime between the tenth and fourteenth centuries) often confuse the history of Celtic poems. The *Myvyrian Archaeology* states that Athraw wrote the poems *Divregwawd Taliesin* (*A Poem of Taliesin*) and *Awdyl Vraith* (*The Diversified Song*). Graves is aware of this confusion and uses it to support the suggestion that "Taliesin" was the pen name of multiple poets.

Not all of Graves's Jewish and Christian sources contain pagan magic. In contrast to *Enoch* and *Tobit*, the *Books of Adam and Eve* contains no allusions to astral magic and addresses Adam's transgression and forgiveness. *Adam and Eve* draws multiple parallels between Adam and Jesus; thereby revealing the late date of its composition. Graves, citing Boswell, dates it to the fifth or sixth century. Another version of *Adam and Eve* appears within *The Apocrypha and Pseudepigrapha* of R. H. Charles and it's likely that Graves read this version as well. The Irish *Saltair na Rann* contains an additional version unique to Ireland and Graves uses this text to support his claim that Celtic bards had enough education to create the complex riddles he credits them with.

Adam and Eve reveals that Adam was buried in the "Cave of Treasures", where he had lived after his exile from Eden. Later generations buried their ancestors there as well and eventually the cave became a sort of oracle; at one point Adam's dead body speaks to his descendants within the cave. Allusions within the text suggest that this cave lies under a hill, which eventually becomes golgotha. This tradition, combined with typical Frazerian ideas, resulted in Graves's merger of this cave with the cave Machpelah. Machpelah was traditionally believed to have two chambers and Graves depicts one of these as a secret pagan oracle containing the jawbone of Adam (Graves 1984, 249–250).

Scattered throughout *White Goddess* are enough heresies to completely rewrite the life of Jesus. In a sense, this is exactly what Graves did when he stopped writing *White Goddess* to quickly draft *King Jesus*. Both books portray Jesus as a Frazerian sacred king condemned to die as a representative of the ultimate deity. Within *White Goddess* Graves struggles to depict Jesus as merely a human leader and to dispel the supernatural aspects of biblical stories. Alternately, the fictional *King Jesus* lets Graves indulge in the supernatural magic, which found no place within his nonfiction works. Together, they reflect Graves's struggle to understand both the realistic and supernatural aspects of Christ's life.

The White Goddess suggests that Jesus was lamed during a secret ritual on Mount Tabor, an idea also found in *King Jesus*. Graves cites two Hebrew sources for this idea and also Jerome's claim that Jesus was deformed. More interestingly, he claims to have found evidence of this in the Gospels but fails to cite this evidence directly. The belief that Jesus was lame or deformed is an obscure one and we must wonder why Graves prefers it.

Perhaps Graves supported this deformed image of Jesus because it helped him to defeat his earlier image of Jesus as the perfected man. Graves's earlier rejection of Christianity may also have included a desire to deface that religion's savior. Perhaps Graves found a lame, small, and frail Jesus easier to abandon than the perfected man whom he had admired in his childhood. Perhaps in some way Graves's image of the crippled Jesus was his parting shot at a religion he now believed to have crippled him in his youth. While Graves saw Jesus as deformed, Yeats followed another obscure tradition, which claimed that: "Christ alone was exactly six feet high, perfect physical man" (Yeats 273). Possibly Graves was taking a shot at Yeats as well as Christianity when he suggested otherwise. Conversely, Graves may have preferred a lame Jesus specifically because he was more human and therefore more approachable.

Graves's argument regarding the sacred limp reveals evidence of Frazer and Murray's research. Frazer cites various taboos involving the king's inability to walk on, or touch, the ground without the use of special footwear. Murray suggests that the role of the god of the witch-cult was often fulfilled by a male who may have been distinguished by special shoes. Graves cleverly connects this suggestion to many myths in his attempt to support his own pre-Christian goddess worship theories. In Graves's hands, Jesus walks with a limp and wears a corrective shoe. This strengthens Jesus' link to the sacrificial kings who Graves claims were nailed through the foot during sacrifice.

Nor is Jesus the only holy man to be linked to the sacrificial kings in this way. Dionysus, Vulcan, Hermes, and Math all become gods with similar corrective or symbolic shoes stressing their sacred feet and their role as sacrificial victims. To support the link between a lame Jesus and Dionysus, Graves cites Plutarch's invocation to Dionysus asking the god to come "rushing with thy bull's foot". By linking these mythic figures and joining them collectively to Murray's symbolic shoe, Graves creates a new relationship between ancient ritual and Murray's witch-cult. Furthermore, he prepares the reader to accept the suggestion that Jesus was only one of many such lame kings and helps place paganism on equal ground with Christianity.

By strengthening links between Jesus and other mythic heroes, Graves lays foundations for revealing the true name of the druidic high god. In chapter sixteen, Graves reveals that the name of "Celtic Dis" was *Oaoueiy — Jievoao* in Roman letters. This name is the secret information that the Amathaonians gave Gwydion's tribe to ensure victory at the battle of *Cad Goddeu*. Yet, there is no evidence of any deities named Oaoueiy or Jievoao within Celtic mythology. Instead, the word appears to derive from *Jehovah*. Clearly, Graves attempts to link Jievoao to Jehovah and establish links between the supreme god of Celtic paganism and the biblical god in the same way he has linked Jesus to various mythic characters. Graves fails to consider that Jehovah is a late word created during the Renaissance by a corruption of the name *Yahweh*. In *King Jesus,* Graves implies that he knows Jehovah is a corrupt variation of the name yet he appears ignorant of its more recent origin and credits its usage to the Hebrews (Graves 1984, 222).

Graves has at least two motives for connecting the high Celtic god to Jehovah. First, he wishes to place druidism on respectable grounds by establishing it as a variation of the biblical faith. Secondly, he implies that Judaism and Christianity were simply deviant variations of an older form of paganism. In a sense, these motives work hand in hand. Both suggestions render Celtic paganism more respectable when placed against Christianity while also placing Judaism and Christianity in their proper contexts against surrounding pagan religions.

As further evidence that the high god of druidism was Jievoao, Graves cites Demetrius, an Egyptian philosopher of the first century BC. Demetrius mentions Egyptian pagans chanting a seven-letter name of their god during their rituals. This name consisted entirely of vowels and Graves claims that this name was none other than the same Oaoueiy or Jievoao. This suggestion allows Graves to unite Celtic and Middle Eastern father gods and create a more unified model of pre-Christian paganism.

In another flurry of name changes, Graves argues that the biblical god whose name is represented by the letters JHWH (from which Yahweh derives) also had an older name drawn from the Cretan dialect. Graves claims this Cretan name is Q're and he links it to the Sabine town of Qures. He then claims that the chief name of this deity was Panemerios, which, according to Graves, means "of the livelong day". This Panemerios was supposedly a god of the solar year and Graves suggests that he was annually shaved bald by the Moon goddess as a way to limit his magical power. Because of this, his male followers sacrificed locks of their own hair and dedicated them to the god at a festival known as the Comyria (Graves 1993, 339-340).

Most of this data derives from Cook's description of the village of Panamara, located in modern Turkey. There archaeologists discovered a temple dedicated to Zeus Panamaros, obviously a variation of Panemerios. Cook suggests that the temple was originally dedicated to a local god before the arrival of Hellenic paganism. Once Zeus was introduced to the temple his name became joined with the name of the earlier deity and Zeus Panamaros was the result. Cook calls Panamaros the god "of the livelong day" and mentions that over 4000 inscriptions exist at the site dedicated to him (Cook 1:18-19).

Additionally, Cook describes the festival of Komyria, which was held in the village of Panamara in honor of Zeus Panamaros. This Komyria is identical to the festival Graves calls the Comyria. However, Cook's description differs radically from that of Graves. Cook claims the Komyria celebrated the return of Zeus Panamaros from the town of Stratonikeia to the town of Panamara. Upon his return, he was believed to enter his temple and perform a sacred marriage to an unnamed goddess. This goddess shouldn't be assumed to be Hera, his traditional wife. Hera had her own temple nearby and celebrated her own sacred marriage on a separate date, which implies that both Zeus Panamaros and Hera were married, but not to each other. Cook claims that the Komyria was celebrated like any other wedding celebration, thus reinforcing the idea that it celebrated the marriage of Zeus to a local goddess.

Cook reveals that another ritual occurred at the temple, the cutting and dedicating of hair to Zeus Panamaros. The purpose of this ritual is unknown but Cook suggests that it was practiced by men of marriageable age. Inscriptions prove that only men dedicated hair in this way and they did so not only at the festival of Komyria but year round (Cook 1:23). Graves, on the other hand, concluded that the Komyria was a festival in which men cut their hair in mourning and to symbolize the cutting of the hair of Panemerios. How Graves arrived at this conclusion based on Cook's description is unknown. Either Graves drew on additional sources or he is guilty of twisting his data beyond belief. The latter is more likely considering the fact that Graves was attempting to assimilate Zeus, Yahweh, and his own Jievoao into a single father god.

This god is the mysterious and vague father god of Graves's hypothetical pagan world and he struggles to prove that this god, in the form of Yahweh, inspired Jesus the rebel son who came not to send peace, but a sword to "destroy the works of the female". Jesus symbolized the divine son of this pagan religion, but rebelled by aligning himself not with his mother but with the Hebrew god. Jesus' rebellion against the pagan establishment is best seen in *King Jesus* during his confrontation with Mary the hairdresser. Jesus continually denies the power of matriarchal paganism and insists that his god is more powerful than the goddess from which he was born. Mary, a representative of the goddess, continually corrects his erroneous interpretations. In their encounter, Mary leads Jesus to an oracular tomb where the priestess laps blood from a bowl before prophesying from a ritual mask made from Adam's jawbone. The connections to *The White Goddess* are numerous.

First, we see the prophetic priestess drinking blood as described in *The White Goddess*. We also have an example of an oracular tomb housing the jawbone of the dead hero. Graves recycled this concept in *The White Goddess, King Jesus,* and *Hercules.* The idea derives ultimately from Frazer's *Totemism and Exogamy*, cited in *Hercules.* The ritual mask itself recalls Harrison's gorgon mask. Yet, none of this is as controversial as the actual confrontation between Mary and Jesus in which they debate the meaning of several sacred images.

A complete description of each image and their meanings as given by Jesus and Mary would be exhaustive. Suffice it to say that within *King Jesus* Graves again assumes an older matriarchal religion was replaced by a newer patriarchal faith which twisted the older imagery to suit its needs. Among the collection of images, Graves postulates, are many which occur in *The White Goddess* and which ring of Frazer. Overall, the suggested images depict Adam as a sacred king. These images include:

1: A triple goddess.
2: The birth of twins from the goddess.
3: Adam as a sacred king who marries the goddess.
4: Adam undergoing a ritual laming.
5: Adam's hair tied to the bedpost and cut off.
6: Adam sacrificed and ritually eaten.
7: Adam reborn from the goddess as the cycle begins again.

Besides these obvious features occur a handful of others, which play no direct part in the seasonal myth of the sacred king, but which still echo *The White Goddess*. These include the three animals symbolic of the goddess. Where we expect dog, roebuck, and lapwing, *King Jesus* instead mentions dog, owl, and camel. Either Graves hadn't solidified his dog, roebuck, and lapwing symbolism when he wrote this passage or he simply modified it to suit the cultural conditions required for the novel.

The dog is a fairly universal symbol and can be made to fit the goddess faith of nearly any culture. In *King Jesus,* dogs are usually seen in the presence of Mary the hairdresser and symbolize protection of secrets and a warning to those who would profane them. Davies's repeated use of dogs to symbolize pagan priests helped strengthen this interpretation in Graves's work. The owl is slightly harder to account for but it was connected to Blodeuwedd and Athena long before Graves wrote and is one of the unclean birds mentioned in Leviticus. The camel is more problematic but is also considered unclean within *King Jesus* and the wearing of camel hair garments was regarded as a token of either prophecy or insanity

(Graves 1984, 229).

The conflict between Jesus and Mary begins when Jesus is confused by the engraved images seen within the tomb. He repeatedly attempts to explain them in biblical terms while Mary constantly corrects him and reveals their true matriarchal meaning. Jesus is confused at what he sees because he believes the images are a mixture of incomplete biblical stories. Mary explains that the confusion is on his part and not in the images. "Here is one story and one story only," she insists (Graves 1984, 251). Here, Mary echoes the opening line of Graves's earlier poem, *To Juan at the Winter Solstice*, a poem written for his son born in 1944; two years before *King Jesus* was published. This line echoes what poet Alun Lewis claimed in a letter shortly before his death earlier that year. The letter, quoted by Graves within *The White Goddess*, refers to the only story a poet can tell: "the single poetic theme of Life and Death" (Lewis, 12). Indeed, 1944 seems to have been the year in which Graves crystallized his poetic system. The death of Alun Lewis, the birth of Juan at the winter solstice, and the research for *Hercules* and *King Jesus* all seemed to have acted as a lens, which focused the mythic images Graves had utilized in his earlier years.

Both Frazer and Graves see Jesus as a divine victim, but they disagree on many minor details. Frazer implies that Jesus was sacrificed by the Jews and that the Jewish faith was based on pagan beliefs and practice. Graves implies Jesus was a sacred victim killed by goddess worshipers. These pagans pulled the strings to ensure his death as their sacrificial victim because his teachings clashed with their pagan beliefs. Although *King Jesus* explained Graves's stance regarding Jesus as he wrote *The White Goddess*, Graves later changed his opinion of Jesus and expressed this in *The Nazarene Gospel Restored*.

Although Jesus is the most prominent biblical figure that Graves attacks, he is in good company. Chapter fourteen of *White Goddess* offers a confused account of Adam and Eve's temptation and the bardic belief that the forbidden fruit was an apple. For once, Graves has chosen to contradict bardic lore and instead implies that the forbidden fruit was originally a fig. He bases this on the fig leaves that Adam and Eve wore after acquiring knowledge. The Bible never names this mysterious fruit and Graves's fig seems a logical suggestion. However, other evidence points elsewhere.

While the Jewish and Christian faiths were still limited to their homeland, the forbidden fruit was commonly thought to be the pomegranate. The pomegranate's many seeds, blood red juice, and oval center made it a natural symbol of female fertility and it symbolized goddess worship in Hellenic times. The Hebrew word for pomegranate is *rimmon*, from the root word *rim*, "to give birth" and symbolic pomegranates adorned the pagan temple called "the house of Rimmon" (2 Kings 5:18). Thus, the pomegranate became the scapegoat in an attempt to discredit the symbols of older pagan goddess worship.

Yet, as Graves observed, the apple is commonly depicted as the forbidden fruit today. What prompted the switch from pomegranate to apple? Possibly, the story of the judgment of Paris. Once the biblical story of the fall from grace had reached Greece, it's likely that the most injurious fruit of Genesis was equated to the most injurious fruit of Greek mythology. This association would then be carried wherever Christianity traveled. If this connection was not made in early Greece, it may have been established at some late point somewhere in Europe after the West became familiar with both biblical literature and Greek classics.

Significantly, another theory exists to account for why the apple has become the forbidden fruit. The apple was to the Celts what the pomegranate was to the ancient Palestinians: a symbol of an older cult. Britain is full of ancient apple lore. King Arthur was borne away to Avalon ("Island of Apples") after his fateful battle, showing how apples were regarded as a magical fruit of the Celtic Other world. The *Black Book of Carmarthen* contains the poem *The Afallennau (Apple Trees)* where Merlin laments the decline of paganism. The *Auraicept* claims that the apple tree is the shelter of the wild hind and bobbing for apples at Halloween is a remnant of a forgotten pagan ritual of either divination or human sacrifice. Examples proving the apple to be sacred to the Celts could be multiplied ad nauseam and Graves believed them to be passports to paradise within Celtic myth. Possibly, the arrival of Christianity in Celtic Gaul and Britain inspired the switch from pomegranate to apple. In order to discredit Celtic paganism the apple became the new scapegoat of Genesis. Graves believes that it was the bards themselves that inspired the change but possibly, it was advocated by Christians wishing to slander the Celtic symbol of fertility and discredit the pagan bards and druids.

The pagan associations of the apple offers further insight into Graves's sources. Graves equates the August 13th feast of Diana to the goddess Nemesis, both of which are often depicted holding apple branches. Cook provides multiple examples from inscribed gems and statuary (Cook 1:270, 274-75). Following Cook's lead, Graves makes all the same associations to Diana, which Cook offers. Both authors equate Diana to not only Nemesis but Isis, Fortuna, and the Celtic Nemetona.

Cook explains that Diana-Nemesis's wheel was akin to the oracular devices used in classical Greek temples. These large wheels, often depicted on vase paintings, worked by means of a rope and once put into motion they delivered oracular answers to visitor's questions. Most likely, this was accomplished by displayed messages, which rotated when the wheel was turned. Such simple divinatory devices were not unknown in ancient or classical times and similar systems with numbers, books, and dice were also used (Lane-Fox 208-13). Cook gives a full description of these wheel devices and, in a footnote, makes particular mention of the few surviving examples still found in some churches (Cook 1: 267). Graves's own footnote emulates Cook's wheel explanation almost to the point of plagiarism but ties the wheel into Irish mythology as well by citing examples from Standish Hayes O'Grady's *Silva Gadelica* (Graves 1993, 255).

The wheel motif was central to Celtic religion and ancient Celts may have used similar divinatory devices. Early Celtic artwork contains many examples of the wheel motif including the Hallstatt sword, which depicts two human figures turning a wheel between them. Other examples include multiple wheel shaped pendants found in Hungary and Bohemia and the male figure supporting a wheel device on the Gundestrup cauldron. Early British coins also contained wheel symbolism, which Davies connected to both stone circles and the zodiac (Davies 1809, 603). If such Celtic wheels do represent divinatory devices, this helps place Celtic religion into a wider Indo-European context. Conversely, if such wheels depict the more archaic religious symbolism of the turning of the heavens around the pole star this implies the survival of earlier Indo-European concepts in Celtic society. The Celts were hardly alone in their notice of this rotation around the celestial axis; Aristotle, Lucan, Ovid, and Virgil all commented upon this phenomenon. Cook was also aware of the wheel symbolism in Celtic art and cites the Gundestrup example (Cook 1:289).

So far, we've seen Graves use his own form of iconotropy to rewrite the myths of several biblical heroes including Yahweh, Jesus, and Solomon. However, Graves isn't content to rewrite the history of these heroes. If their lives must be rewritten then Satan must also be reinterpreted in light of his new relationship with these revised biblical characters. Chapter nineteen of *White Goddess* attempts to humanize the image of Satan found within Revelations. Graves begins by attacking the riddle, which has puzzled biblical experts for generations, the infamous cryptogram found in Rev 13:18: "Here is wisdom. Let him that hath understanding count the number of the beast: for it is the number of a man and his number is six hundred threescore and six".

Experts have long known that ancient Hebrew used letters to represent numbers in much the same style as Roman numerals. Thus, 666 has been interpreted variously as either the name of the coming antichrist, or his initials. Initially it appears that the encoded word could only contain three letters and that logic dictated that all three letters were identical. Yet, the mathematical process used to arrive at 666 may not be identical to either the common numerological system used by astrologers today or the cabalistic methods known as gematria and temurah. In a footnote, Graves illustrates the most commonly accepted formula and mentions variants in spelling which affect the solution. Possibly, the author used an unknown variant of the Hebrew system or had even committed an error in his spelling or math. Graves rightfully observes that the possible combinations are nearly endless.

He mentions that the two most widely accepted solutions to the puzzle are "Nero Caesar" and "Lateinos" (the Latin one). Both answers imply the belief among early Christians that the antichrist will be of Roman descent. Graves arrives at his own solution by translating 666 into Roman numerals (DCLXVI) and then reading it as an acronym. His final answer suggests that Revelations was written, or rewritten, in the reign of Domitian and the puzzle attempts to equate Nero with this later emperor. Our interest, however, lies not in Graves's solution but in how he reached it.

Graves's solution came to him unbidden, suddenly, and complete in a single blast of inspiration. This is poetic inspiration at work. It's the force which Welsh bards labeled *awen*, a flash of supernatural insight akin to divine revelation. This is the very trance state that Graves has attempted to describe for years and chapter nineteen of *White Goddess* is perhaps the most revealing look at exactly what analeptic thinking is. Unfortunately, Graves's description of the process is vague and we suspect that he's trying to express the inexpressible.

The implication is that poets use a certain type of logic or thought pattern, which can't be explained. Whether we call it poetic trance, divine inspiration, awen, or analeptic thinking we never truly capture the event in words. This trance state must be experienced to be understood. Graves explains that he visualized the letters D.C.L.X.V.I. and "looked at them slantwise" to gain deeper insight.

He never explains what slantwise means but simply says that poets will understand his meaning (Graves 1993, 345). This slantwise vision is identical with his analeptic method and comparable to Lewis Carroll's "mental squint" cited by Graves in chapter twenty-five. He firmly denies any supernatural qualities of this trance state but he is one of the few poets to do so. Many poets believe inspiration is supernatural and, considering Graves's interest in the occult, we suspect that he may secretly entertain similar ideas, which he refuses to admit. Certainly, he developed his trance theories from earlier mystics who believed in the supernatural aspect of inspiration.

One such source was John Dunne, whose book *An Experiment with Time* is a forerunner of Graves's analeptic trance theory. Dunne's study suggests that precognitive dreaming was inherent in everyone rather than only a few selected psychics. However, few people realized their prophetic ability because they failed to remember their dreams, failed to make the connection between dreamed events and real events, or the revealed information was so trivial as to be easily overlooked or mistaken for coincidence. Similar claims had been made before but Dunne was one of the first to attempt a controlled dream experiment and correlate the findings to his theory. Dunne's conclusion, much simplified, is that our sleeping consciousness transcends time and dreams of both past and future events. From this, Dunne suggests that the waking mind can also do this once our usual perceptions of time had been overcome. Ultimately, Dunne's theory suggests that we can predict future events but, unfortunately, our accuracy can't be measured until after the event has occurred. The uses of such precognitive ability are limited by the triviality of those events that are revealed and the fact that they can only be evaluated in retrospect.

Dunne's theory that we can project our consciousness both forward and backward sounds suspiciously like Graves's proleptic and analeptic trances. Graves had been developing his trance methods since at least 1922 and the publication of Dunne's book in

1927 may have attracted his attention. If so, Graves had over twenty years to incorporate *An Experiment with Time* into his analeptic methods before publishing *The White Goddess*. Yet, from his comment, it's difficult to tell when Graves read Dunne's work, or if he had merely depended on second hand accounts. *An Experiment with Time* was popular enough that Graves could have found his information nearly anywhere. The *Times Book Review* of December 3, 1939 reviewed Dunne's works and Graves was an avid reader of literary reviews. Additionally, William Seabrook's *Witchcraft* provides a lengthy quote from the *Times Book Review* in question (Seabrook 332). Seabrook's *Witchcraft* was published in 1940 and it's possible that Graves had read it shortly after its publication.

A less mystic explanation is that Graves's mind is simply recalling sources which he no longer remembers reading but whose facts have remained in his memory none the less. Most people have had similar experiences of remembering a fact but not remembering where they read it. Graves doesn't simply fabricate results from the wishful thinking of an uneducated man. All of the needed elements to arrive at the answer are already in his head and his trance method only works on problems with which he has already encountered most of the underlying knowledge. This is exactly what he does while pondering the 666 cryptogram. He finds a meaning and then plows his way to it disregarding established history, mythology, and etymology. For a fleeting moment, Graves understood the solution and then it vanished and his rational mind was left to ransack his brain for the connections, which inspired the vision in the first place. It's the process of connecting these facts which is mysterious, not their discovery. Somewhere in his mind, Graves has the needed knowledge. During the analeptic process these elements gel in a way that even he doesn't fully understand. It transcends time because it skips steps in the logical thinking process to arrive directly at an answer, which is somehow based on the preexisting knowledge.

As a confirmation of Graves's method, he inserts into brackets what appears to be newly found supporting evidence. Graves writes,

"Excellent: I now find that this is the conclusion of Dr. T.W. Crafer in his recent work on the *Apocalypse*" (Graves 1993, 347). Although Graves never fully cites this source it seems that Crafer had independently reached the same solution to the 666 problem, which Graves claims to have reached by trance. Graves inserts this notice into *The White Goddess* as a paragraph unto itself and within square brackets, creating the impression that these words were hastily added as an afterthought. However, it's possible that Graves had read Crafer's works before reaching his analeptic solution and perhaps, unknowingly, he had incorporated this earlier reading into his own poetic trance. If so then Graves's analeptic solution wasn't a feat of supernatural insight but rather an inaccurate memory which was only refreshed after reexamining the sources. Either way, it's interesting to note that it's now commonly accepted that Revelations was written during Domitian's reign rather than Nero's and the author intentionally equated the two men (Myers 956).

Graves uses the explanation of analeptic trance in chapter nineteen to prepare us for the conversation offered in chapter twenty. This conversation is the most unusual part of *The White Goddess* and without an understanding of Graves's trance method we may wonder why he has chosen to present it in a fictional dialog. However, armed with this understanding of analeptic thought we may wonder if the conversation presented is fictional at all or if Graves has reconstructed an authentic dialog. Graves has impressed us with his solution to the puzzle of Revelations. Now he is preparing to take an extended trip into altered states in order to reconstruct a conversation between Theophilus and Lucius Paulus nearly 2000 years ago.

To fully appreciate the debate between Theophilus and Lucius we must peer into their characters and the location where their encounter occurs. In *Acts 13:6-12* Paul and Barnabas preach Christianity to Lucius Paulus, the Roman proconsul of Cyprus. The supposed year of his conversion is 45 AD, a scant two years after Graves's fictional conversation. Inscriptions at Antioch confirm the existence of Paulus, lending support to the biblical story. Incidentally, this falls within the rule of Claudius, who ruled from 41-54 AD. Graves has cleverly placed his conversation in exactly the era he was most familiar with via his own novel *I Claudius*. No less important, he has placed the conversation during the early conflicts between Christianity and pagan religions. As if to erase any doubt as to the identity of this Paulus, Graves makes him recite his encounter with Paul and Barnabas.

Theophilus appears in Luke 1:3. Graves has intentionally chosen this minor character because his lesser status makes him easier to mold into a needed role for historical fiction. Theophilus was supposedly a historian and this fits well both with Graves's comment that he was a famous Greek historian and that Luke is one of the more historically accurate gospels and may have been written to appeal to the historically inclined Theophilus. As further evidence, Luke implies in his gospel that the Theophilus he addresses is familiar with Jewish scripture and Graves's Theophilus has read Jewish scripture.

Thus, before the conversation begins we know that we're about to overhear the thoughts of two minor biblical characters in the town of Paphos. This town, on the southwestern coast of Cyprus, had once been a capital city and home to a temple of Aphrodite. Frazer repeatedly mentions this site was one of the most famous temples in the world and Aphrodite was worshiped there in the form of a white cone shaped stone (Frazer 381, 383, 384). Altogether, Paphos seems a fitting place for two pagans to meet and discuss the relationship between Christianity and paganism.

With these factors established we understand exactly what Graves wishes to convey. Perhaps the most important point is Theophilus's opening statement regarding the migration of tribes on the South coast of the Black Sea. Here Graves speaks through the mouthpiece of Theophilus as he explains these periodic tribal movements and sums up several points already raised in *White Goddess*, including the identity of the Sea People and the wave of migration their movements caused.

Paulus plays the part of Graves's critics. He questions Theophilus's theory and must have each aspect explained in detail. This method allows Graves to expound his ideas in depth and also creates a character who can play devil's advocate much as his real life critics had done. Yet, Paulus is no fool; he gives intelligent answers to many of Theophilus's questions.

Other typically Gravesian ideas within the conversation include the concept that kings retain their office by marriage to the queen and that male royalty depends on marriage to the proper woman (Graves 1993, 356). Graves advanced this theory earlier in *White Goddess* and Briffault suggests similar marriage traditions in *The Mothers* (Briffault 228). Graves ties this concept into the story of the *Odyssey* and cleverly uses it to explain the suitors who sought the hand of Penelope. These men not only wanted to marry Odysseus's wife; they wanted the kingship that came with it. This explains why Odysseus's son, Telemachus, never becomes king. To do so he must marry his own mother and this was forbidden.

Lastly, Graves offers another example of iconotropy in the form of heroes riding upon dolphins. He mentions such examples as Arion, Icadius, Enalus, Theseus, and Coeranus. Doubtless, Graves was familiar enough with Greek mythology to provide these examples directly from classical accounts. However, it's interesting to note that Cook provides a nearly identical list when he writes, "Many well-known figures in classical mythology are said to have been saved from the sea by riding on the back of a dolphin (Arion, Eikadios, Enalos, Koiranos, Phalanthos, Taras, Theseus, etc.)" (Cook 1:170). It may be unfair to say Graves copied his list of characters directly from Cook but it's obvious that Cook's *Zeus* inspired Graves's own dolphin symbolism.

Overall, the message of chapter twenty is that erotic pagan matriarchy was slowly being replaced by a patriarchal faith, which sought to limit female power and sexuality. Graves had expressed this idea at the opening of the chapter with his unfinished *englyn* beginning:

> Circling the circlings of their fish,
> Nuns walk in white and pray;
> For he is chaste as they,

Upon the completion of the chapter, Graves feels he can supply the ending, which makes his poem meet its needed form and also express the intended idea:

> Who was dark-faced and hot in Silvia's day,
> And in his pool drowns each unspoken wish.

The meaning is clear. Nuns, the descendants of pagan priestesses, circle their placid fishponds and deplore their lost power and sexuality. They are "bricked up alive", as Graves had claimed in an earlier poem and their "cat-like longing" is ignored (Graves 1961, 155). They pray to Jesus, the modern incarnation of their fertility hero, yet he is powerless to help. He has been systematically stripped of masculinity to become a feminized prince of peace unable to satisfy even his symbolic wives. If, at this point, anyone remains unsure of Graves's opinion of Christianity he has neatly summarized his views here. Christianity was no alternative for the poet who is bound to express nature's erotic and violent cycle of life and death.

Nor is this Graves's only treatment of fish and sexual symbolism. He expands on this connection when discussing the mermaid in chapter twenty-two. The combined symbolism of fish and sexuality merge flawlessly in the image of the mermaid, which graces more than one of Graves's poems. Mermaids had recurred in Graves's works ever since he had spoken with a Welshman who claimed to have seen one. Other listeners might have scoffed at the story but the man's firm belief and sincerity disturbed Graves for years (Norris 3). The sexual aspects of the mermaid unite with the chastity of the Virgin again in *To Juan at the Winter Solstice* (Graves 2000, 405).

Graves ends this chapter with an unusual twist on the common tale of virgin women sacrificed to sea monsters. In Graves's hands, the virgin chained to the rocks is no longer a human sacrifice but is an aspect of the sea monster itself. Later he suggests that this same sea monster is identical with the creature that supposedly swallowed Jonah and that this swallowing and spitting out of the prophet symbolized a spiritual rebirth via the goddess in fish form. The virgin in these later legends symbolizes the monster once it has been defeated and chained by the male deity embodied by the mythic hero. Once again, Graves has shifted the meaning of the story to produce a tale of a male hero usurping female power.

A careful reading of Graves's works illuminates his ability to reconstruct the Paphos conversation. In *King Jesus,* Graves states that many of his controversial theories on Christianity evolved from his reading of the *Acts of the Apostles* (Graves 1984, 419). In particular, Graves notes that Sergius Paulus was impressed with Paul and Barnabas. Graves questions why a Roman Procurator of Cyprus would be impressed by early Christians and this contributed to the trance state which inspired chapter twenty of *White Goddess*. Graves sought to express this problem in poetic form and then threw himself into a trance state to recover lost evidence. The result was the conversation and poem already discussed. Significantly, the Historical Commentary appended to *King Jesus* was written in South Devon and therefore confirms that chapter twenty of *White Goddess* was an early part of the book and not one of the many additions quickly slipped in during the editing stage.

This begs the question of which was written first, chapter twenty of *White Goddess* or *King Jesus*? *King Jesus* was published in 1946 and if it was inspired by the same trance state, which inspired chapter twenty of *White Goddess* then it proves that Graves didn't write *White Goddess* in a few weeks of brainstorming. If he wrote the *White Goddess* chapter first, then it could have served as inspiration for *King Jesus*. In fact, this chapter of *White Goddess* may have originally been part of an early draft for *King Jesus*, which Graves later edited.

Then, upon writing *White Goddess,* he found an opportunity to include the conversation as a means of illuminating his trance methods and as a way to include the controversial theories within the conversation. Graves felt the material within the conversation was too valuable to simply discard; he resolved the issue by placing it within *White Goddess.* This could explain the unusual appearance of a fictional chapter in a nonfiction book and the appearance of Jesus' contemporaries within a book, which has little to do with Jesus.

Conversely, Graves could have written *King Jesus* first and later entered the trance state, which produced chapter twenty of *White Goddess.* The fact that *King Jesus* was published before *White Goddess* implies that it was written earlier. However, it was typical of Graves to have several projects brewing at once and much of the writing and sources of *White Goddess* and *King Jesus* must have overlapped in the same way that *White Goddess* overlapped with *Hercules.* Regardless of which was written first, the fact that pages of *King Jesus* appear within the first typescript of *White Goddess* reveal their close connection and imply that material and research common to both was shuffled between them (Firla 114). Ultimately, the question of which was written first is irrelevant. The important thing is that Graves undoubtedly read the *Acts of the Apostles* and began his speculations early enough to include the reconstructed conversation within *White Goddess.*

In all, chapter twenty provides further insight into the analeptic method. Graves began with a partial poem, which he couldn't finish and wrote a historical situation which supplied the needed answer. Did Graves imagine this conversation or did it come to him in poetic trance state? If we believe Graves, the conversation came to him as a record of an actual conversation. The possibility that these two minor biblical characters held such a conversation is unrealistically slim. Yet, can we discount it, or Graves's trance ability to recover such a conversation if it happened? Literary critics and historians say we can safely dismiss analeptic trance and its findings. On the other hand, this is exactly the sort of supernatural experiences for which pagans strive. Even if he is merely deceiving himself, Graves enters a productive mental state and gains results. This state is synonymous with pagan ritual. The experience is subjective, but its effects are obvious. Using such methods and his feminist slant on pantheism made Graves one of the earliest founders of the pagan revival.

These explanations of trance states are explored in later pagan texts such as Stewart Farrar's 1971 *What Witches Do*. Farrar makes no mention of Graves's trance work but devotes an entire chapter to clairvoyance; recapitulating arguments which we have applied to Graves's work. Farrar's explanations of clairvoyance include the use of supernatural powers and the possibility that clairvoyance may simply be a heightened sense of intuition, which anyone can achieve. This higher intuition is identical with the poetic intuition, which Graves examines within *White Goddess*. Farrar admits that this intuition may be either supernatural or a simple matter of recalling past data (Farrar 1971, 94). Either way, he believes that sharpening this power allows the user to predict the future more accurately and relates these visions to dreaming much as Dunne before him. Farrar also believes that certain physical items serve as triggers to inspire a clairvoyant state.

This explains Graves's fascination with those knickknacks he surrounded himself with while witting. Graves's dislike of mass production and industrialization lead him to write in a room furnished with only handmade items. Everything, from the bookcases to the chairs and picture frames, must be handmade in order for Graves to write comfortably (Kersnowski 152). Besides these larger items, Graves immersed himself in decorative trinkets which he often handled while lost in thought. In the Postscript to *White Goddess* Graves mentions a few items which inspired the writing of the book: a small humped back figure playing a flute, a decorative brass box, a figurine of an African priest, an engraved Roman gemstone, and several small gold weights. Graves follows his train of thought and establishes a connection between all these things and the triple goddess. Other sources mention that Graves enjoyed picking up odd pebbles from the beach and even bent nails and broken glass, which caught his eye. One visitor noted that Graves had removed a curiously twisted stick from a fire and saved it for later consideration. After a few minutes of silently handling the stick, Graves snapped back to awareness and confessed, "I like to know the reason for everything" (Kersnowski 47). It seems that any handmade or naturally formed item could inspire Graves's trance. Proof of this theory comes from Graves's poem *To Bring the Dead to Life*, where he advises the reader to "assemble tokens" and mentions "a seal, a cloak, a pen" (Graves 1961, 144). Graves was thinking of Claudius when he wrote the poem and a dreamy contemplation on a similar array of trinkets had probably inspired the trance for *I, Claudius*.

Sixteen years after the publication of *White Goddess*, Doreen Valiente had similar trance experiences, which she believed to be visions of earlier witchcraft practices. Between 1964 and 1966, Valiente experienced a series of visions centering around a man named John Breakspeare whom she believed practiced witchcraft in early nineteenth century Surrey (Valiente 100). Valiente admits that her impressions of Breakspeare and his friends may be the result of her own wishful thinking; yet even if this is true her experiences are interesting in light of Graves's analeptic methods.

From Valiente's visions, we learn that John Breakspeare was a witch of the late eighteenth or early nineteenth century. Members of his coven included his wife, two men, and a woman. Their initiation ritual involved an oath sworn at knifepoint and their rituals used a black handled knife, cords, cakes and ale, and magic circles (Valiente 101-02). Breakspeare revealed that he had changed his name from John to Nicholas as a parody of the other famous Nicholas Breakspeare, better known as Pope Adrian IV. Besides his frequent attacks on the church Breakspeare also opposed the merger of Eastern mysticism with Western witchcraft. He denied the Saracen impact on witchcraft, which later authors suggested and warned: "Do not mix up East with West and end nowhere" (Valiente 112, 114). He also admonished literary occultism and detested occult texts such as the *Key of Solomon* and Agrippa's works. To Breakspeare witchcraft was distinctly unliterary and derived from direct observation of nature. Lastly, he admits that his coven often dressed as "gypsies or tinkers" and favored a feminist interpretation of Arthurian legends.

It's hardly surprising that most of Breakspeare's philosophy reflects that of Valiente herself and Valiente admits that her visions of Breakspeare came during a time when she was highly critical of Wicca's future. Breakspeare's dislike of occult literature is paralleled by Valiente's attitude towards Gardner's use of the *Key of Solomon* and Crowley's works within his rituals. Likewise, Breakspeare's attacks on Saracen impact upon witchcraft may derive from Valiente's dislike of Eastern ideas within Wicca and the close association between Gardner and Sufi Idries Shah. By the time of these visions Gardner had worked with Shah for at least five years and it's rumored that Shah had ghost written the Gardner biography *Gerald Gardner: Witch* (Kelly 169).

Breakspeare's beliefs and rituals are the key to deciphering Valiente's visions and reveal their probable origin. The black handled knife likely derives from Valiente's training with Gardner; no mention of such knives appears in authentic witch trial records. Ironically, Gardner had taken the idea from the *Key of Solomon*, the very book Breakspeare detested. Breakspeare's ritual garb, intended to mimic "gypsies or tinkers", rings of Leland's works. It was Leland who popularized the connection between witchcraft and gypsies and recorded the dying slang language used by Irish tinkers. Likewise, Breakspeare's feminist interpretation of Arthurian legends smacks of Dion Fortune and his description of ritual dances derives directly from Murray. In short, nearly all of Breakspeare's details derive from Valiente's favorite authors and post date the period of Breakspeare's supposed existence.

These factors undercut any claim to the historical existence of John Breakspeare and instead reveal how someone such as Valiente or Graves may concoct their visions based on earlier reading. At first Valiente was critical of her visions and wondered if they were merely her imagination or products of her subconscious (Valiente 115). Like Graves, Valiente denies being a medium or psychic but admits that Breakspeare's rituals resemble modern spiritualist meetings (Valiente 99, 103, 110). Yet, as the visions increased, she became convinced of their truth. One factor, which motivated this belief, was that she was unaware of Pope Adrian IV's real name of Nicholas Breakspeare until after receiving the vision in question. Yet, it's possible that she had read this name somewhere beforehand and forgotten it just as Graves may have read Crafer's analysis of the apocalypse before resolving the 666 reference. In both instances, the poet had perhaps become intimately familiar with the appropriate sources beforehand; Valiente with pagan and occult works, Graves with obscure Jewish and Christian texts.

Graves favors pagan spirituality but continually embraces these obscure texts and occult aspects of mainstream religion. The Gnostics, Essenes, Masons, and other mystical Christian groups appear repeatedly throughout *White Goddess*. Graves's brief treatment of the Masons warrants special attention as a possible bridge between Christian mysticism and later Wiccan ritual. In chapter eight Graves mentions the "five-fold bond" which binds wrists, neck, and ankles and reveals that this ritual binding was a prelude to the divine consort's murder. He alludes to this five-fold bond when discussing the ritual conditions of Llew's death and states that similar bindings occurred in pagan rituals of human sacrifice and modern Masonic initiation rituals. While describing the Masonic ritual, Graves quotes an unidentified source which claims the participant must be "neither naked nor clothed, barefoot nor shod, deprived of all metals, hood winked, with a cable-tow about his neck" (Graves 1993, 404). The similarity to the five-fold bond implies a connection between Masonry and ancient paganism.

A clue to Graves's sources and intentions lies in the fact that the two Masonic references only appear in later editions of *White Goddess*. Therefore, Graves discovered the link sometime between 1948 and 1966. Based on his 1964 article on witchcraft we can be more specific. In this article, Graves mentions "a mystical Saracen free-masonry" which merged with European witchcraft (Graves 1964, 557). Apparently, Graves's interest in the relationship between Masonry, paganism, and the Saracens dates to at least 1964. This interest led him to mention Masonry in the witchcraft article and to revise at least two passages of *White Goddess*.

This interest was spurred by the 1961 meeting between Graves, Gardner, and Sufi mystic Idries Shah. Gardner was a Mason before he promoted Wicca and had commented on the similarity of the rituals in 1954 (Gardner 1954, 94, 134). His suggestion that suspected medieval witches associated with Masons allowed him to explain this similarity without revealing that Gardner based Wiccan ritual on Masonry. Graves wasn't concerned with modern Wicca but the idea that an earlier witch-cult possibly influenced Masonry appealed to him. By adding the Masonic references to *White Goddess* Graves reverses the chronology. Rather than admit that Wiccan ritual was drawn from Masonry Graves implies that Masonic ritual was derived from an earlier witch-cult. This indirectly supports not only his own theories but also those of Gardner and Murray.

Graves's view after meeting Gardner can be compared against his Masonic references before 1961. *King Jesus* contains at least one Masonic reference in the description of Jesus' initiation into the Essene community. Graves portrays the initiation ritual as similar to Masonic initiation: Jesus is regarded as a postulant who is brought into the group by a sponsor, his name is asked, he undertakes vows of secrecy and he is given a white apron, leather girdle, and trowel (Graves 1984, 205-206). These symbols undoubtedly imply connections between the secret traditions of the Essenes and Masonry. Whether or not Graves believed the Masons possessed Essene teachings, is irrelevant. The important feature of this passage is

Graves's limited knowledge of Masonic initiation ritual. *King Jesus* makes no mention of the "five-fold bond"; nor does it depict Jesus as hood winked (blindfolded) or wearing the cable-tow despite the fact that the Masonic initiation ritual had been published decades earlier. Apparently, Graves didn't associate blindfolding or ritual binding with Masonic initiation until after his meeting with Gardner.

This allows us to theorize on the creation of Gardner's Wiccan initiation ritual. Gardner began with knowledge of Masonic initiation traits: those mentioned above and also loose fitting bindings, exposed chest, and threats at weapon point. Graves was unaware of the ritual binding but he coins the term "five-fold bond" to label the modes of ritual death shared by various divine consorts. Later, when Gardner fleshes out Wiccan initiation ritual he borrows from both Masonry and Graves's description. When Graves, Gardner, and Shah finally meet Gardner reveals the similarity between Masonic initiation ritual and the five-fold bond and mentions that Wiccan initiation is similar to both. Graves is impressed and includes the similarity in the revised edition of *White Goddess*. It never occurs to him that the similarity between Wicca, Masonry, and sacrificial rituals exists mainly because Gardner had streamlined them himself.

As a final consideration, we may even have a slight indication of Shah's contribution. Shah's Sufism inclined him towards Eastern sources and it's possible that he suggested the similarity between Graves's five-fold bond and the account by Suleyman, an Arab merchant, who witnessed a similar ritual in China in 851. This Arabic reference only occurs in later editions of *White Goddess* and Gardner's failure to mention it may imply that he was also ignorant of it until the three men met.

Graves's use of Masonic references is typical of his desire to paganize esoteric groups. This desire leads him to reinterpret Essene and Gnostic history as well. The Essenes first appear in chapter eight, where Graves connects them with Pythagoras, the philosopher who possibly refused to record his beliefs. In chapter nine, Graves expands on both Pythagorean and Essene beliefs; the lack of credible sources regarding either group allowed Graves to accept typical assumptions and stress their pagan associations. Graves suggests that Pythagorean Essenes enforced a form of baptism before its acceptance into mainstream Christianity. Other historians had suggested this long before Graves and his acceptance of the theory conforms with popular contemporary theories regarding both Pythagoreans and the Essenes. All of these historians, including Graves, wrote before the discovery of the Dead Sea scrolls and much of their data is based on classical writers such as Pliny and Josephus, now known to be inaccurate.

Yet, the Masonic and Pythagorean connections with the Essenes is only part of Graves's belief. He also credits the Essenes with faith healing, magic circles, invocations, and a secret alphabet. *King Jesus* reveals that the Essene community was built in concentric circles of huts. This model taught the wheel of the year concept to Essene initiates and each circle is named for a letter of the Essene alphabet. A comparison between the Essene alphabet within *King Jesus* and the ogham in chapter six of *White Goddess* reveals our suspicion; Graves credits the Essenes with a Hebrew variant of ogham. Graves clarifies the matter by listing the Essene ogham in chapter nine of *White Goddess*.

Graves's treatment of the Gnostics is similar and probably derives from the confusion between Gnostics and Essenes, which was common before the discovery of the Dead Sea scrolls. Again, Graves cites ancient and classical sources, now known to be inaccurate, and chooses to focus on their pagan traits. Just as the Dead Sea scrolls were discovered too late for Graves's research; so were the texts of Nag Hammadi, the most revealing Gnostic collection known to date. Graves was aware of their discovery, in 1947, but their slow translation and publication denied him access to their material.

Ultimately, Graves's treatment of the Bible and other Christian sources leads him to ask if Christianity is a suitable religion for poets. His answer is no, at least to Christianity as it's practiced today.

He laments that Christianity is the only serious religion remaining in Europe and therefore the only religious choice for European poets.

In the same chapter, Graves includes another sly blow to Christianity. While lamenting the death of various pagan religions Graves mentions that Emperor Constantine had reluctantly endorsed Christianity after increased pressure from the Roman army, which was "recruited from the servile masses that had responded to the Church's welcome for sinners and outcasts" (Graves 1993, 424). Here he implies that Christianity was a religion of the uneducated masses, the lower class from which the grunts of the Roman army were drafted. This Christian folly of accepting the uneducated masses was reiterated in his *Crane Bag* and his Oxford lectures. Graves agrees with Frazer and Gibbon's implication that Rome's acceptance of this foreign work force and their foreign religion was a step in the weakening of the Roman Empire. Graves expresses similar ideas in *King Jesus* when he complains that Christians recruited from the "dregs of society" who couldn't qualify for membership into the more elegant Greek paganism or even "an ordinary drinking-club". He shrewdly observes that Messianic religions are favored by "the idle, ignorant and impatient" (Graves 1984, 283, 333). The idea that early Christianity appealed to those of limited education and led to the downfall of the Roman Empire is echoed today in the works of some pagans.

The wide range of religions tolerated within the Roman army is well documented and answered the need to pander to the various nationalities within its ranks. Here, among outsiders, the lower class and the uneducated, Christianity laid down its roots and spread, sending out shoots with the movements of the Roman army. Christianity is a religion of the masses and the masses are, to Graves, invariably uneducated. Much of *The White* Goddess (and Graves's other works) decries the loss of classical education and the pagan philosophy which often accompanies it.

In chapter twenty-five, he complains of the decline of classical education and laments the loss of a common literary canon. This statement brings to mind the required reading lists often encountered in the pagan community. Many pagan groups do have a common canon of pagan texts. This canon is far from universal but can at least be applied to each separate group and the high degree of repetition between such groups creates an unofficial canon of pagan classics.

Graves never published a complete list of his suggested canon but *White Goddess* mentions three titles, which he includes in his personal canon. Modern Graves fans may be surprised to learn that none of the three are pagan works and one of the three authors was even canonized by the church. These titles are William Langland's *Piers Ploughman*, Thomas More's *Utopia*, and John Lyly's *Euphues*.

Graves's use of *Piers Ploughman* has already been noted. Roughly a century later More's *Utopia* (1516) also satirized English society and called for better education and religious tolerance. More hailed from Oxford and was highly critical of his government; matching Graves in both respects. More's claim that he wrote *Utopia* as a satire allowed him to disavow any controversy the book might cause. Graves makes a comparable disavowal in the forward to *White Goddess* where he offers no suggestions to the reader but merely states his interpretation of facts. In all three cases, we suspect the authors are hedging their true intent.

More's desire to distance himself from his works via satire reveals his good sense. He realized that a book as short as *Utopia* could never detail a truly perfect society; it can only capture a few isolated traits. Readers must take from More's works with whatever little pieces they could incorporate into their own lives. Like both *Piers Ploughman* and *Lambspring*, More preaches personal perfection amid societal corruption. It was this message which most appealed to Graves, the truth inspired poet who detested the industrialization and corruption around him.

Utopia's central character, Raphael Hythlodaeus, is depicted as a globetrotting philosopher well educated in Greek classics and highly impressed with Plato's *Republic*. This latter fact contrasts with

Graves attacks on Plato early in *White Goddess* but a close look at Raphael's character dispels any contradiction. Early in *Utopia* Raphael declares that he's obligated to speak the truth, even if it makes him unpopular in the royal courts. He claims philosophers shouldn't tell lies and concludes that he has no desire to model society directly upon Plato's *Republic* (More 64). In all, Raphael is exactly what Graves believes a good philosopher should be, well educated, honest, humble, and balanced between poetic and scientific approaches.

Lastly, *Utopia*'s religious views deserve notice in relationship to *The White Goddess*. The islanders of More's perfect society include both moon and sun worshipers as well as Christians. Others follow a Deism, which equates the Supreme Being with nature. Many Utopians offer conflicting definitions of this deity but all use the name Mythras when speaking of him. Religious tolerance is mandatory and over zealous Christians are deported as trouble makers. Utopian funeral practices involve the belief in ghosts, another item, which surely caught Graves's eye. Regardless of the various religions, all Utopians worship on the same days and their calendar consists of a solar year divided into lunar months; thus, they have merged the two systems, which Graves attempts to combine within *White Goddess*.

In all, More's Utopian religion is a merger of Deism and druidic concepts taken from Greek and Roman authors. More reveals that Utopian children are entrusted to the priests for their education and these priests wield the ultimate punishment of excommunication, which all citizens fear. During war, Utopian priests retreat and pray for victory. Should a priest enter the battlefield he has the power to part combatants and spare the lives of either Utopian soldiers or their enemies. Their churches are great gloomy enclosures devoid of any idols or graphic depictions of their deity. All of these ideas derive from Caesar and Pliny's accounts of druidism.

Nor is Utopian religion without its mysticism. Their priestly robes are adorned with feathers in cryptic shapes, which conceal religious concepts. This, and the simple Utopian alphabet More uses to present Utopian poetry, probably increased Graves's interest in the book. More's fictitious alphabet looks nothing like ogham but, like ogham and Tolkien's tengwar, is a logical progression of simple symbols. In all, it resembles the sort of secret codes schoolchildren devise for passing notes in class or the numerical symbols of *Barddas*.

Later in the same century, More's friend, John Lyly, published *Euphues, or the Anatomy of Wit* and *Euphues and His England*, in 1578 and 1580 respectively. These works are considered high points in sixteenth century literature. Although Lyly's place in the English literary canon is undisputed, we wonder why Graves mentioned him in lieu of better known authors. Graves may be indulging in a little favoritism; Lyly, like More and Graves himself, was also an Oxford man.

If Graves's canon favored More and Lyly for their Oxford affiliations, then perhaps we can also understand Graves's biased treatment of John Milton within *White Goddess*. Milton had attended Cambridge; "the other place" as Graves scornfully called it (Seymour 349). Milton's alma mater, his emulation of Virgil's epic style, his attack on Nennius, and his negative attitude towards pagan inspiration are all contributing factors to Graves's dislike of him. Graves paints Milton as a narrow minded, censorious Christian who would ban the very books, which Graves would place in his canon. Milton's most famous prose piece, *Areopagitica*, is taken out of context by Graves and depicted as a censorious work rather than an appeal for freedom of the press. Milton had the poor taste to suggest that John Skelton's *Poems* and the novel *The Recognitions* deserved eternal suppression. Graves enjoyed both of these books and Milton's attacks upon them marked him for Graves's special abuse. Chapter twenty-two of *White Goddess* opens with Graves cleverly citing Skelton to illuminate Milton's *Paradise Lost* and Graves's treatment of *Areopagitica* is typical of his style. He frequently uses his sources in unorthodox ways, often turning the citation against the author to support a contradictory claim. Such creative use of his sources has led to heavy criticism but is simultaneously a tribute to his ability to twist intended meanings into new ideas, which question their own origins. This method of breaking down sources to question their most fundamental assertions was a trait of the Celtic bards whom Graves emulates and is also found in another of Graves's preferred authors Lewis Carroll; another Oxford man.

CHAPTER XVI

LAURA RIDING AND THE MOON GODDESS

Graves wasn't the first poet to be simultaneously inspired and tormented by his loyalty to the goddess. His entire argument is based on the concept that all poets are subjected to this love-hate relationship. We've already seen this dynamic relationship exposed in Graves's works and in Keats's *La Belle Dame Sans Merci*; neither poet was alone in his torment or dedication. John Skelton had been mocked for expressing his love of the Muse by appearing publicly in a gown embroidered with the name Calliope, the Muse of epic poetry (Graves 1962, 15). Roughly a century earlier the fourteenth century Welsh poet Dafydd ap Gwilym suffered the same combination of torment and love, and captured it perfectly in his confession to a friar:

> I was always in love with a white-faced black-browed girl, and that from her who slew me I had neither profit nor reward from my lady; only that I loved her long and lastingly and languished greatly for her love ... and failed to win her for all that (Jackson 213).

Gwilym's image of a pale faced, dark haired Muse was clearly the forerunner of Graves's own Moon goddess and the recurring motif of paleness in Keats's *La Belle Dame Sans Merci*. Pallid white skin and jet-black hair provided two of the three colors sacred to the Celts. Blood red lips or rosy cheeks were the only lacking features to complete the image. It was this combination of white, black, and red, which symbolized the other world to pagan Celts and beauty to generations of European poets.

Graves first mentions these color attributes in chapter four of *White Goddess* where he explains that white symbolizes the new moon, red for the full moon, and black for the old moon. This lunar interpretation reappears in *The Greek Myths* (Graves 1992, 76, 306). Both books rely on the tenth century lexicographer Suidas for descriptions of the cow goddess Io and on Hyginus's fable of a similar red calf. White for the new moon and black for the old moon seem understandable and is commonly found in pagan rituals, but red for the full moon is more obscure. Critics suggest Graves took his color symbolism from Suidas, but this is only a partial explanation (Vickery 39).

The full moon has been associated with menstruating women since time immortal and Graves's footnote proves he was fully aware of the fact (Graves 1993, 166). Briffault mentions the belief that menstruation was caused by intercourse with the moon and argues that lunar cults are universally female institutions (Briffault 252). Both the moon and women have an average twenty-eight day cycle and it became natural for the roundness of a full moon to be linked to the fertility of women in ancient times. Thus symbolically linking the color red to the full moon becomes appropriate.

Some critics deny that Graves found his color symbolism in Frazer, but Frazer devotes considerable time to the moon's links to women. He doesn't elaborate, but implies connections between women and the moon and stresses the phases of a goddess's life in relation to her sacred crops. He also mentions the course of human thought and compares it to a web of three colors, "the black thread of magic, the red thread of religion, and the white thread of science" (Frazer 826).

The primary source for Graves's color symbolism is Celtic myth. These three colors symbolize the Celtic other world and can be magical when combined. The combination of white, red, and black is usually used to describe an attractive woman and such women appear frequently enough in Celtic myth to suggest that this was their idea of beauty. This description recurs in the tales *Peredur*,

Deirdre, and *Snow White* and spans from the mid-fourteenth century to Grimm's 1812 book. Graves's color usage in *The Bards* proves that he was aware of this theme by the early 1930's.

In Celtic literature, these three colors frequently cause magical trance; the characters in *Peredur* and *Snow White* were both entranced by them. This trance could come from the colors themselves or from the beauty of the woman, whom Graves considered a manifestation of his White Goddess. White, red, and black also play major roles apart from each other in Celtic myth, but it would be tedious to enumerate examples. The white and red dragons mentioned by Geoffrey of Monmouth and by his source, Nennius, are typical examples. Their color symbolism and their link to similar dragons in *Lludd and Lleuelys* (and Revelations' four horsemen) is left for others to discover.

Regardless of other sources, such as Suidas, Frazer, or Grimm, Graves was intimately familiar with Celtic mythology since childhood. He had even mastered the difficult Welsh poetic form of the *englyn* as early as 1912 (R.P. Graves 1986, 83). He had probably encountered the white, black, and red symbolism in *Peredur Son of Evrawg* or another Celtic source in early reading. Suggesting that he took this color scheme exclusively from Frazer or Suidas is unrealistic in light of Graves's Celtic disposition.

Graves has ample justification for choosing these colors for the three aspects of the goddess. Yet, as Vickery observes, Graves feels free to change this at will and at one point, he calls Caridwen the "white lady of death". All of this color symbolism is odd for a poet who frequently attacked the use of colors in poetry (Graves 1922, 76). Graves had once warned that poems of a "mere versifier" resembled a bad painting of a tropical sunset (Kersnowski, 4). Here we see not only Graves's dislike of color adjectives but also his continual resentment of the "mere versifier".

Another indicator that Graves and Gwilym followed the same tradition is their conflict with the church. Both poets challenged mainstream religion and Graves once commented that his works would kill Christianity (Kersnowski 24). Gwilym also viewed his poetry as heretical but held no illusions of ultimate victory. It's significant that his above poem is framed as a confession to a friar. Gwilym realized that his languishing for the "white-faced black-browed girl" placed him in conflict with Christianity. Gwilym places all hope for life and salvation in a woman who symbolizes the goddess and unites human love, physical desire, and intellectual companionship with a mystical or spiritual love usually directed towards Jesus. He knows that it's wrong to base his spirituality on worship of a female and confesses his sin openly. The friar advises Gwilym to lessen his future punishment by abandoning poetry and turning towards prayer. In short, the friar believes that salvation comes from identifying with Jesus' suffering rather than languishing for an earthly female, no matter how beautiful or noble.

The dangers of loving this female archetype include more than spiritual suffering; it may lead to death. In the medieval and Renaissance eras, when the inquisition raged, heretics were hunted and executed *en masse*. Poets who directed spiritual love towards anything other than Jesus or Jehovah were often censored, imprisoned, and occasionally executed. Combining such heretical views with contemporary Neoplatonic thought was a sure formula for persecution. It's significant that Giordano Bruno, the sixteenth-century philosopher, wrote poetry in this vein.

Bruno is best remembered for advocating Copernicus's helio-centric universe, insisting that the earth circled the sun rather than vice versa. This refusal to place earth at the center of creation led to conflicts with the Church, but Bruno challenged the Bible in verse as well. His collection of love poems, *De gli eroici furori*, depicts the universe as an archtypical female and Bruno as her lover. Bruno paints himself as the suffering romantic questing after his lover. He pleads for her attention and strives for direct experience of her love despite the possibility that such a revelation could kill him. Eventually, his flaunting of Christianity brought him to the inevitable end of all poets, kings, and heroes in Graves's system.

Bruno, like Hercules, was forced to mount the pyre and was burned alive. His death stands midway between the works of Gwilym and Graves and went on to inspire poet Sir Philip Sidney.

Another source of Graves's goddess imagery was the 1566 Adlington translation of Apuleius's *The Golden Ass*, a book Graves knew by 1926. In chapter four of *White Goddess*, Graves quotes the book's most famous passage, the detailed and majestic description of the goddess as seen by Lucius in his prophetic dream. Two interesting features stand out. The first is that Lucius views the magical power of the waxing and waning moon much as pagans understand it today. Such an idea was not alien to either Apuleius, or to Aldington when he translated the work. The belief that moon phases are alternately lucky and unlucky is widespread in pagan literature and the earlier sources it draws from. Besides Apuleius and Graves, identical ideas regarding lunar phases can be found in Leland and Briffault (Leland, 46; Briffault, 250). The Bible likewise contains many references to moon worship, celebrations, and lunar sacrifice.

Other early writers, which helped develop the multifaceted lunar goddess, include seventeenth century cabalist Robert Fludd, Frazer, Briffault, and Harrison. Fludd, a devotee of both Apuleius and Bruno, imagines the world soul as a nubile female as early as 1617. His accompanying illustration depicts a giant nude female bridging the space between man on earth and God in heaven. This goddess conceals her breasts behind solar and lunar symbols; significantly, the moon hides her left breast and thereby suggests the typical polarity, which connects the left side of the body with feminine lunar aspects and the right with masculine solar attributes. Another crescent moon, concealing her sex organs, reinforces the connection between lunar and feminist symbolism.

Frazer's contributions are literary rather than graphic. He repeatedly refers to the belief in a "corn mother" in Northern Europe who is viewed as either maiden, mother, and old woman. His examples indicate that few (if any) cultures viewed her as all three successively; although Frazer himself uses *Maiden, Corn-*

mother, and *Old Woman* together in a single sentence in his summary (Frazer 477).

Harrison's *Prolegomena* links a double goddess, who is both Mother and Daughter, with the moon and suggests that a triple goddess later evolved from this double goddess image (Harrison 262, 286, 537). Harrison later describes a double goddess who bears a hero son and applies the terms "Maiden, Bride and Mother" (Harrison 562, 647). Briffault's contribution is even more interesting. He claims the three lunar phases are seen in New Britain as a "White woman" whose two sons are locked in eternal conflict (Briffault 296, 335). The genesis of Graves's goddess and her two lovers and sons derives from the same British tradition. After publication of Graves's work, the concept of a great goddess was given psychological support by Erich Neumann's *The Great Mother* and eventually found its way into feminist writing.

While attempting to streamline goddess worship Graves struggles to unite all goddesses into one. His selective claims of iconotropy enable him to disregard conflicting aspects of various goddesses and merge goddesses of differing cultures into a single female deity. The goddess's triple aspect allows Graves to resolve more significant personality conflicts by regulating particular goddesses into either maiden, mother, or crone category. Hecate can't be equated to Persephone, but each can be made into single aspects of the multifaceted goddess who supersedes both. Once Graves has established the goddess is omnipotent and omnipresent it becomes natural for specific goddesses to depict only portions of the larger whole.

In doing this, Graves may have drawn inspiration from a minor source found within Davies's *Mythology and Rites*. Davies repeatedly quotes long passages from Faber's *Mysteries of the Cabiri*, another supporter of Bryant's Arkite theory. In these quotes Faber equates Venus, Derceto, Isis, Ceres, Proserpine, and Latona to the moon and suggests that this composite goddess was viewed as mother, daughter, and consort at different times (Davies 1809, 178). Davies himself stated that "the attributes of the mother and daughter, in the Bardic mythology, as well as in that of other heathens, are so much confounded together, as not to be easily distinguished" (Davies 1809, 205).

By merging these goddesses, Graves attempts what most religions fail to do. He tries to reconcile opposites in reality, which imply opposites in the divine. Hecate is the vicious hag of black magic whose worshipers meet nocturnally at the crossroads. Persephone is the innocent, bright-eyed virgin violently abducted into the underworld. Yet each becomes an aspect of the other and they are united in a larger goddess. The implication is that this larger goddess can show no favor to either Hecate or Persephone. She may be Hecate and Persephone, each in turn, but she can never complete forsake one for the other. The goddess is all things at all times and therein lies the paradox.

Graves tries to reconcile opposite traits in the goddess yet insists that the goddess has a will of her own, which mankind chooses to ignore. Supposedly, man has turned from the goddess to her son and tainted the world with patriarchal corruption while the goddess passively allows this to happen. In suggesting this, Graves has confronted another paradox which plagues many conservative Jews and Christians: how can anything happen against the will of an omnipotent deity?

Jehovah expresses his will repeatedly throughout the Old Testament yet his followers frequently stray from the path and invoke his anger. If Jehovah is truly all powerful then their straying becomes impossible. Judaism and Christianity resolve the issue by introducing mankind's free will and Satan's temptation. Supposedly, we are always at liberty to choose between obedience or rebellion and Satan utilizes man's free will to tempt him into rebellion. Yet, an omnipotent god can surely foresee when humans will falter and easily intervene or completely destroy Satan. His refusal to do either is considered evidence that he values human free will beyond his own will.

Supposedly, Jehovah will only destroy mankind after their repeated failure has proven their inherent corruption. Upon that fateful day, the elect followers will ascend to heaven and those who have strayed will be punished. Yet, we're left with the lingering suspicion that all is predetermined and Jehovah knew the names of the faithful beforehand. From his perspective, everything is predetermined; humans are left to blunder onward as best they can and question whether or not real free choice is possible.

The paradox between the ultimate deity and human free will is stated more elegantly in Graves's pagan goddess worship but, as with mainstream religion, the question remains unanswered. Where Christianity claims that man may invoke God's anger Graves merely suggests our punishments are automatic responses to our choices. The goddess appears to have no part in our punishments. We stick our hand in the fire and we are burned; the goddess needn't take an active part. The biblical god punishes us with a foreboding scowl; the goddess watches with a bemused smile as we punish ourselves. Graves's goddess appears more human but still fails to resolve the paradox.

The advantage to Graves's system is the elimination of Satan or any tempting force to weaken man's morals. Graves realizes that humans are fallible enough without Satan. The king or hero of his goddess religion does have a rival, or tanist, but he seldom serves as tempter. The rival weakens the hero not through temptation but via direct competition for the goddess's affection. He may even use methods identical to the hero's and lure the goddess toward him with poetry or magic ritual. In turn, the hero-poet mounts no counter attack but instead increases his own degree of competition. He strives to write better poetry, to be more heroic, a better lover, and basically, a better man in general. This competition drives him further along the upward spiral path as he attempts to stay one step ahead of his tanist. He could directly assault his competitor with satire or black magic but this violates the rules of fair play which the goddess respects and thereby makes him the dark tanist and pushes the rival into favor.

Graves downplays the flaws inherent in his goddess worship but he knew of them and this leads him to discourage goddess worship as an actual religion. Unlike Shelley, Calvert, and Lovecraft Graves builds no altars. His Oxford lectures warn against rebuilding goddess shrines and he later complains that Wicca "attracts hysterical or perverted characters" and is torn by "schisms and dissolutions" (Graves 1964, 553). The reasons for this are that the relationship between the goddess and the individual has become too private to tolerate public ritual or dogma. With the diversification of Western culture, the large ecstatic group ritual is no longer acceptable and *orgy* lost its sacred connotation even before Rome collapsed, to become vulgarized by the decadent. Graves believes that attempts to reinstate large-scale public goddess worship are either pedantry or morally dangerous.

Nor does it seem that Graves wishes a return to the matriarchal era even if it were possible. In the same lecture series, Graves labeled the matriarchal era a "female monopoly" controlling all significant aspects of life. Men escaped from this domination only by amazing strides of intelligence and Graves wholly commends our male ancestors for their intellectual efforts. Modern men, he says, could never return to the "collective slavery" of the prehistoric matriarchy (Graves 1962, 88). Although he often calls for a renewed respect for females and spiritual equality, Graves is in no hurry to unite his beliefs to religious rituals. His poetry often focuses upon the horrible end poets come to and Graves sees no reason to live out this destiny in the most literal sense.

Above all else, Graves believes poetry and religion both require spiritual homage to females, rather than dogma. Men may be physically superior to females but they must acknowledge her superiority in intellect and spirituality. Man may not rely on woman for his physically survival but he depends on her fulfillment of his intellectual and spiritual life. Without her, he is dangerously incomplete. The power of the female over the male, and the rest of creation, is almost magical. It leads to reverence of the female both in person and in ideal, which then leads to religion and poetry.

All of this can be compared against what Harrison claims in *Prolegomena*:

> Such myths are a necessary outcome of the shift from matriarchy to patriarchy, and the shift itself, spite of a seeming retrogression, is a necessary stage in a real advance. Matriarchy gave to women a false because a magical prestige. With patriarchy came inevitably the facing of a real fact, the fact of the greater natural weakness of women. Man the stronger, when he outgrew his belief in the magical potency of woman, proceeded by a pardonable practical logic to despise and enslave her as the weaker. The future held indeed a time when the non-natural, mystical truth came to be apprehended, that the stronger had a need, real and imperative, of the weaker. Physically nature had from the outset compelled a certain recognition of this truth, but that the physical was a sacrament of the spiritual was a hard saying, and its understanding was not granted to the Greek, save here and there where a flicker of the truth gleamed and went through the vision of philosopher or poet (285)

Graves would probably shudder at this passage. While the under-lying idea that man needs woman in a more than physical sense is stated, it's nearly lost amid statements that would make Graves cringe. Harrison supports real women, not idealized goddesses. Women who are seen in light of Graves's ideas are full of "magical prestige", which exalts them but also limits their humanity. To Harrison the "natural weakness of women" can't be ignored. Once this weakness is realized and the magical prestige vanishes a new sort of progress begins based on "a pardonable practical logic" which no longer holds the female as sacred. Yet, it's exactly this magical prestige which *The White Goddess* intents to restore.

Graves's goddess serves to explain the relationship between

poetry and romance. Poetry and love are both vague and undefined, yet both are real and bound by equally vague rules and conditions. Both are subject to personal interpretation and both offer extreme self-expression. Both require devotion and the willingness to take chances. Thus, they can have the same effect. Graves simply takes the next step and merges the spiritual aspects of both to form a pagan religion. The connecting factor is the goddess, a female archetype that man strives towards on multiple levels. Merging images of Mother Nature, the three graces, and the muses gives Graves an omnipotent goddess whom merges romantic, erotic, and spiritual love and becomes infinitely more lovable than Blake's old Nobodaddy.

Graves believes that the entire natural world reflects this goddess but man is her highest achievement and is best suited to understanding her complexities. Humans were created to contemplate the divine as no other creature can. Yet, even humans must fail to understand the totality of creation. After all, they are only a cog in the wheel, which is attempting to understand the whole.

In each romantic relationship, the man struggles to serve the woman although he can never serve her as well as he desires to, or should. The same can be said of a poet serving the goddess. His service is never enough and eventually the relationships burns itself out from its own intensity. This is why most poets are young; young men are more concerned with love's intensity. They are young, hopeful, and energetic because they are new to the service of the goddess. Poets can only write beyond this young and energetic period if they continually strive for new insights into their poetic relationships. Graves says virtually the same thing in the opening of *White Goddess's* first chapter when he admits to a lifelong adhesion to poetic principles and a constant interest in "outstanding poetic problems" (Graves 1993, 17).

There is a definite backlash against Graves's idea that all women are aspects of the goddess. Critics argue this view is sexist because it ranks women too highly over men in a position they can never

actually achieve and thus women are doomed to fail in the role
Graves assigns them. These critics contend that Graves's system is no
better than the false magical prestige, which Harrison attacks. Even
if women do succeed in this role, they are made useless by doing so.
To fulfill this role women would simply become useless items, a
symbol, or an icon of the goddess but debarred from everyday
society. Their very sanctity would reduce women to mere archetypes
rather than individuals and they would fall into the same trap, which
Graves believes Jesus fell victim to.

Granted, Graves has made sexist sounding remarks in *The White
Goddess* but it's unlikely that Graves was intentionally sexist and
these lines are often quoted out of context. It would be more accurate
to say that Graves simply may not realize the implications of what he
says. He believes his opinions on women are correct and that it's
spiritually healthy for others to agree. He believes that any other
opinions would decrease our respect for women and lead to other
forms of moral decay.

For Graves, this merger of romance, eroticism, and spirituality
manifested in a series of romantic relationships in which he played
the role of the hero-king serving his lover, the goddess. Laura Riding
was the most competent and literary of the women who personified
the goddess for Graves, but for all her ability, she was only human.
Eventually, Graves became more conscious of her human faults and
the stress of their relationship began to outweigh the advantages to
either of them. After Riding's departure, Graves married a loving
wife but maintained a series of rocky relationships with younger
women representing the Muse in his poetic system. Each of these
women was expected to inspire Graves in ways similar to those
established by Riding.

Although Riding was disliked by many, she was a positive
influence on Graves. Under her influence, he found himself able to
focus on something other than morbid flashbacks of World War I.
His love poems increased in quantity and quality under Riding, as
did his understanding of poetry. Riding was the strict schoolteacher

and Graves was the infatuated schoolboy. At one minute, she could inspire the most beautiful poetry and smile approvingly of it. At the next minute, she could bring the ruler slamming down on his fingers to drive home a lesson he may have missed. Graves never knew which reaction to expect, but he knew he was improving in her company and this made him idolize her even more.

In a sense, Riding became the Muse personified. Nancy may have instilled Graves with a large part of his respect for the feminine, but it was Riding who was the first prototype of the goddess. Often her actions and statements appeared as melodrama (or even psychodrama) in which Graves played the part of the dying god in her service. Many men would have been disturbed by this facet of Riding, but Graves was attracted all the more. Their partnership provided Graves with the emotional and intellectual challenge, which he demanded from personal relationships. These melodramatic tendencies served Graves as well as they served Riding and he saw no reason to shun them. After all, melodrama was central to those inspirational sources Graves favored: Greek and Roman mythology, the Bible, and early English ballads. On one level, Riding's embodiment of the goddess is comparable to the Wiccan ritual of "Drawing Down the Moon" in which the priestess delivers spiritual advice after a ritual shift in consciousness. Riding used no circle dance, candles, or pentagrams but she did dispense philosophical advice derived from the goddess archetype.

Graves's acceptance of Riding's supernatural status is revealed in chapter nineteen of *White Goddess* where he offers his poem *On Portents*. Graves mentions that the poem is referring to the Muse but in reality, the poem refers to Riding in the Muse's role. *The White Goddess* merely admits that Graves wrote the poem several years beforehand. The exact date of publication was 1931, during Graves's involvement with Riding. It's noteworthy that Graves offers the poem as a commentary on the Muse but he refuses to mention Riding's name until chapter twenty-five of *White Goddess*.

Predictably, his first mention of Riding comes in a paragraph concerning the poet's devotion to the Muse. Graves depicts the Muse as never fully satisfied and reveals that originality must be tempered with a simple style. The Muse detests overblown bombast and worn clichés. Only simple and honest assertions are acceptable and even most of these fail to please her. Graves's claim that the Muse is never satisfied can be traced back to the exacting standards Riding demanded from herself and her literary circle.

It has often been said that Riding was the model for Graves's White Goddess right down to the physical description of a thin, pale, fair-haired woman with a hooked nose. We could substitute "fair hair" with "raven haired" and describe her to the letter. Although these terms fit Riding, we can't over simplify. It's more appropriate to say that Riding was the most impressive of a series of women who personified the goddess for Graves. Graves's description of the goddess was a composite of many women and it has been suggested that this image was also heavily influenced by his friend Irene Gay (Hutton 194). The same description also fits the majority of the Greek and Roman goddesses and it would be error to think Graves drew only from Riding or Gay when developing his goddess.

In truth, the goddess was a combination of nearly every woman (and some men) whom Graves knew and admired. Although she contains strong elements of Nancy Nicholson and Laura Riding, she just as easily contains traces of men, including literary influences that Graves never knew personally. Frazer immediately comes to mind. Graves was also influenced by an early reading of Freud (O'Prey 262). Critics such as Randal Jarrell have also suggested Jungian influence but Graves refused to utilize Jung and denied his impact until the end.

The three aspects of the White Goddess reveal three approaches to female sexuality; two of which are at odds with typical Christian morals. To Graves, and other pagans, all three are acceptable within their correct contexts. The goddess isn't all flowers, milk, and honey; nor is the dewy eyed virgin draped in a toga her only manifestation. Her sexuality ranges from the shy innocence of Persephone to Queen

Medb, who never slept alone and never without a tanist waiting in the shadows. At her most extreme, she can become the "black screaming hag" of *The Tempest*. As a poet, Graves honors all three aspects of the goddess but often he seems obsessed with the darker aspects of her sexuality.

His treatment of Mary reveals Graves's attitude towards virginity and the submissive female. Within *King Jesus*, Mary is depicted not as a virgin but as a woman secretly married and impregnated before her marriage to Joseph. Both marriages are arranged by others and, although Mary obviously loves her first husband, she plays little part in her own betrothal. Throughout *King Jesus*, Mary is sensible and intelligent but always piously submissive. Graves portrays her as the "good mother" and possibly, she was Graves's favorite manifestation of the young virgin aspect of the triple goddess. Graves's suggestion that Mary was secretly married and impregnated is tantamount to heresy to Christians but allows Graves to retain his image of Mary as innocent, pure, and kindly while at the same time eliminating the supernatural element of Jesus' birth. Graves may have been reluctant to abandon his unsullied image of Mary much as he hesitated to abandon Jesus as the perfect man. A direct attack on Mary's image would also assault over a thousand years of literature and art, which depicted Mary as immaculate. Graves was loath to deny this respectable tradition. Even his beloved Celtic bards had worshiped Mary and he quotes Nash in his treatment of the subject:

The Christian bards of the thirteenth and fourteenth centuries, indeed, repeatedly refer to the Virgin Mary herself, as the cauldron or source of inspiration, to which they were led, as it seems, partly by a play on the word, on assuming the soft form of its initial "mair," which also means Mary. Mary was "Mair," the mother of Christ, the mystical receptacle of the Holy Spirit, and "Pair," the cauldron or receptacle and foundation of Christian inspiration. Thus we have in a poem of Davyd Benvras, in the thirteenth century,

Crist mab Mair am Pair pur vonhedd,-
Christ, son of Mary, my cauldron of pure descent. (Nash 196)

Graves offers this as evidence that Celtic bards equated Mary with Brigit and preserved goddess oriented paganism within their poetry. Ironically, Nash cites the same lines as evidence of the bard's Christian faith. It's amusing to notice that Graves has cleverly chosen exactly the right spot to end his quote. Nash's following line reads: "But all this is Christian, and not Druidic mysticism, and an adaptation of popular ideas, which forms another phase in the employment of this symbol". The popular ideas which Nash claims these Welsh bards used is the well documented increase of Mary worship from the twelfth century onward. Nash uses the line from Davyd Benvras to prove the bard was Christian following standard Mary symbolism. This contradicts earlier statements from Davies that medieval bards were concealing a system of paganism. Then, after the fact, Graves comes behind both Davies and Nash and reverses the meaning of the statement again. Granted, there is nothing wrong with debating the meaning of something so personal and subjective as poetry. Yet, Graves is flying directly in the face of better research and contradicting it without serious consideration.

In chapter twenty-two of *White Goddess*, Mary's image diverges from the immaculate mother of Jesus to a more sexually assertive woman. This new Mary has passed the initiation stage and embraces sexuality with greater acceptance. Yet, Graves hesitates to openly attack the mother of Jesus and instead merges her with St. Mary of Egypt. This Egyptian Mary appears in one of Graves's sources, *Book of the Saints*, as a prostitute who offered herself to the entire crew of a ship bound for the Holy Land. Skelton's *Laurel* mentions this Mary as Mary Gipsy and likely served as further encouragement for Graves's decision to include her.

Eventually Graves equates Mary to Marian and the mermaid, and lists her attributes in a simplistic fashion resembling today's mass-market paperbacks on paganism. Most of the description is a long chain of consciousness linking various images, names, trees, and colors back to various incarnations of Marian. We are told that Marian is the mermaid and can be equated to Aphrodite and:

> ...the tunny, sturgeon, scallop and periwinkle, all sacred to her, as aphrodisiacs... The myrtle, murex and myrrh tree were also everywhere sacred to her; with the palm-tree (which thrives on salt), the love-faithful dove, and the colours white, green, blue and scarlet. (Graves 1993, 395).

Anyone who has read even a handful of introductory pagan books can see the similarity between this sort of symbolism and current pagan thinking. Countless books today offer listings of various gods and goddesses and their corresponding symbols, animals, colors and plants in a comparable fashion. Such tables of correspondences are usually placed at the back of such books for easy reference for those wishing to construct rituals around a central theme. Here, Graves has applied the same system to his own work. His way of presenting the goddess and linking her symbolically to various plants, colors, and symbols was one of the early inspirations for later pagan authors who wished to organize their own goddess images into a coherent system. As evidence, Starhawk quotes a dozen lines taken from the same paragraph in her own classic Wiccan text *Spiral Dance* (Starhawk 38).

The last aspect of the goddess is the malicious crone who combats sexuality with death and infertility. *The White Goddess* cites several examples of this archetype. In every example, she turns sexuality into a weapon; either by excessive and self-destructive indulgence or via direct attacks on fertility. Her hostility towards the poet marks the last of the five life stages as her mood darkens and her interest turns to the tanist. This shift from lover to betrayer is often a quick one; the line between Morgan le Fay and the Morrigan is thin and blurred.

When discussing these aggressive aspects of female sexuality Graves cites Malinowski's *Sexual Life of Savages in North-Western Melanesia*. Graves compares the females of European pagan culture to those of the Melanesian islands, whom supposedly sexually assaulted men who dared to break certain female taboos. The implication is that Melanesian men could be raped for violating customary female rights and that this was once the attitude in Europe as well. Yet, an examination of Malinowski's commentary suggests that no such examples of male rape were known in Melanesia.

The comparison between European and Melanesian women revolves around the alleged behavior of the women of the island of Vakuta and the mythic island of Kaytalugi. Melanesia tradition stated that any man who trespassed in the gardens of Vakuta was subjected to sexual assaults of the most degrading type. Allegedly, men were attacked by groups of rabid women, restrained by force, and repeatedly raped by each woman in turn. To modern ears such legends sound like sadomasochistic fantasy but Melanesian men regarded this legend with real horror and disgust. A similar fate awaited any man who landed on the mythic island of Kaytalugi. This mysterious island was supposedly inhabited only by females. Men who dared to trespass there could expect to be repeatedly raped, without food or rest, until they died of exhaustion (Malinowski 423).

However, these stories were merely legends and Malinowski never witnessed these offenses first hand. The natives couldn't recall a single victim of this custom or even remember when the last rape had occurred (Malinowski 274, 276). The island of Kaytalugi itself was entirely mythical and while there were stories of men who had supposedly visited it long ago, there was no real evidence and the island itself was never located. Thus, this island of aggressive females is comparable to similar tales of Amazon women. Such islands of female savagery are a common device in myth and legend but their existence should not be taken as fact.

In reality, rape among the Melanesians resembled rape in the Western world. Women were the victims in all known cases and punishment for infidelity was often the motive. Additionally, women could be murdered for adultery (Malinowski 273, 324). Thus, the reality is exactly opposite of what Graves implies. Rather than citing factual record, as Malinowski does, Graves draws from Melanesian legends to uphold Rousseau's romantic image of the noble savage, an idea that Malinowski repeatedly denies in his work.

The death aspect of the goddess can manifest itself in others ways, apart from the aggressive sexuality of the Amazon. As Hecate, she is worshiped nocturnally at crossroads by those wishing to curse others or wishing protection from curses. As Caridwen, she hunts and punishes those who have drunk the cauldron of inspiration against her will. Her war on life and fertility knows no bounds and her methods include blighting crops and throwing children to the sea.

The death goddess as child killer appears in *White Goddess* as Black Annis, the legendary nocturnal hag who ate Leicester children. Exactly where Graves encountered this legend is unknown but her tale is mentioned by E. M. Hull, one of his sources. Nor should we rule out the possibility that he had encountered this legend first hand. Tales of Black Annis had been circulating since the eighteenth century and were well established by the time Graves wrote. However, it seems that Graves was unaware of the origin of these legends. If he had known the truth, he most likely wouldn't have mentioned her.

Agnes Scott had been a monastic Christian living in caves of the Dane Hills, near Leicester, in late medieval times. How this pious anchorite became the Black Annis who carried children away to her cave by night is unknown but it has been suggested that the legend spread in the wake of Protestant Reformation and the resulting backlash against monastic Christians (Hutton 274). It's interesting that Graves mentions the image of her, donning a nun's habit, at the

Swithland Church and claims this image is a later corruption of earlier legends. This church is Agnes Scott's final resting place and doubtless, the image of her in the nun's habit is a more realistic depiction of her than the legend surrounding her name. Obviously, Graves was unaware of the true history of Black Annis despite the fact that at least some of the locals knew the truth. Nonetheless, Graves retained his image of Black Annis for years and she reappears in the same guise in his *English and Scottish Ballads*.

The archaeological evidence Graves cites for the existence of the triple goddess include Sir Robert Mond's excavation at Tresse, Brittany, which was examined in depth by V.C.C. Collum in his 1935 book *The Tresse Iron-Age Megalithic Monument*. Graves, like Collum, was impressed by the site's series of megalithic uprights bearing sculpted breast-like protrusions. The first upright displayed two pairs of young "breasts", the second upright displayed a larger pair of protrusions which Collum interpreted as mature breasts. Although the third upright was broken and missing, Collum suggested that it had originally displayed a pair of withered breasts, representing old age. Collum, like other historians under the sway of Frazer and Harrison, supported theories of a prehistoric mother goddess cult and considered the megalithic breasts as evidence of its existence in Brittany.

Graves's belief that the goddess predates the god is expressed again in *Hercules*, where he depicts all pagan religions before the mid-second millennium as exclusively matriarchal and refuses to introduce male deities until at least the thirteenth century BC. Exactly what evidence brought Graves to this conclusion is unknown, but there are earlier sources, which support similar models from which he could have drawn. Briffault makes a similar sweeping statement when he claims there were no male "idols" in the Neolithic Mediterranean. Later Briffault clarifies this statement by claiming no male idols have been found in Crete and only two examples of male gods, depicted on seals, were known (Briffault 86, 371). In Europe, Rhys observed that Celts worshiped their ancestors and traced descent through their mothers. Therefore, at some point they logically favored goddesses over male deities (Rhys, Brynmor-Jones 54). The sum total of Rhys and Briffault's works appear to substantiate Graves's theory but, as all archaeologists know, the absence of evidence can't be accepted as evidence of absence. Our inability to find something does not imply that it never existed and the existence of the Cretan seals proves that Cretans were at least familiar with male deities despite the fact that no idols survive.

CHAPTER XVII

LEGACY

Readers of *The White Goddess* eventually realize that the battle of *Cad Goddeu* is simply a framework from which Graves supports his own poetic models. Despite his attempts to justify the historical argument, we suspect that Graves was fully aware that he was placing his own values on the legend. Theoretically, Graves was free to choose any myth, legend, or tale he desired to support his poetic model and even if he insisted on a Celtic framework, his choices were almost infinite. It seems that if Graves was truly aware of what he was attempting to do he would have fully formulated his poetic system and then searched Celtic history for a myth which could be made into the appropriate metaphor.

The fact that Graves chose the battle of *Cad Goddeu* and even struggled to include an obscure version, which required further explanation reveals that perhaps Graves wasn't completely aware of his own creative process. It seems Graves had brilliant flashes of insight into his poetic system but simultaneously he was having insight into what he considered authentic Celtic history and attempting to converge both revelations. This accords well with his own claim that he wrote *White Goddess* in a three-week brainstorm and then spent years revising the draft.

Incidentally, it also reveals that he considered much of his argument historically valid. Graves struggles to graft his poetic system onto a myth, which does not perfectly fit his needs. Obviously, he stuck to the *Cad Goddeu* framework, including the lapwing, because he felt it was more than poetic metaphor. He chose *Cad Goddeu* as the central theme partly because it corresponded to the metaphor he wanted to create, but also because he felt there was a kernel of historical fact to the story, which couldn't be dismissed.

This belief in historical accuracy explains why he went to such pains to include the obscure reference to the lapwing. Graves believed that this kernel of truth had to be accounted for in the poetic system he was trying to create. *The White Goddess* had to prove that historical truth and poetic truths were fully compatible. After all, the magical power of truth is central to Celtic literature and to Graves's own work.

Of course, *The White Goddess* is not unique in attempting to match reality to spiritual idealism. This is the core of most religious writings and both the Bible and *White Goddess* strive to express spiritual ideas through a historical argument and, incidentally, both books fail. However, each book fails in a different way and to a different degree. Earlier critics have expounded the Bible's failures *ad nauseum* and this isn't the place to expand on their arguments. On the other hand, the failure of *White Goddess* is much more subtle and interesting.

Both the Bible and *The White Goddess* begin in the remote past and end with a warning of a near future of impending disaster. *Revelations* is a detailed description of the apocalypse complete with seas of blood, angles armed with sickles, and a seven-headed dragon. Few Christians interpret these images literally. Yet, if these are metaphors, we are at a loss to understand exactly what they symbolize. Graves's warning is more conservative and draws no elaborate pictures of world doom. He simply warns that we have lost our way and unless we heed nature's warnings, we will eventually destroy ourselves. The details are left to our imagination.

Just as the two books differ in promises of world destruction, they also differ in accounts of mankind's creation. The Bible denies scientific evidence and argues that mankind was made in God's image. God's active part in mankind's creation is a vital premise to biblical ideas of salvation. God made mankind, God will destroy mankind, and mankind's only hope for salvation is through God.

Just as Graves refuses to concoct visions of world destruction, he refuses to speculate on human origins. To him the question is irrelevant. Regardless of how we arrived here, we still owe a debt to the goddess, Earth personified, or Mother Nature herself. He firmly believes the spiritual and the material worlds can be aligned but he refuses to take any such alignment based on faith or hypothetical theory. Graves's spirituality only extends to what he can prove to himself and (hopefully) to others without contradicting the reality he knows. In his pagan theology, it is a prerequisite that the mundane world reflects spiritual truisms.

This insistence on historical and scientific support for spiritual concepts is precisely what leads him to cite so many fellow authors and researchers. Granted, Graves believed his historical claims and wished to support them with citations from the usual suspects but his desire to match spiritual tenets with the real world extend beyond the historical aspect. Graves draws on other sources to support more than his historical argument. He supports his own brand of pagan spirituality by drawing on the works of mathematician and astronomer William Hamilton, inventor and engineer J.W. Dunne, and nineteenth-century physicist James Maxwell. To Graves, the discoveries of such men do not threaten his private beliefs but enhance and confirm them, proving once again that Graves's poetic system is expressed in the very fabric of the universe.

Biblical authority pales by comparison and most biblical arguments for God's power rest on circular logic. The Bible claims to be true because it is the word of God and anyone questioning this statement is encouraged to find proof within the Bible itself. Biblical authors refused to openly acknowledge any preexisting sources and the impact of ancient paganism on early Judaism or Christianity is conveniently ignored. Rather than seeking the nature of divinity in reality, the Bible attempts the impossible by seeking to define divinity and then limiting the reader's input to only those sources, which confirm biblical views. Overall, this strategy allows the educated reader to reveal the division between Christian beliefs and actual reality much easier than the division between Graves's theology and reality in *The White Goddess*. Frankly, *The White Goddess* comes closer to bridging the gap between the spiritual and the real, and where it fails it's more able to conceal its failure.

Like *Witch-Cult*, *The White Goddess* was shunned by experts and championed by lay readers. However, *The White Goddess* won popular support quicker than Murray's theories because Graves appealed to a wider audience of both historian and poets. Graves's work rode the tide created by Murray and *The White Goddess* slid easily into the growing niche of pagan literature. The book became one of the few titles, which both fell into the witchcraft genre and expanded this genre to include the modern spiritual practices, which nontraditional Westerners searched for.

A vital contributing factor to this acceptance was Graves's implicit belief in the supernatural and magic. *The White Goddess* is a far cry from modern pulp pagan spell books and offers no step by step instructions for ritual magic. However, Graves refuses to condemn magic and recounts many ancient magical practices without derision. The result is that Graves subtlety and indirectly implies the reality of magic. This subtle favoring of magic begins on the first page of the Forward, where Graves defines poetry as a "magical language". Here Graves is not using *magical* in the usual poetic sense of beautiful, captivating, or whimsical. He means magic in the same sense which Aleister Crowley used *magick* to differentiate between literary metaphor and actual acts of supernaturalism such as invocation, divination, spell casting, and all that these things imply.

Graves's favoring of this type of magic appears again as early as the second paragraph of the first chapter as he attempts to explain the unusual prestige which poetry still receives. This respect, Graves argues, derives from the fact that the public is still vaguely aware that poetry derives from magic; again using the word to indicate some form of occultism. Graves is a poet and has been dedicated to the study of poetry since his teens, poetry is based upon magic; therefore Graves implies his own belief in (and support of) magic. A glance at his poems confirms his belief.

Graves's interest in history and magic lead him to investigate the history of magic itself. He searches Celtic literature for hints of magical formulas, he extracts the alchemical references from Skelton, and he reads obscure works such as *Lambspring* and the *Steganographia*. It seems that when Graves states that "magic is disreputable" he's not stating his own belief, he's lamenting the fact. It's Graves's desire to reconcile magic and reality which leads him into historical error and many later pagan authors, missing this point, fall into the trap which Graves attempts to conceal and ignore.

Despite the rising education level of the pagan community, many popular authors still commit to the errors found within *The White Goddess*. The belief that witchcraft descends from Europe's legendary matriarchal era has been echoed as late as 2002 in Hans Holzer's definitive *Witches*. Holzer claims that witchcraft existed alongside Celtic druidism and eventually amalgamated with it (Holzer 13, 16). Indeed, Holzer seems to support most of Murray's claim that witchcraft was a pagan survival stomped out by the church and driven to a secret underground existence carried out in hereditary traditions (Holzer 30, 32, 50). He goes on to say that Graves's works contributed to the rituals of witchcraft and therefore simultaneously supports Murray's witch-cult theory and illustrates Graves's role in the pagan revival.

Holzer is not alone in his continued support of Graves and Murray. Many popular Wiccan authors follow suit. Gardner believed Wicca descended from a matriarchal Stone Age religion (Gardner 1991, 43). Slater supports the idea of witches driven underground to exist secretly throughout the Middle Ages (Slater II). Ann Moura declares that Wicca developed in ancient Europe when local paganism merged with religious ideas brought from Pakistan and echoes portions of Murray's witch-cult theory (Moura 121, 243). Buckland is more cautious at first and backs away from Murray's theories on the first page of his best-known work, yet he seems to support her repeatedly in the later text (Buckland 1). Overall, the pagan authors of the last half of the twentieth century supported

Murray's claims much like Graves.

Perhaps the most interesting development to spring from pagan interpretation of *The White Goddess* is the creation of what historian Peter Ellis despairingly labeled the Celtic "tree zodiac". Once Graves had reinforced the connection between ogham characters, the trees attributed to them, and the lunar months those trees thrived in it became relatively easy to construct a zodiac system. This is exactly what Graves has done, but his readers have taken the argument even farther. They have linked each tree month to a personality type and thereby developed an astrology system which classifies people based on their ogham sign and corresponding tree. It's important to understand that although Graves established the connection between ogham and lunar months he never publicly endorsed its use as a astrological system. Nowhere in *The White Goddess* does Graves suggest drawing up horoscopes or predicting the future based on the ogham tree of your birth month. The concept of dividing humanity according to lunar cycles smacked too much of Yeats's *A Vision* for Graves to ever endorse it.

However, we've already seen that what Graves publicly stated and what he privately believed were sometimes at odds. Graves read his horoscope frequently, showed an interest in numerology, and consulted the I Ching. His use of ghosts in his fictional works imply more than a passing interest in the matter and his experiences at Charterhouse, the séance, and the Egyptian flat reinforced his belief in the supernatural. Publicly Graves demurred from personal statements regarding the supernatural but privately he courted the supernatural with at least some degree of sincerity.

In a letter dated April 15, 1946, Graves offers conclusive proof that he experimented with ritual magic. Doctor George Simon and his wife Joanna, a married couple Graves had known since 1944, had suffered three miscarriages and asked Graves for advice. Graves's reply is revealing:

Magical instructions. Clear out all rubbish from the house (backs of drawers, under stairs, etc., between May 14 and June 14) and burn it, unless classifiable as salvage, in the backyard. A bunch of primroses would please the Goddess and, when nobody is snooping, and handful of pearl barley laid on a raised stone ... To show that you really are cultivating her, not the Holy God of the immaterial universe, the following charm will gratify her exceedingly. It is chockful of astrological magic (O'Prey 47).

These instructions were accompanies by a circular charm written by Graves in Latin. Here, finally, is evidence that Graves took his magic seriously. In one deft move, he creates a fertility charm based on Latin invocations, the magic circle, and concrete poetry akin to that of Gertrude Stein. What else could we expect from a man who twenty-four years earlier had written that the poet was a "highly developed witch doctor" and that "poetry is not a science, it is an act of faith" containing "rhythmic mesmerism" (Graves 1922, 13, 19, 50)?

The Simons followed Graves's magical advice and, to the credit of pagans everywhere, the magic worked. The Simons wrote to Graves announcing the birth of their daughter Helena and Graves wrote back another revealing reply. He advised the new parents, "Dress her plainly because she's going to be beautiful and a danger to men, with a nativity so close to midsummer" (O'Prey 49). Obviously, Graves believed that the girl born under a magic spell must be protected by astrological magic.

It's unlikely that later pagans knew of this incident and it seems that later authors made the leap from Graves's tree zodiac to full blown "Celtic astrology" independently. Such pseudo-Celtic astrology systems didn't appear until a few years after the publication of *The White Goddess* despite the fact that Graves was using similar methods to assist the Simons before 1948. Thus, we can conclude that Graves didn't publicly advocate any sort of astrology based on his ogham system. Instead, readers were making these connections themselves and various hybrid systems were appearing in pagan circles.

The White Goddess was popularized by groups such as Fred Adams's Feraferia and Graves's ogham calendar appeared in pagan writings by at least the middle of the 1960's. Graves's impact on Adams was enormous and drove Adams to visit Graves in 1959. Feraferia literature and rituals are steeped with references to Graves's works and Adams admits that both *The White Goddess* and *Seven Days in New Crete* were inspirations for his group (Holzer 382; Adler 239). Other Feraferia rituals utilize thorn, oak, holly, ash, alder, and willow, mention the "Duir Oak Month", and quote Blake. Furthermore, the ogham tree calendar used by Feraferia exactly matches that of *The White Goddess* and their tree associations to the letters are also identical (Holzer 380).

Several other pagan authors have utilized Graves's tree calendar despite occasional qualms regarding its authenticity. Ellen Hopman's *A Druid's Herbal* cites Graves's ogham calendar while admitting that Graves may have created the entire system himself (Hopman 1995, 11). Pauline Campanelli's *Ancient Ways* cites Graves and her "Celtic tree calendar" is obviously drawn from his works (Campanelli 105, 173). A deeper examination comes from Jane Raeburn's *Celtic Wicca*, which touches on both Macalister and O'Flaherty's ogham theories and adopts Graves's dating scheme to date ogham's creation (Raeburn 127). Raeburn has also followed up on Graves's sources such as *Flora Scotica* and *The Book of St. Albans*.

Other pagan works utilizing *The White Goddess* include *The Magician's Companion* by Bill Whitcomb. Whitcomb links ogham letters to lunar months via Graves's calendar and uses the terms "unhewn dolmen" and "stations of the year". *The Magician's Companion* also reproduces a hand chart similar to that of Graves (Whitcomb 189-190). Richard Webster's *Omens, Oghams and Oracles* cites *The White Goddess* in the bibliography, provides a system of divination based on Graves's ogham calendar, and devotes a full page to each of the ogham character's interpretations. D.J. Conway's *Oak, Ash and Thorn* claims the ogham contains a magic system for the initiated and refers to the letters of the forfeda as "the crane bag", presumably after Graves's ogham article of the same name (Conway 185, 187). Conway is unsure if ogham letters are linked to the months but is inclined to believe they are. Lastly, Edred Thorsson's *Book of Ogham* rejects Graves's calendar and questions Graves's historical accuracy.

Ross Nichols, the Chosen Chief of the Order of Bards, Ovates and Druids between the years 1964 and 1975, also cherished Graves's works. Records reveal that Nichols utilized Graves's ogham calendar within the Order (Matthews 1996, 345). Nichols also mentions Graves, *The White Goddess,* and the tree calendar in his *Book of Druidry.* In all, Nichols reproduces a significant amount of Graves's ogham material including the relationship between the tree calendar and the *Song of Amergin* and the chart of ogham letters transposed onto the unhewn dolmen (Nichols 289).

In his *Taliesin,* John Matthews suggests that the known ogham inscriptions are ancient and that ogham was used by bards to speak secrets in full view of others. He questions what pagans have done with ogham and states that Graves never intended ogham to serve as a framework for goddess worship (Matthews 2002, 211, 220). His wife, Caitlin Matthews, has released an attractive box set of ogham staves intended as divination tools. The accompanying booklet offers divinatory meanings for each of the ogham characters and although she doesn't adopt Graves's tree calendar she recommends *The White Goddess* in her bibliography. Matthews's method of drawing and casting ogham staves is quite independent of Graves's ogham system. Graves's late usage of the I Ching implies that he never developed his own method of ogham casting.

Significantly, Gerald Gardner retains ogham's traditional Irish origin and bypasses most of Graves's ogham theories entirely (Gardner 1991, 60). Nonetheless, much of Gardner's work depends on Graves's reconstruction of pagan Europe and Gardner favors Graves's Belgic invasion theories. Indeed, it can be difficult to trace the impact of Robert Graves within paganism because Gardner's own works are so saturated with Graves. It is often a moot point to ask whether a later pagan author is drawing directly from Graves or receiving Graves's ideas via Gardner.

In January of 1961, Gardner visited Graves's home on the island of Majorca and the two men held a long conversation in which Idries Shah was also present. There is no record of what the three mystics spoke of but Gardner had visited Graves with the intent of learning how ogham and goddess worship influenced European paganism. Graves, on the other hand, probably wanted to extract from Gardner any information regarding the growing phenomenon of Wicca. Shah favored Eastern mysticism and was interested in how both men's ideas could be compared against his own philosophy.

We may not be able to use Graves's analeptic method and hear these men speaking in the way Graves hears Theophilus and Paulus but certain points can be reconstructed with a high degree of proba- bility. Three years after meeting Gardner Graves published an article entitled *Witches in 1964*. In the article, Graves mentions aspects of Gardner's religion which no casual reader could know and we must conclude that Graves had obtained this material directly from Gardner.

The first interesting point is that Graves accepts Gardner's expla- nation that *witch* derived from the earlier Anglo-Saxon *Wicca*. Even more interesting is that Graves expands the definition of Wicca to include "a magician who weakens the power of evil" (Graves 1964, 551). By doing so, Graves enables modern day Wiccans to deny charges of evildoing leveled against them. Graves, still wishing to uphold Murray's romantic concept of witchcraft as a pagan survival, was cleverly supporting Wiccans as the descendants of authentic British paganism.

The same article quotes seven lines of a chant beginning: "Queen of the Moon, Queen of the Sun" and ending: "When the Sun shall come up early". This same chant appears in Gardner's *Witchcraft Today* and in his article, Graves is unclear whether he received the chant from Gardner's book or from their conversation. Comments from Graves indicate that he had read Gardner's book by at least

1964, however, other evidence suggests that the two men also discussed this chant in 1961.

Graves calls this chant "a modern witch chant", but nowhere in *Witchcraft Today* does Gardner reveal this chant as modern. On the contrary, Gardner attempts to depict his source as authentic pagan survivals. How did Graves know this was a modern chant if Gardner refused to label it as such in his books? Two solutions can be suggested. Either Gardner admitted in conversation that the chant was written recently, or Graves's poetic ability allowed him to spot a piece of modern forgery when he saw it. Graves was enough of a poet to know hack poetry on sight. Yet, if this poem were honestly a pagan survival of a secret religion of the uneducated masses, we would expect it to be hack rhymes of exactly this nature. Therefore, it seems that Gardner admitted to Graves that this poem had only been recently written by a member of his coven.

By way of confirmation, Doreen Valiente admits that she wrote the poem in the early 1950's (Farrar 1981, 148). Thus, Valiente wrote the poem and Gardner included it in *Witchcraft Today* with no indication of the date, but upon his conversation with Graves Gardner apparently confessed its true origin. Gardner knew he couldn't fool Graves. Ultimately, we see Gardner confessing that at least part of his religion had been authored by his own students.

This admission may be damaging to his claim that Wicca was a true pagan survival, but it relieved Gardner of charges of fraud, which were frequently leveled against him. Given a choice between the two, Gardner would rather admit that his coven had reworked preexisting material than face charges of outright deception. Such an admission of Valiente's role was becoming increasingly important to Gardner after their separation. After breaking with Gardner, Valiente was free to admit her own contributions to Wicca and Gardner was forced to hedge earlier statements to avoid embarrassment.

Graves also mentions another issue which occasionally embarrassed Gardner; Gardner's questionable credentials. In two separate newspaper articles, Gardner billed himself as Dr. Gerald Gardner.

Graves knew these claims were bogus. His article says of Gardner, "his doctorate came from no University". How did Graves know this? Either Gardner freely admitted that his earlier claims were false, or Graves had read Gardner's biography *Gerald Gardner: Witch*, which had been published a year before their meeting. Regardless of his source, the fact that Graves knew the truth implied that Gardner was moving towards a new public policy. His disputes with Doreen Valiente had led to questions of his honesty and Gardner was discovering that complete truth was his best option. Furthermore, if Shah truly did ghost write Gardner's biography, as is rumored, then Gardner may have found it difficult to lie in the presence of his biographer.

The next item of interest in Graves's article is the mention of witchcraft authors Christina Hole and Charles Williams. Here is positive evidence that Graves's interest in witchcraft extended well beyond Murray and ventured into the more lurid pulp authors who exploited the traditional witch image. Hole's works include *Haunted England*, *Witchcraft in England*, and *A Mirror of Witchcraft*. The first two titles were published before *The White Goddess*, but if Graves had read them, he found nothing helpful. In her works, Hole superficially distances herself from Murray's witch-cult theory but repeatedly uses the theory's corollaries and supporting evidence. Ultimately, we are given the impression that Hole's work was quickly produced in the wake of Murray as a means to cash in on the witch craze. Williams's works included *Descent into Hell* and *Witchcraft*. Like Hole, Williams likely added nothing new to Graves's perspective if Graves had read his works before 1948. Conversely, if Graves had read both Hole and Williams after the publication of *The White Goddess* we must wonder if he did so in an attempt to follow up in his interest of traditional witchcraft, which *The White Goddess* began. Possibly, Graves had only read both author's works between meeting Gardner in 1961 and the publication of his 1964 article.

According to the article, Hole and Williams ignore the fact that the witch-cult came to Europe via the Saracens. During the Middle

Ages, *Saracen* was a much abused term and signified anyone of Middle Eastern descent or a Muslim of any nationality. Thus, the statement that the witch-cult originated from the Saracens implies that European witchcraft had roots in Islam. Undoubtedly, Hole and Williams ignored this theory because it's untenable to even a moderately trained historian. The similarities between European witchcraft and Islam are few and depend more on the commonalties shared by all religions than on any real importation. Significantly, Murray fails to note any similarity between her witch-cult and Islam. Gardner lightly dismisses the Saracens in *High Magic's Aid* and omits them completely from *Witchcraft Today*. Possibly, the connection between the witch-cult and the Saracens was suggested to Gardner by Shah, whose interest in Middle Eastern philosophy was well known. If Shah did suggest this idea to Gardner, he probably did so between the publication of *Witchcraft Today* in 1954 and Valiente's visions of John Breakspeare in 1961. Breakspeare's criticism of Saracen theories was probably Valiente's reaction to Gardner's increased interest in Shah's claims.

Not all of the pagan authors who have been influenced by Graves have chosen to embrace ogham. Victor Anderson, founder of the Faery Tradition of Wicca, explained during an interview that the three prime goddesses of druidism were, "Anna, Nimue and Mari" (Hopman 2002, 79). These three goddesses are, coincidentally, the three aspects of the triple goddess found in Graves's *Watch the North Wind Rise*. Each of these goddesses is recorded in sources outside of Graves's works. However, the obvious implication is that Anderson drew directly from *North Wind* rather than searching out the minor character of Nimue concealed within Spenser's *Faerie Queen*.

Other pagans who utilize Graves but avoided ogham include Robert Cochrane, who worked closely with Doreen Valiente for a short time. In the 1960's, Cochrane and an assistant working under the name Taliesin attempted to found a pagan group based on *The White Goddess* (Hutton 313). Cochrane often drew from Graves but rejected Gardner and sought to establish his own brand of paganism distinct from Wicca. Cochrane's group experimented with belladonna and hallucinogenic mushrooms and this suggests that they were reading the enlarged edition of *The White Goddess*, which included Graves's mushroom material.

Interestingly enough, some pagan authors reveal little, if any, influence from Graves. Ray Buckland shows little interest in Graves's work in his superb *Complete Book of Witchcraft*. Like many pagan authors, Buckland provides a recommended reading list, which includes our usual suspects in addition to Gardner, Starhawk, Valiente, Leland, and the Farrars. Graves isn't included and while Buckland does mention ogham he gives an incomplete version containing only twenty three characters and erroneously places the forfeda in the middle of the alphabet (Buckland 177). Apparently, Buckland uses ogham sources other than Graves. Yet Buckland undoubtedly discovered Graves's works at some point because *The White Goddess* appears in the bibliography to his *Witchcraft from the Inside*.

Graves's work has affected non-pagan historians as well. In 1976, ogham was given another publicity boost with the publication of Barry Fell's *America BC*. Fell, a marine biologist turned amateur archaeologist, calls for a radical reevaluation of America's prehistory and claims to have discovered several ogham inscriptions in the United States. Fell suggests that ancient Celts visited the Unites States roughly 3000 years ago, bringing their druids, building megalithic structures, and inscribing ogham (Fell 5-6, 142). These Celts worked with Phoenician traders to erect a monolithic temple to Baal, whom Fell depicts as a sun god. Fell bases his evidence almost exclusively on crudely defaced stones bearing a superficial resemblance to ogham. While Fell's theories sound revolutionary, we must remember that an inscription of the name Baal written in ogham would lack the vowels and consist simply of B and L for a total of three-letter strokes placed against the stem line. This is hardly conclusive evidence for a Phoenician temple and most professional archaeologists have refuted Fell's claims.

Nowhere in *America BC* does Fell cite *The White Goddess*, but we feel the presence of Robert Graves and Edward Davies throughout Fell's works and Graves's grandfather, Charles Graves, is cited early in the book (Fell 37). The highly fantastic interpretation of ogham inscriptions, the suggestion that Phoenicians and Celts left joint ogham inscriptions, and druids worshiping Baal all ring of Graves's model of pagan Europe and Davies's merger of Phoenician paganism and druidism. Like Graves, Fell pushes the creation of ogham deep into Celtic prehistory. Yet, conversely, Fell refutes Graves's assumption that ogham existed in Gaul (Fell 58, 92). In short, Fell uses amateur ogham research to produce questionable theories of Celtic migration in much the same way Graves had done before him.

Other endeavors include Patrick Crampton's 1967 *Stonehenge of the Kings*. Crampton's book quotes selections of Graves's *Greek Myths* and reconstructs Britain's monolithic culture in light of the matriarchal ideas found within *The White Goddess*. Key feminist authors such as Riane Eisler, Mary Daly, and Merlin Stone have also relied on Graves's works for their historical perspective.

Fiction has also benefited from *The White Goddess*. Graves's romantic paganism inspired dozens of fiction authors in a way, which few other nonfiction works can do. Comparisons between *White Goddess* and *Golden Bough* frequently mention the flood of literary output these books inspired. More interesting is the comparison between *White Goddess* and Burton's *Anatomy of Melancholy*. Martin Seymour-Smith, J. M. Cohen, and Daniel Hoffman have all noted similarities (Day 1963, 96, 157; Hoffman XII). Graves easily emulates the eye for detail and depth of knowledge displayed by Frazer and Burton and all three men devote considerable space to the Celtic traditions, which later authors revived.

By 1964, Lloyd Alexander was drawing on the *Mabinogion*, and perhaps directly from *The White Goddess*, to write *The Prydain Chronicles*. Alexander's bards spell out secret alphabets with their fingers, spit beans at ghosts, and use "letter sticks" for divination. The evil queen Achren dwells in the Spiral Castle and her consort

Arawn raises an army of undead via an evil cauldron. Alexander was not alone; much of his work emulates fantasy master Tolkien. Tolkien's works may possess no direct debt to *The White Goddess* but his warring Ents are highly reminiscent of the battle of the trees and his utilization of complex alphabets and inscriptions has already been noted. These authors echo ideas from *The White Goddess* as they spin tales of long ago and far away. Yet, Graves's works could just as easily be incorporated into visions of the future.

The works of science fiction author Frank Herbert bear the familiar marks of not only *The White Goddess* but also Graves's Middle Eastern influences such as *Seven Pillars of Wisdom* and *Travels in Arabia Deserta*. Herbert's *Dune* chronicles abound with ancient languages and secret finger spelling. The religions of his futuristic universe are closely monitored by the Bene Gesserit, an order of witch priestesses seeking to produce a male hero-savior. Arrakis, the central planet of a universal power struggle, lies in the hands of this male savior, his mother, wife, and daughter. Here Herbert has intentionally imitated the world of the triple goddess, who is both creator and destroyer, and her hero son-consort. Behind this power struggle is an ecological battle reflecting the real life ecological awareness, which many pagans advocate.

Herbert revealed further pagan tendencies in *The White Plague*. When a synthetic plague devastates Ireland and Great Britain it kills only females and threatens to drive mankind to extinction. In the aftermath of this holocaust, women become scarce, revered figures who inspire various fertility rituals in their male worshipers. Herbert plays on the tensions of Northern Ireland to supply his plot with countless references to both ancient and modern Celtic culture and merges Celtic lore to a Gravesian pagan model. In a particularly pagan scene, young virgins are impregnated beneath rowan trees during lunar worship (Herbert 1983, 304).

Philip José Farmer embodied concepts from *The White Goddess* and *Watch the North Wind Rise* in his 1960 science fiction novel *Flesh*. Farmer paints a picture of a post nuclear future in which America has reverted to a pagan culture reminiscent of Frazer and Graves. In this world, a returning astronaut is crowned as the sun hero, the divine son of the triple goddess. In their post collapse society, the new Americans have chosen to name their three goddesses Virginia, Columbia, and America. These three embody the three aspects of the Great White Mother and rule over lavish fertility rituals. Farmer clearly revels in the humorous descriptions of sexual rites and invokes images of nubile virgins anointed with red, white, and blue paint. Yet the underlying message is identical to that of *North Wind*; blind obeisance degrades even the most well meaning beliefs. Like the pagans of *North Wind*, the pagan of *Flesh* have carried their rejection of science too far and sunken into superstition and ignorance.

Hints of *The White Goddess* even occur within George Lucas's *Star Wars* series. Lucas's musical composer, John Williams, revealed in an interview that the music for *The Phantom Menace* was inspired by a reading of *The White Goddess*. Williams had Nash's translation of *Cad Goddeu* translated from English into several other languages. Then, picking the one that sounded the most cryptic, he developed a chanting chorus of the words and incorporated them into the soundtrack (Hanson). It's a far cry from the original Welsh text, or even from Nash's translation, but the effect is the same mysterious sounding nonsense.

Among pagans, Marion Zimmer Bradley's *Mists of Avalon* is easily the most popular fictional work to be influenced by *The White Goddess*. Bradley's Arthurian Britain depicts a slow decline of matriarchal paganism under the growing threat of Christianity. In one passage, Igraine observes the night sky, watching the constellation called the Wheel as it circles the North star. Igraine reflects on the fact that the constellation symbolizes "the endless Wheel of Birth and Death and Rebirth" and believes that only pagans are reincarnated. Christians and other lesser people are merely "once-born" (Bradley 59). Throughout the story the priestesses of Avalon are depicted as the three aspects of the triple goddess and the words maiden, mother, and crone are occasionally used in their descriptions (Bradley 169).

By now, it becomes obvious that many critics of *The White Goddess* can be divided into two groups; the historical critics who misunderstand the poetic side of the book, and the poets who misunderstand the historical side. Peter Ellis's attack on Graves's ogham theories is typical of the first group. Ellis attacks Graves for his historical inaccuracies but makes historical mistakes of his own when discussing Graves's biographical details, incorrectly stating that *White Goddess* was published in 1946 and claiming that Graves attended St. John's College before World War I. His article reveals valid reasons for banning *White Goddess* from the college syllabus but by sidestepping the poetic contributions of the book, Ellis is missing at least half the point.

Margot Adler's defense of Graves's metaphorical argument is typical of the second group. She defends his rights as a poet and suggests that some pagans have taken Graves too literally (Alder 59-60). Pagan author Nigel Pennick sides with Adler when he calls *The White Goddess* "a poetic interpretation of facts the author didn't fully understand" and claims, "it would be a mistake to read it as history" (Pennick 170). Pennick and Adler evaluate *White Goddess* based upon literary standards and allow historical questions to remain unanswered.

Other critics have pursued an identical path and this has often led to their own inaccuracies. John Vickery conjectures that Graves selected the trees of the ogham from his earlier poetry and that Graves found his color symbolism in Suidas. He misses the facts that the ogham tree symbolism was established in the *Auraicept* centuries before Graves wrote and that black, red, and white are traditional combinations of Celtic poetry. Poet and critic Grevel Lindop mistakenly claims that both *Hanes Taliesin* and *Jubilate Agno* contain alphabets and that a recent publication of Smart's works may have inspired Graves's examination of Taliesin's riddles (Firla 26-28). However, neither *Hanes Taliesin* nor *Cad Goddeu* contain alphabets in any way; the belief that they do is itself a creation by Edward Davies and Robert Graves. Nor do we have any evidence that Graves read the recent edition of Smart's works. Rather, it's more likely that Graves was inspired by Middle Age acrostics such as those within Bede's *History*, *Piers Ploughman*, and Skelton's *Garland of Laurel*, three of his known sources. Poe's *Gold Bug* cypher, mentioned in Graves's *On English Poetry* may have also served as inspiration. Vickery believes that a well-documented historical fact is merely a creation by Graves while Lindop states that a creation by Graves is an actual fact. The line between Graves's facts and the conclusions he builds with them is often blurred by such literary critics who examine the book solely from a literary standpoint.

Where Ellis has dodged the poetical question, Adler and Pennick have dodged the historical questions of ogham and medieval Welsh bardism. All of these authors have acted stereotypically for their respective groups. Both parties have used *The White Goddess* as a sharpening stone for the particular ax they wish to grind but, apart from documenting Graves's sources, little has been accomplished and the book remains unintelligible to many readers. Authors in both camps should be reminded that Graves attacks exactly this sort of departmentalization in chapter thirteen of *White Goddess*.

The truth is that *The White Goddess* is not primarily a historical book or primarily a poetic book. It is primarily a spiritual book and Graves depends on both poetry and history to uphold his spiritual ideas. Behind the search for ogham's origins and Graves's definition of "true poetry" is a simple claim that man owes spiritual homage to woman. Graves truly believes this. He expresses it in his poetry. He lived it in his life. This is the concept that *The White Goddess* truly supports. Poetry and history are merely tools to uphold the claim that man should devote his life to woman. *The White Goddess* is a testament of Graves's belief and he plunders both literature and archeology to support his claim. He believes wholeheartedly in this tenet and he's willing to distort both poetry and history to make the reader believe it too.

If *The White Goddess* was merely a history book it would contain no poetry. If Graves only wanted to prove the existence of a prehistoric matriarchy, he wouldn't have cited Keats, Coleridge, Alun Lewis or his own poems. If he was arguing only for the connection between ogham and goddess worship there would be no need to ask "must all things swing around for ever" or to record his astonishment at watching a heron catching fish. None of this supports a primarily historical argument and this proves that Graves wasn't solely out to prove a historical point or uphold his model of prehistoric Europe. Graves intended to uphold the prehistoric model created by authors like Frazer and Harrison, but only because they indirectly supported his claim of woman's spiritual superiority.

On the other hand, *The White Goddess* isn't intended solely as a poetic primer. The insignificant amount of poetry quoted and Graves's treatment of his fellow poets proves this. Nowhere does Graves offer his own poetry for criticism or emulation. Never once does he break down a poem showing its strong and weak points. If the book was mainly a poetic book it would be pointless to track invading warrior tribes from the Black Sea to Ireland, it would be unnecessary to consult with Macalister regarding ogham, or cite Sir Robert Mond's excavations, or Blackstone's legal commentaries. Graves cites portions of poetic tradition, but only because they support his own religious beliefs regarding the Muse.

Graves holds religious beliefs, which contradict mainstream biblical religions and puts him at odds with society. This belief drove him to abandon a conventional lifestyle. He gave up working a "normal" job and left his homeland so that he could live with his own beliefs in a Majorcan village. He knows exactly what he did and why. He hints at it when he compares himself to Don Quixote. *The White Goddess* was intended to justify this decision and the beliefs, which inspired it. We can almost hear Graves saying: "Look here, I'm not crazy. Here are other people who think like I do. Here are some poems that make the same point. Here are some historical records that show people once thought like I do now. I have archaeological evidence that this culture once existed and here is proof that invaders destroyed it. It was common once and it's still found in the best poets even now."

A quick look at *Cad Goddeu* and *Hanes Taliesin* reveals exactly how Graves uses poetry to support his views. Nowhere does Graves review Taliesin's works as poems or criticize them by artistic standards. Instead, he cites them as evidence of his pagan model. He never claims they are good poems or that future poets should emulate their style. Poetically speaking, *Cad Goddeu* is a horrible poem hardly worth the time Graves spends on it and modern readers can sympathize with Davies's claim that Taliesin wrote "without an atom of poetical merit" (Davies 1809, 273). Yet, it hints at historical evidence, which supports Graves's spiritual ideas. These two poems are not examples of what Graves considers good poems, they merely point the way towards the historical model of Europe that he favors. Graves has taken two obscure poems and bent them to support his views. Then he pillaged literature to find other poems that express the concepts, which he claims originated in this model. Graves bends the rules then stacks the deck to match his game.

However, we can forgive him to a degree simply because he finds so much supporting evidence in our literature. Perhaps there never was a worldwide matriarchal goddess culture that used ogham. Yet, there exists countless poems expressing the same spiritual concepts, which this culture would have expressed if it had existed. The concept of man's spiritual homage to woman is everywhere in poetry, regardless of whether or not Graves bends evidence to support matriarchy. Graves could have cut all historical evidence from *The White Goddess* and rested his spiritual beliefs solely on the works of other poets, but this wasn't good enough for him. He wanted to prove his case to poets who would accept poetical evidence but he also wanted to prove himself to non-poets requiring historical evidence. This meant that Graves had to supply a historical argument, even if he had to bend facts to reach it. He wanted to show how both history and poetry supported his spiritual claim. As already stated, Graves very nearly succeeds in putting a square peg into a round hole. Zeta and Gamma did not perfectly kiss but their match was so close that nobody has completely separated them since. The final product is so awe inspiring that few people have even made the attempt.

EPILOGUE

Ending our chase of *The White Goddess* we may wonder if we are any closer to our goal than when we started. Like so many Celtic heroes, we kept our prey constantly in sight and were nonetheless robbed of the final kill by otherworldly forces. We are in good company. Pwyll did no better. What did we expect? We had been pursuing the Muse on her own grounds.

Yet, the chase must be renewed by each generation of artists. Literary tradition renews the pursuit of the Muse whenever a new school of literature is established. Individual poets join the chase when they abandon these schools and begin hunting for their own voice. Graves began stalking the goddess in earnest when he left the Georgian school of poets and began hunting for his personal Muse. Nor will the hunt end with the advancement of our technological society. In an essay entitled "How to Keep and Feed a Muse" science fiction author Ray Bradbury reveals that poetry is one of his primary inspirations. His test of poetic quality is reminiscent of Housman's and demands that the hairs of the arm stand on end (Bradbury 39).

The battle of *Cad Goddeu* still rages today both inside the pagan community and beyond it. The constricting tenets of mass-marketed religion are still being challenged by an undercurrent of more enlightened paganism. Today's freethinking pagans draw their inspiration from nature just as Gwydion once did and they focus their power against the shadowy forces of monotheist religions who still believe theirs is the only way. The oppressive regime may appear as fifteenth century Inquisitors, Orkish armies, or futuristic Sith lords but their somber black uniforms always betray their intentions. In contrast, the supporters of the ecstatic nature religions wrap themselves in the forest colors of green and brown whether they are Wiccans, Druids, Ents, or Jedi. Each side experiences their losses and gains and, although the mystics are always the minority, somehow they are never completely annihilated. The dog, roebuck, and lapwing remain in their service.

Finally, we realize that *The White Goddess* is a unique book, which could only have been written at a unique point in history; in the few years between the decline of Frazer's theories and the rise of contemporary paganism. Had *The White Goddess* appeared five years earlier few people would have been interested. Had it appeared five years later, nobody would have believed it. The discovery of carbon-14 dating, the Essene's Dead Sea scrolls, the gnostic texts of Nag Hammadi, and the decipherment of Linear B would have destroyed its argument. *The White Goddess* rode upon the cutting edge of historical research immediately before these discoveries and depended upon Graves's ability to speculate upon these subjects. In a sense, *The White Goddess* was the last of the "druidic revival" literature, which could flaunt its conjectures without evidence. Robert Graves was the last of a long line of such revivalists including Iolo Morganwg, Edward Davies, and Lewis Spence.

Nonetheless, *The White Goddess* was the catalyst for the rise of paganism. It was Graves who revived and extended the ideas of the these authors and if this new life lasted only a few years it was still enough to popularize them and familiarize the average reader with them. It's unlikely that paganism would have developed as it did without Graves's work. Had Gardner not read *The White Goddess*, or any of Graves's other works, Wicca might have a considerably more Hermetic or Masonic appearance. Without Graves's works, Gardner would have relied more upon the Golden Dawn, Aleister Crowley, and older occult authors such as Barrett and Levi.

In short, Graves found no religious school to give his allegiance to and was forced to create his own system. He hoped that other poets would incline towards this system but he never considered that his poetic paganism would appeal to the general public. Ironically, *The White Goddess* is now more popular with non-poets practicing paganism than with serious poets wishing to utilize Graves's style. Graves's works revealed spiritual truisms, which were recognized by those Europeans seeking a new form of spiritual expression, which would put them in touch with their native roots. Their devotion to Graves's pagan theology will ensure that *The White Goddess* will continue to sell "quietly" for generations.

BIBLIOGRAPHY

Adler, Margot. *Drawing Down the Moon.* Boston: Beacon, 1986

Alexander, Lloyd. *Prydain Chronicles, The.* New York: Henry Holt, 1973

Bonewits, Isaac. *Real Magic.* York Beach: Weiser, 1993

Bradbury, Ray. *Zen in the Art of Writing.* New York: Bantam, 1992

Bradley, Marion Z. *Mists of Avalon, The.* New York, Knopf, 1982

Briffault, Robert. *The Mothers.* New York: Atheneum, 1977

Bromwich, Rachel. *Trioedd Ynys Prydein.* Cardiff: U. Of Wales Press, 1961

Brownlow, F. W. *Book of the Laurel, The.* Newark: U. Of Delaware Press, 1990

Buckland, Raymond. *Buckland's Complete Book of Witchcraft.* St. Paul: Llewellyn, 1990

Calder, George, ed and trans. *Auraicept na N'Eces.* Edinburgh: Four Courts, 1995

Campanelli, Pauline. *Ancient Ways.* St. Paul: Llewellyn, 1991

Campbell, Joseph. *Hero with a Thousand Faces, The.* New York: Princeton UP, 1973

Carmichael, Alexander. *Carmina Gadelica.* 2 vols. Edinburgh: Oliver and Boyd, 1928

Cohen, J.M. *Robert Graves.* New York: Barnes & Noble, 1967

Conway, D.J. *By Oak, Ash and Thorn.* St. Paul: Llewellyn, 2002

Cook, A.B. *Zeus.* 3 vols. New York: Biblo & Tannen, 1964

Crowley, Aleister. *Magic in Theory and Practice.* Secaucus: Castle, 1991

Davies, Edward. *Celtic Researches.* London: J. Booth, 1804

Davies, Edward. *Mythology and Rites of the British Druids.* London: J. Booth, 1809

Day, Douglas. *Swifter than Reason.* Durham: U of North Carolina Press, 1963

Doughty, Charles. *Travels in Arabia Deserta.* New York: Random

House

Ellis, Peter. *Dictonary of Celtic Mythology*. New York: Oxford, 1994

—.*Druids, The*. Grand Rapids: Eerdmans, 1995

—.*The Fabrication of 'Celtic' Astrology*. March 6, 2003 http://cura.free.fr/xv/13ellis2.html

Evans, J. G. *Poems from the Book of Taliesin*. Tremvan: Llambedrog, 1915

Farrar Janet., Farrar Stewart. *Eight Sabbats for Witches*. Custer: Phoenix, 1981

—.*The Witches' Way*. Custer: Phoenix, 1984

Farrar Stewart. *What Witches Do*. Blaine: Phoenix, 1991

Fell, Barry. *America BC*. New York: Pocket, 1989

Firla, Ian., Grevel Lindop. *Graves and the Goddess*. Selinsgrove: Susquehanna U.P., 2003

Fitch, Ed. *Magical Rites from the Crystal Well*. St. Paul: Llewellyn, 1992

Ford, Patrick, ed and trans. *Mabinogi, The*. Berkeley: U of California, 1977

Frazer, James. *Golden Bough, The*. New York: Collier, 1963

Frew, D. Hudson. *Crafting the Art of Magic: A Critical Review*. Dec. 16, 2003 www.wildideas.net/temple/library/frew.html

Gardner, Gerald. *High Magic's Aid*. London: Pentacle, 1994

—.*Meaning of Witchcraft, The*. New York: Magickal Childe, 1991

—.*Witchcraft Today*. New York: Magickal Childe, 1991

Geoffrey of Monmouth. *History of the Kings of Britain, The*. Trans. Lewis Thorpe. New York, Penguin, 1966

Goodridge, J. F. *Piers the Ploughman*. Harmondworth: Penguin, 1984

Graves, Beryl., Ward, Dunstan., ed. *Robert Graves: The Complete Poems*. Manchester: Carcanet, 2000

Graves, Richard P. *Robert Graves, The Assault Heroic*. London: Weidenfeld, 1986

—.*Robert Graves and the White Goddess*. London: Weidenfeld, 1995

Graves, Robert P. *Life of Sir William Rowan Hamilton*. New York: Arno Press, 1975

Graves, Robert, Alan Hodge. *Long Week-End, The*. New York: Norton,

1963

Graves, Robert, Raphael Patai. *Hebrew Myths.* New York: Anchor, 1989

Graves, Robert. *5 Pens in Hand.* New York, Doubleday, 1958

—.*Claudius the God.* New York: Random House, 1962

—.*Collected Poems.* New York: Doubleday, 1961

—.*Collected Short Stories.* New York: Doubleday, 1964

—.*Crane Bag, The.* London: Cassell, 1969

—.*Crowning Privilege, The.* Garden City: Doubleday, 1956

—.*English and Scottish Ballads.* London: Heinemann, 1969

—.*Fairies and Fusiliers.* New York: A.A. Knopf, 1918

—.*Goodbye to All That.* Garden City: Doubleday, 1957

—.*Greek Myths, The.* London: Penguin, 1992

—.*Hercules, My Shipmate.* New York: Creative Age, 1945

—.*King Jesus.* New York: Farrar, 1984

—.*On English Poetry.* London: Heinemann, 1922

—.*Oxford Addresses on Poetry.* New York: Doubleday, 1962

—.*Poems of Robert Graves, The.* Garden City: Doubleday, 1958

—.*Watch the North Wind Rise.* New York: Farrar, 1976

—.*White Goddess, The.* New York: Noonday, 1948

—.*White Goddess, The.* New York: Creative Age, 1993

—.*Wife to Mr. Milton.* New York: BOMC, 1991

—."Witches in 1964." *The Virginia Quarterly Review.* Vol. XL, No. 4, 1964

Guest, Charlotte, ed and trans. *Mabinogion, The.* London: Dent, 1913

Guirrand, Felix., ed. *Larousse Encyclopedia Of Mythology, The.* Trans. Richard Aldrington. New York: Barnes & Noble, 1994

Hanson, Scott. *The Phantom Lyrics.* May 20, 2003 www.classical-recordings.com/johnwilliams/phantomlyrics.htm

Harding, M. Esther. *Women's Mysteries Ancient and Modern.* London: Longmans, Green & Co., 1935

Harrison, Jane. *Prolegomena to the Study of Greek Religion.* Princeton: Princeton UP, 1991

Hawkins, Gerald. *Stonehenge Decoded.* Garden City: Delta, 1965

Herbert, Frank. *Dune.* New York: Berkley, 1984

Herbert, Frank. *White Plague, The.* New York: Berkley, 1983

Hoffman, Daniel. *Barbarous Knowledge.* New York: Oxford UP, 1967

Holtzer, Hans. *Witches.* New York: Black Dog, 2002

Hopman, Ellen. *A Druid's Herbal.* Rochester: Destiny, 1995

Hopman, Ellen and Bond Lawrence. *Being a Pagan.* Rochester: Destiny, 2002

Hubert, Henri. *Greatness and Decline of the Celts, The.* New York: Dorset, 1988

—. *Rise of the Celts, The.* New York: Dorset, 1988

Hutton, Ronald. *Triumph of the Moon, The.* New York: Oxford UP, 1999

Jackson, Kenneth. *Celtic Miscellany, A.* New York: Barnes & Noble, 1995

Jones, T. Gwynn. "Bardism and Romance." *Transactions of the Honourable Society of the Cymmrodorion.* London, 1915. 205-310.

Joyce, Patrick Weston. *A Social History of Ireland.* 2 vols. New York: Benjamin Blom, 1968

Kelly, Aidan. *Crafting the Art of Magic.* St. Paul: Llewellyn, 1991

Kernowski, Frank., ed. *Conversations with Robert Graves.* Jackson: UP of Mississippi, 1989

Kieckhefer, Richard. *Magic in the Middle Ages.* Cambridge: Cambridge UP, 2000

Lane-Fox, Robin. *Pagans and Christians.* New York: Knopf, 1989

Leland, Charles. *Aradia, Gospel Of The Witches.* Washington: Phoenix, 1990

Levack, Brian, ed. *Witchcraft, Magic and Demonology.* Vol. 4. New York: Garland, 1992

Lewis, Alun. *Ha! Ha! Among the Trumpets.* London: Allen, 1946

Llywelyn, Morgan. *Bard.* Boston: Houghton Mifflin, 1984

Macalister, R. A. S. *Ancient Ireland.* New York: Arno, 1978

—. *Secret Languages of Ireland, The.* Amsterdam: Philo, 1976

MacCulloch, John Arnott. *The Religion of the Ancient Celts.* London: Studio Editions, 1992

Markale, Jean. *Celts, The.* Rochester: Traditions, 1993

Matthews, Caitlin. *Celtic Wisdom Sticks.* Lodon: Connections, 2001

Matthews, John., ed. *Bardic Source Book, The.* London: Blandford, 1999

— .*Celtic Reader, The.* London: Thorsons, 1995

— .*Druid Source Book, The.* London: Blandford, 1996

— .*Encyclopaedia of Celtic Wisdom, The.* New York: Barnes & Noble, 1996

— .*Taliesin: The Last Celtic Shaman.* Rochester: Inner Traditions, 2002

Mehoke, James. *Robert Graves: Peace-Weaver.* Paris: Mouton, 1975

Milton, John. *Paradise Lost.* New York: Mentor, 1961

More, Thomas. *Utopia.* Trans. Paul Turner. New York, Penguin, 1985

Moura, Ann. *Origins of Modern Witchcraft.* St. Paul: Llewellyn, 2000

Murray, Margaret. *God of the Witches, The.* New York: Oxford, 1970

— *Witch-Cult in Western Europe, The.* New York: Barnes & Noble, 1996

Myers, Allen., ed. *Eerdman's Bible Dictionary.* Grand Rapids: Eerdmans, 1987

Nash, David William. *Taliesin: Or, The Bards and Druids of Britain.* London: John Russell Smith, 1858

Nichols, Ross. *The Book of Druidry.* London: Thorsons, 1992

Norris, Leslie. "Where the Crakeberries Grow." *The Listener* 28 May 1970

O'Prey, Paul., ed. *Between Moon and Moon.* London: Hutchinson, 1984

Pennick, Nigel. *Magical Alphabets.* York Beach:Weiser, 1992

Piggott, Stuart. *Druids, The.* New York: Thames & Hudson, 1985

Powell, T.G.E. *Celts, The.* New York: Thames & Hudson, 1994

Raeburn, Jane. *Celtic Wicca.* New York: Citadel, 2001

Rhys, John, David Brynmor-Jones. *Welsh People, The.* London: T. Fisher, 1902

Rhys, John. *Hibbert Lectures.* London: Williams and Norgate, 1888

Richardson, Alan. *20th Century Magic.* St. Paul: Llewellyn, 1991

Robbins, Rossell Hope. *Encyclopedia of Witchcraft and Demonology, The*. New York: Crown, 1981

Robinson, James., ed. *Nag Hammadi Library, The*. New York: Harper, 1988

Roszak, Betty, and Theodore Roszak. *Masculine/Feminine*. New York: Harper, 1969

Russell, Jeffrey. *Witchcraft in the Middle Ages*. London: Cornell UP, 1984

Rutherford, Ward. *Celtic Mythology*. London: Thorsons, 1995

Seabrook, William. *Witchcraft: Its Power in the World Today*. New York: Harcourt, 1940

Seymour, Miranda *Robert Graves, Life on the Edge*. New York: Holt, 1995

Seymour-Smith, Martin. *Robert Graves, His Life and Work*. New York: Holt, 1982

Skeat, W. W. *Langland's Piers the Plowman and Richard the Redeless*. 2 vols. London: Oxford UP, 1965

Skene, William. *The Four Ancient Books of Wales*. Edinburgh: Edmonston and Douglas, 1868

Slater, Herman. *A Book of Pagan Rituals*. York Beach: Weiser, 1993

Squire, Charles. *Celtic Myth and Legend*. New York: Portland House, 1994

Starhawk. *The Spiral Dance*. New York: Harper, 1989

Summers, Montague. *History of Witchcraft and Demonology, The*. Secaucus: Castle, 1992

Taylor, John. *The Witchcraft Delusion*. New York: Gramercy, 1995

Thorsson, Edred. *Book of Ogham, The*. St. Paul: Llewellyn, 1994

Tolkien, John R.R. *Return of the King, The*. Boston: Houghton, 1965

Tolstoy, Nikolai. *Quest for Merlin, The*. Boston: Back Bay, 1985

Tyson, Donald, ed. *Three Books of Occult Philosophy*. St. Paul: Llewellyn, 2003

Valiente, Doreen. *The Rebirth of Witchcraft*. Custer: Phoenix, 1989

Vickery, John. *Robert Graves and the White Goddess*. Lincoln: U of Nebraska Press, 1972

Webster, Richard. *Omens, Oghams and Oracles*. St. Paul: Llewellyn, 1995

Whitcomb, Bill. *The Magician's Companion*. St. Paul: Llewellyn, 2002

White, Gilbert. *Natural History of Selborne, The*. Harmondsworth: Penguin, 1987

Williams, Charles. *Witchcraft*. New York: Meridan, 1971

Williams, Ifor. *Beginnings of Welsh Poetry*. Cardiff: University of Wales Press, 1980

Wilson, Colin. *The Occult*. New York: Random House, 1971

Yates, Frances. *Giordano Bruno and the Hermetic Tradition*. Chicago: University of Chicago Press, 1991

Yeats, William B. *A Vision*. New York: Collier, 1966

Moon Books, invites you to begin or deepen your encounter with Paganism, in all its rich, creative, flourishing forms.